BREWERS MOTOR SERVICES
&
LLYNFI MOTOR SERVICES

'THE MAESTEG RIVALS'

Incorporating

Cream Line (Maesteg) Ltd

William John, Maesteg

F. J. John, Nantyffyllon

Griffith Hughes, Caerau

M. E. Pratt & Son, Caerau

By Vernon Morgan

The Maesteg Rivals

Published by Vernon Morgan Books

January 2025

ISBN: 978-1-0685699-0-6

© Copyright Vernon Morgan (2025)

All rights reserved. No part of this book may be reproduced or transmitted in any form, or by any means, electronic or mechanical, including photocopying, recording or by any information storage and retrieval system without permission from the publisher in writing.

Other titles published by this author:

James of Ammanford.	(The history of J. James & Sons Ltd., Ammanford).
SWT 100.	(The South Wales Transport Co. Ltd., centenary).
Images of Old Llanelli & District.	(Historical views of Llanelli & District).
Saml. Eynon & Sons, 'The Hero', Trimsaran.	(The history of Samuel Eynon & Sons).
Silcox Motor Coach Co. Ltd., Pembroke Dock.	(The history of Silcox Motor Coach Co. Ltd).
Davies Bros (Pencader) Ltd.	(A history of the Davies Bros. group of companies).
Rees & Williams Ltd., and West Wales Motors Ltd. 'The Friendly Rivals'.	(A history of both companies).
Ffoshelig Coaches Ltd., Carmarthen.	(The history, and centenary of Ffoshelig Coaches Ltd).
The Laugharne Rivals, 'Williams Bros. and Ebsworth Bros. Ltd.'	(A history of both companies).
D Coaches of Swansea. Inc. 'Diamond Holidays'.	(A history of the 'D' Coaches group of companies).

Cover Picture: Depicts Brewer's Motor Services' AEC 'Reliance' **278 TNY**, working an excursion to the seaside resort of Porthcawl, in Mid-Glamorgan. Fitted with Weymann B53F bodywork, it was new to Brewer's in April 1963, and was their first 36 feet long service bus. It was still in excellent condition when photographed here at Sandy Bay, Porthcawl, on 25th July, 1976, after 13 years continuous service. An absolute credit to the maintenance staff at Brewer's, who looked after it prestigiously for 25 years, until the business passed to United Welsh Holdings Ltd., in Jan. 1988. *(Copyright John Jones)*.

Rear Cover: Llynfi Motor Services' 1961 Leyland 'Titan' PD3/6, **LHG 537**, was photographed at the company's Maesteg depot, on 25th May, 1982, about to depart on one of their numerous school services. This East Lancs bodied vehicle was new to Burnley Colne & Nelson Joint Transport Committee (Lancashire), in April 1961, but was acquired from Lancaster City Transport (537), in October 1978. It served Llynfi for four years, before onward sale to Bevington Motors Ltd., a car sales outlet, at Margam, Port Talbot, where it was used as a static all-over advertisement, parked alongside the M4 Motorway, near Port Talbot. *(Copyright, John Jones)*.

Title Page: Pictured here outside 'The Duffryn Hotel', Caerau, was the entire 1924 fleet of A.E. & F.R. Brewer, Caerau. From left to right, NY 4610, a Leyland 36/40 hp (RAF type), with Leyland bodywork, seating 30 passengers; L 5492, a 1919 Napier 25 hp; and NY 2484, a Maxwell 20 hp, which was their first bus, acquired new in 1923. *(B. Gage collection)*.

AUTHORS ACKNOWLEDGEMENTS

This publication has been published to commemorate the 100th anniversary of the well renowned, and much loved omnibus business, of Llynfi Motor Services, Maesteg.

It has been an enormous challenge to produce this publication in time for the company's centenary, due to the vast amount of research undertaken, to collect substantial information regarding the numerous competitors that challenged one another in the Llynfi Valley, during the inter-war period.

Nevertheless, as always, I have enjoyed compiling this interesting publication, and I am indebted to numerous people for their sincere help and assistance in compiling it.

First of all, I would like to single out and thank my very sincere friends, John Jones, and Byron Gage, for their genuine enthusiasm, and extremely sincere help. They have supplied me with most of the photographs, and much of the information contained within.

My sincere thanks also to Mike Taylor, for allowing access to 'The Cardiff Transport Preservation Group' Archive, and to the dedicated voluntary staff of 'The Bus Archive' at Walsall, for allowing access to their extensive collection of material, and supplying me with numerous monochrome photographs.

Additionally, I would like to thank my friends and fellow bus enthusiasts, John Bennett, John Martin, Steve Powell, Robert Edworthy, Richard Evans, Simon Nicholas, Alistair Douglas, Don Jones (LTBPS), G. Mead, Andrew Jarosz, D. Gwyn John, Kevin Lane, P.S.A. Redmond, the late Roy Marshall, Peter Yeomans, John Wiltshire, R.H.G. Simpson, and Robert Mack, for use of their photographs and/or information.

Much other valuable information has come from material in the care of The National Archive, Companies House records, Glamorgan Archives, The PSV Circle, and the 'Welsh Bus & Coach monthly newsletter', with kind permission from David Donati.

Whilst every effort has been made to ensure the accuracy of the contents of this publication, no assurance is given or implied by the compiler, that complete accuracy has been achieved.

I must also point out that it has not always been possible to identify individual photographers. No discourtesy is intended through lack of acknowledgement, in view of which, I trust they will accept my sincere thanks.

CONTENTS

INTRODUCTION	9
A.E. & F.R. BREWER. 'BREWER'S MOTOR SERVICES Ltd'	19
THE 'NEW' A.E. & F.R. BREWER Ltd. UNDERTAKING	99
BREWER'S MOTOR SERVICES, VEHICLE DETAILS	133
BREWER'S MOTOR SERVICES, VEHICLE DISPOSALS	142
BREWER'S MOTOR SERVICES, PHOTOGRAPH INDEX	146

++++++++++++++++++++++++++

W.G. THOMAS. 'LLYNFI MOTOR SERVICES'	147
LLYNFI MOTOR SERVICES, VEHICLE DETAILS	237
LLYNFI MOTOR SERVICES, VEHICLE DISPOSALS	246
LLYNFI MOTOR SERVICES, PHOTOGRAPH INDEX	251

++++++++++++++++++++++++++

D.J. THOMAS. 'CREAM LINE (MAESTEG) Ltd'	252
WILLIAM JOHN. MAESTEG	260
FREDERICK JAMES JOHN. NANTYFFYLLON	261
GRIFFITH HUGHES. CAERAU	266
M.E. PRATT & SON. CAERAU	269
OTHER MAESTEG & DISTRICT COMPETITORS	271

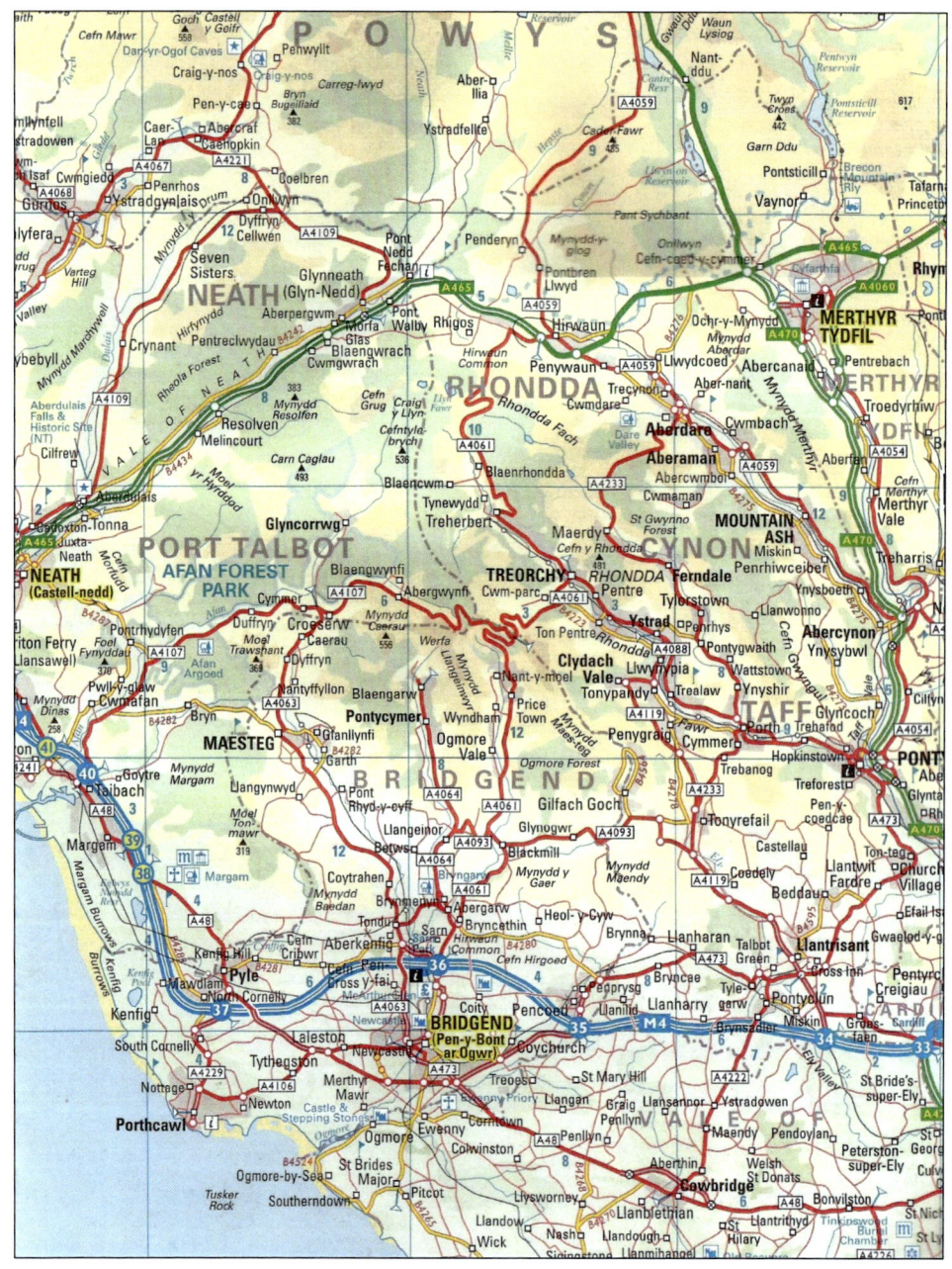

Above: This map shows the location of Maesteg, and the surrounding area mentioned in this story.

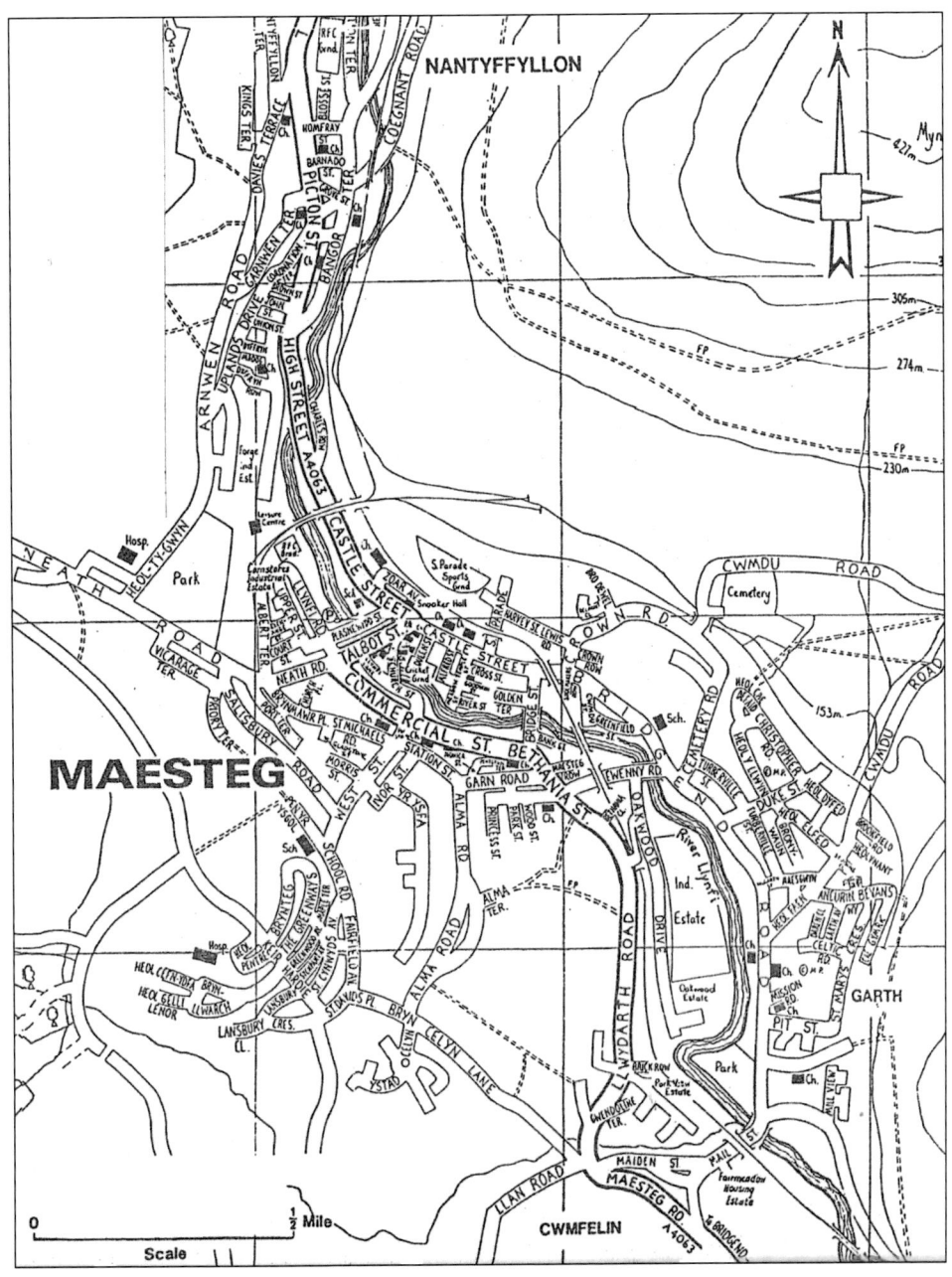

Above: Street map of Maesteg, and the district of Nantyffyllon.

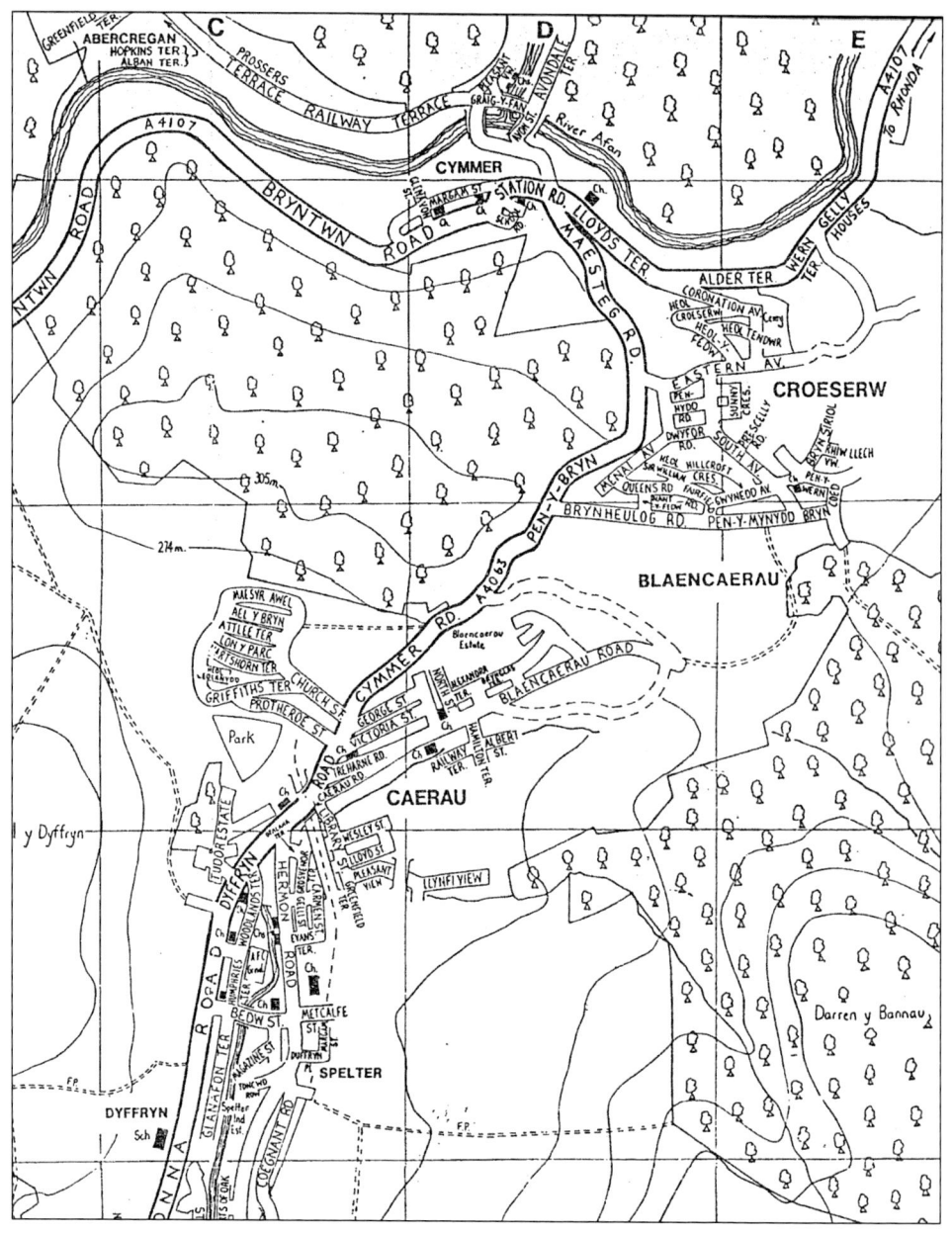

Above: Street map of Caerau, and the districts of Dyffryn, Blaencaerau, Croeserw, and Cymmer.

INTRODUCTION

The historical market town of Maesteg is situated at the northernmost end of the Llynfi Valley, in Mid-Glamorganshire, South Wales, surrounded by the neighbouring villages of Caerau, Dyffryn, and Nantyffyllon to the North, with Garth, Cwmdu, Llangynwyd (Llangonoyd), and Cwmfelin, to the South.

The surrounding mountains pay tribute to the valley's historical past in the mining industry, which sustained the inhabitants of the valley. By 1908, there were six collieries in the Maesteg area, Garth, Oakwood, Coegnant, Caerau, Maesteg Deep, and St Johns (Cwmdu), which was the last pit to close in the Llynfi Valley in November 1985.

A seventeen mile horse drawn railway called the Dyffryn Llynvi and Porthcawl Railway Company (DL&PR), was built between Pwll-Cawl (which became Porthcawl), and Garnlwyd (near Brynllynfi Colliery), in Caerau, and was completed in June 1828. The railway opened up the district, and in conjunction with transporting coal to the newly constructed Porthcawl Harbour, led to the formation of an Iron Foundry in the town. Maesteg soon became a prosperous industrial town with the collieries, two Ironworks, a Tinplate Works, and a Spelter (Zinc) Works. However, Iron making at Maesteg ceased in 1885.

The non-standard, 4ft 6inch gauge DL&PR railway introduced passenger traffic as early as 1836, which in turn offered local citizens, day excursions and holidays, to the Victorian seaside town of Porthcawl. In 1848, the DL&PR changed its title to Llynfi Valley Railway, and in 1861, the railway was converted to broad gauge, and became steam hauled.

The Maesteg Urban District Council was formed in 1894, after the Local Government England & Wales Act 1894, was introduced, and carried out their duty to licence Hackney Carriages and Omnibuses plying in their district, which was controlled by the local police inspector.

However, the Hackney Carriage and Omnibus licensing system adopted by the Maesteg UDC, was quite unique. Only two other local authorities are known to have had similar licensing practices for Hackney Carriages. The Maesteg Authority had licensed all private hire motor cars (taxis), of *any* seating capacity, as 'Omnibuses', until March 1920, together with charabancs, vans, and even lorries, provided they were equipped with bench type seating.

There was also no restriction to the amount of motor cars or drivers plying within the district, and the Licensing Authority's conditions stated that each motor car (taxi), was to operate on a registered stage carriage service route, and would operate the journey in the same way as an omnibus – to travel all the way to the end of the registered route, even if the passengers had already alighted, and upon arrival at its terminus, to form a queue, and in sequence pick up passengers for their return journey. Returning empty was not allowed.

In 1914, there were just two licenced Omnibus operators in the town, Edgar Thomas, of 19 Bridgend Road, Maesteg, and Messrs E. Morgan & Sons, of Caerau, who both paid the Council's Omnibus licence fees of 5 shillings (5/-), and a further 5/- each for Omnibus drivers licences. They were joined in April 1915, by David John Thomas, of 28 Talbot Street, Maesteg, who later formed 'Cream Line Services' in Maesteg. He was the elder brother of William George Thomas, of Llynfi Motor Services fame.

There were inevitably numerous anomalies and prosecutions in the early days, ranging from overloading, to unlicensed vehicles, and unlicensed drivers, besides racing, and 'short-cutting' the route.

By 1919, the demand for public transport in the Llynfi Valley had significantly increased, and a few more operators appeared on the busy Maesteg to Caerau route, i.e., David John Hamer of Caerau, Thomas Buckley of Maesteg, and Henry Charles Herbert & Sons, 100 Commercial Street, Maesteg.

In the meantime, the Great Western Railway Company refused the Council's request to put on extra late night trains, and retrospectively, the Council looked into the possibility of running their own electric tramcars in July 1919, but the plan was aborted due to its high cost. There was no alternative, the public had to be conveyed by road.

However, on 27th September, 1919, a national rail strike started, leaving the villagers of nearby Bryn, completely isolated. The 'Port Talbot' railway was their only means of transport within the valley, so William George Thomas, of 4 Exchange Street, Maesteg (brother of David John Thomas, operator of the Maesteg to Caerau service mentioned earlier), appeared on the scene with a motor car, and provided the villagers with an 'unlicensed' service between Bryn and Maesteg.

At this point in time, the village of Bryn had no direct road access to Cwmavon and Port Talbot. That road was still at planning stage. W.G. Thomas became a 'lifeline' to the villagers, who continued to support him when he began running the service legally after the rail strike was over. The story of W.G. Thomas' business, 'Llynfi Motor Services', is told on page 147.

Meanwhile, men that had learnt to drive whilst in World War 1 Army service, saw the potential to put their new skills into practice, and entered the transport business with an assortment of vehicles, including surplus World War 1 stock, to challenge their competitors. Most of them took out the necessary licences to operate the services legally, but the Council's strange bye-laws, combined with fierce competition, quickly finished them off. It became 'the survival of the fittest'. New operators were appearing and disappearing on a regular basis, and in 1920, there were no less than twenty licenced operators in the town, mostly single vehicle owners.

In June 1920, Griffith Hughes, of Llwydarth Road, Maesteg (later Blaenllynfi Hotel, Caerau), and Martha Ellen Pratt of Caerau, were two of the twenty new operators working the Caerau route. Martha Pratt had acquired the licence previously granted to David John Hamer. The Hamer family were closely linked to the Pratt family, and at one point shared the same address.

The list of operators increased annually until the trade depression of 1926-1938. During that period of acute poverty and large scale unemployment, the population of the Llynfi Valley decreased by almost a third, as many residents left the district to seek employment elsewhere.

On 15th February, 1921, the South Wales Commercial Motors Ltd., asked for permission to stand at the Town Hall Square, Maesteg, with a service emanating from Bridgend through to Caerau. Their offer to pay a mileage rate of 2d a mile was willingly accepted by the Council, and the Licensing Committee gave them permission to fix fare table, and timetable boards at their stand in Maesteg Bus Station, and stated 'they would give them assistance in the matter'.

H. R. EVANS & SONS'
Chars-a-bancs
SCALE OF CHARGES
FOR THE SUMMER SEASON 1920

The Char-a-banc is booked on the assumption that it is in order on the day booked, and the Proprietor does not accept any responsibility for loss, etc., due to unforseen breakage of any mechanical part.

	s.	d.		s.	d.
Tondu	2	6	Merthyr	14	0
Bridgend	3	0	Newport	14	0
Pencoed	5	6	Llanelly	15	0
Porthcawl	6	0	Chepstow (direct)	20	0
Ogmore, Garw & Nantymoel	6	0	Carmarthen	21	0
Garw to Ogmore	6	0	Wye Valley	22	6
Southerndown & Ogmore	6	0	Symonds Yat	24	0
Gilfach	6	0	Brecon	25	0
Cowbridge	6	0	Symonds Yat & Wye Valley	26	6
Cefn Cribbwr	6	0	Hereford	27	0
Llanharran	6	6	Gloucester	28	6
Aberavon	6	6	Builth	30	0
Llantwit Major	7	0	Cheltenham	31	0
Llantrisant	7	0	Aberystwyth	32	6
Tonyrefail	7	6	Bristol	40	0
Llwynypia	8	6	Fishguard	40	0
Neath	9	0	London	60	0
Cardiff, Penarth & Barry	10	0	Ascot	60	0
Pontypridd	10	0	Derby	70	0
Swansea	11	0	Blackpool	100	0
Glyn Neath	11	0	North Wales (tour 7 days)	100	0
Cardiff and Barry	12	6	Fortnightly Tours	160	0
Mumbles	12	6	Abergavenny	21	0
Mountain Ash	12	6			

Chars-a-bancs to be home by 10 p.m., if not 6d. per hour per passenger will be charged for waiting.

ENQUIRIES FOR BOOKINGS:

Central Garage, 15 Talbot St., Maesteg
Telephone 23.

Above: Charabanc operator, Henry Evans, bought a new AEC YC, 30 seat charabanc in July 1919, registered L 5048, and a Napier 20 seat Wagonette, registered L 5492, in October 1919. His last recorded vehicle was a Talbot Darraq, 5 seat motor car, registered NY 1289, acquired new in May 1922. However, after refusal of a licence to operate circular tours around Porthcawl, in May 1922, Mr. Evans terminated the charabanc business, and sold the Napier to A.E. & F.R. Brewer, Caerau, in July 1923. Porthcawl Council would only licence Hackney Carriage proprietors residing in that Parish. *(Courtesy Byron Gage).*

At the same time, the brothers Albert Edward Brewer, and Frederick Roland Brewer applied for their first omnibus licences. They were not exactly newcomers to the passenger carrying business, as they had been 'giving lifts' to people on their lorry, when they travelled between Caerau and Maesteg on their 'milk round' business. 'Brewer's Motor Services' soon became the largest passenger vehicle operator in the Llynfi Valley, and their history is dealt with separately, beginning on page 19.

Not far behind A.E. & F.R. Brewer on the Maesteg to Caerau route was William George Thomas of 'Llynfi Motor Services', who 'claimed' to have operated the Caerau route for a short while in 1921, but gave it up due to fierce competition. However, there is no record of W.G. Thomas licensing any routes, or vehicles, before March 1924, but it was known that he operated an unlicensed service from Maesteg to Bryn, during the railway strike of 1919.

Sydney T. Jenkins

(Nephew of the late Mr William Jenkins, Ironmonger), who has recently been Demobilised after FOUR YEARS SERVICE in the MOTOR TRANSPORT SECTION wishes to announce that he is

OPENING A

MOTOR GARAGE

FOR HIRING AND REPAIRS IN

Church Street, MAESTEG.

At the Rear of Mr Griffiths, Chemist.

THE

CHAR - A - BANC

HAS ARRIVED,

and is one of the finest on the road. As comfortable to ride as a private car.

Until Further Notice a TWICE DAILY Service will be run to PORTHCAWL as follows:

Leave Maesteg (Town Hall) **10** o'clock
Return Porthcawl **7 p.m.**

Leave Maesteg (Town Hall) **1.30** o'clock.
Return Porthcawl **9 p.m.**

Fare 5s. Children Half-Price.

Please Book Early.

Also open to arrange for Picnic Parties and Long Day Trips and Tours.

Apply at Messrs. JENKINS, 44 Commercial St., Maesteg

S. T. JENKINS'

Char-a-banc Trips

Saturday, July 9, BARRY Island
6/- return.   Leave Square 10 a.m.

Sunday, July 10,   Special Tour of Brecon & Abergavenny
Route—Via Neath, Pontardawe, Craig-y-Nos Cray Waterworks.
Return via Crickhowell, Gilwern, Abergavenny, Pontypool and Newport.
17/6 return.   Leave 7.30 a.m.

Tuesday, July 12,   PORTHCAWL
3/- return.   Leave Square 10 a.m.

Wednesday, July 13, WYE VALLEY
12/6 return.   Leave Square 8 a.m.

Book your seats at 18 Alfred Street.

The Glamorgan Advertiser.

Six months later in August 1921, an established Maesteg operator, Sydney Jenkins, of 18 Castle Street, Maesteg, asked for a Hackney Carriage licence for his 1919, AEC YC, 30 seat charabanc, registered L 5052. Jenkins, who changed his address continuously, did not operate local services, only charabanc outings as shown in the advertisements above.

Above: Hackney Carriages at Talbot Street, Maesteg, awaiting passengers outside Maesteg Town Hall, circa 1924. Left to right, **NY 3125** of D.J. Thomas, Maesteg, **NY 1879** of Elias Williams, Caerau, **NY 2485** of Thomas Lloyd, Maesteg, and **MC 7435** which is unidentified. The bus in the backdrop is probably a South Wales Commercial Motors' vehicle, working from Bridgend to Maesteg. *(Cardiff Transport Preservation Group collection).*

Above: This motor car, probably an Austin, fitted with a 'Stepney Spare Wheel' and acetylene lighting, was another example of the numerous motor cars running as 'Omnibuses' between Maesteg Town Hall and Caerau in the 1920s. *(Courtesy Byron Gage).*

Above: This unidentified Ford 'TT', was another vehicle licensed by the Maesteg UDC Licensing Authority, for service in the Maesteg area.
(Courtesy of Byron Gage).

Above: This 1920, Commer RC, **BO 3023**, owned by South Wales Commercial Motors Ltd., is seen here in 1921, receiving a thorough examination by the local police inspector, prior to its licensing by the Maesteg Licensing Authority.
(Byron Gage collection).

Another operator granted a licence to operate the Caerau route in February 1922, was Elias Williams, of Greenfield Terrace, Caerau, with a new Chevrolet, 5 seat tourer registered NY 1879. Elias only operated motor cars, and cancelled his licence (TGR 445/1), in April 1934.

In the meantime, the battle on the Caerau road intensified, and by mutual agreement with South Wales Commercial Motors, in October 1923, Brewer's asked the Licensing Committee for transfer of SWCM's licence, for the Maesteg to Caerau route. At the same meeting, M. David Morgan, of The Mason's Arms, Bryncethin, applied to run a bus service between Bridgend and Maesteg. That application was rejected, but in September 1924, he was granted a licence to run a new 26 seat bus between Bryncethin and Maesteg. A year later, David Morgan complained to the Licensing Committee that the SWCM were illegally running buses on his timetable. The Hackney Carriage Inspector investigated and no action was taken.

The battle for licences inevitably extended to an area West of Maesteg in February 1924, when William George Thomas, of 4 Exchange Street, Maesteg (later known as Llynfi Motor Services), applied for his first licences with the Maesteg, and Port Talbot Councils. His intention was to provide an omnibus service between the towns, when the long awaited new road between Bryn, and Ynysygwas (Cwmavon), near Port Talbot opened.

The Clerk of Port Talbot BC, immediately contacted Maesteg UDC, stating that his council favourably entertained the long standing application of The South Wales Transport Co, to ply for hire between Port Talbot and Maesteg. The Clerk also stated that W.G. Thomas' application was deferred, as they thought it a mistake to grant a licence to an individual who only had one or two conveyances.

The Maesteg Licensing Committee replied stating their council consider that licences should be granted to all applicants who undertake to maintain a regular service according to their respective timetables, and deferred the application of South Wales Transport, asking W.G. Thomas to submit his timetable. The issue was resolved in good time for the 'Grand Opening of Bryn Road'. Licences were granted to both applicants for a jointly operated service.

The operations of 'Llynfi Motor Services' are dealt with separately on pages 147 to 236.

On 3rd May, 1924, the new 'Bryn Road', classified B4282, was officially opened by the Minister of Transport, Mr Harry Gosling (January 1924 - June 1929). Civic dignitaries from Maesteg and Port Talbot local authorities were present at the ceremony, together with a local band, who were paid £5-0-0 for their services by Maesteg Council.

June 1924, saw a new Hackney Carriage Inspector take over at Maesteg, who modified the arrangements for 'standing cars and buses' plying for hire in the town. [1] The number of cars permitted to stand in Town Hall Square was limited to six, and a reserve stand for about twenty cars, in single file order, was formed in Castle Street. [2] Only two buses were allowed to stand in front of the Town Hall, others were to remain in Church Street, and when one bus departed, another would be allowed in front of the Town Hall. The system did not bode too well with the car drivers, who unsuccessfully met the council to discuss the new regulations.

Eleven months later in May 1925, a group of local bus proprietors asked the Council not to issue further licences for buses running between Maesteg and Caerau. The matter was ignored, and six weeks later another four new operators were granted licences for that route. Three of them fell by the wayside within twelve months, but Frederick James John, of 36 Barnardo Street, Nantyffyllon, quickly established himself, and much to the disappointment of SWCM Ltd, successfully gained a licence to run between Maesteg and Bridgend, in December 1925. Fred continuously defied everyone, including the Licensing Committee, and was constantly in trouble. His brother William John of 25 Alfred St, Maesteg, had established himself on the Maesteg to Caerau route since August 1920. More about them on pages 260-5.

Another newcomer in June 1925, was David William Griffiths of Llangynwyd, who traded as Griffiths Bros. The three brothers only ran motor cars, on a route between Maesteg Bus Station and Llangynwyd, and a workmen's stage carriage service to Cwmdu Colliery, 3 shifts daily.

The Licensing Committee then received an application from Joseph Jones & Co, of Huntspill House, Pontycymmer, asking to run a Friday and Saturday only bus service, from Blaengarw, in the adjacent Garw Valley, to Maesteg. The application was rejected on 15th December, 1925.

On 18th January, 1927, established omnibus operator, Thomas Buckley, of Caerau, asked for a licence to ply for hire between Maesteg Town Hall, and the Rose & Crown at Cwmfelin, via Castle Street, and Bridgend Road, with a 14 seat Crossley bus registered NK 5524, purchased from Premier Coaches, of Watford, Herts. That licence was also refused.

Fifteen months later, the Council's Sub-Committee met to consider new regulations and charges, to use the 'new' Bus Stand in the Market Ground. It was approved that [1] the stand be for BUSES only. [2] The Stand to be open as from 30th April, 1928. [3] A charge of 7/6d per week to be made for each bus. [4] The sub-committee were vested to make other necessary regulations for control of the new bus stand during the first fortnight. [5] The Market Inspector would supervise the stand, and be responsible for collection of tolls for the first fortnight. [6] A police sergeant to be posted on the stand on Monday, Friday, and Saturday of the first week.

In the meantime, the licensed 'Car Proprietors' were complaining about the new bus station arrangements, and the Sub-Committee met a week later to make further recommendations, which were approved and adopted on 15th May, 1928. They were [1] A charge of 1/6d per day to be made for any additional bus using the stand for the purpose of 'duplicating' the service of any particular proprietor. [2] That a charge for small cars using the stand to be 1/6d per car, per week. [3] That an account of fees owed by The South Wales Transport Co. Ltd., and the South Wales Commercial Motors Ltd., be forwarded to them.

Two days later, another meeting was held to discuss the new bus stand, where complaints were made by The South Wales Commercial Motors Ltd., Cardiff, and The South Wales Transport Co, Swansea, stating they considered the charge of 7/6d per bus, per week for the use of the bus stand, excessive. The Committee then recommended [1] that as from 21st May, 1928, the charges for buses using the stand be 5/- per bus, per week, and 1/- per bus, per day, for extra buses. [2] The charge for cars not carrying more than 7 passengers, be 1/- per week. [3] The amounts paid over and above these fees since inauguration of the parking place be refunded.

Further recommendations were made five days later: [1] that an alternative site for cars be sought after, within reasonable proximity of the Town Hall, and at Nantyffyllon. [2] that the accounts of The South Wales Transport Co Ltd., and South Wales Commercial Motors Ltd., be rendered monthly. [3] Charges for cars to be considered at next meeting (ongoing issue). Amendments [1 & 2] were approved and adopted at a meeting held on 5th June, 1928.

On 6th August, 1928, the Licensing Committee received an application from the Great Western Railway Company, to run omnibuses between Bridgend, Maesteg, and Caerau Railway Station. After consideration by the committee, the application was refused due to the fact that the applicant refused to provide a timetable.

The next two licence applications on 25th September, 1928, came from 'the rivals' F.J. John and SWCM. Frederick John asked to run a service over the Bwlch Mountain, from Maesteg to Treorchy, whilst SWCM asked to extend their existing Bridgend to Maesteg service to reach Treorchy and Upper Rhondda, or a separate service between Maesteg and Upper Rhondda via the Inter-Valley Road. Both operators were asked to submit timetables, and on 21st November, 1928, SWCM withdrew their application, in view of the gradient and nature of the ground on the Cymmer side of the mountain. It appears that F.J. John made the same decision!

At this particular point in time, however, Maesteg UDC agreed with Glyncorrwg Council, to bear half the cost of the preparation of plans for a proposed road from Caerau to Cymmer. As for the road within the Glyncorrwg Council's area, they were not prepared to bear any cost, as the proposed scheme would be of greater benefit for the residents of Glyncorrwg.

In May 1929, D.J. Thomas, Talbot Garages, Maesteg, applied for permission to run a bus service between Maesteg and Bridgend. At the same meeting, he complained of difficulties in obtaining satisfactory settlements for the issue of interchangeable return tickets from certain other operators on the Caerau route. Consequently, a meeting was called between the joint operators, where it was decided to abolish return tickets, in favour of reduced single fares.

However, the ongoing issue regarding bus stands, and car stands was revived on 16th July, 1929, when the Council's Sub-Committee recommended that the action of the Market Inspector, not enforcing charges to small cars using the stand, be approved, and confirmed that there was lack of suitable accommodation for cars on the stand. Fourteen days later it was decided that cars be allowed to stand at the lower end of Church Street.

On 1st August, 1929, a new company, Western Welsh Omnibus Co. Ltd., with headquarters at 253 Cowbridge Road West, Cardiff, was registered. This company was an amalgamation of South Wales Commercial Motors Ltd; Great Western Railway Co. Ltd., (Road Motor Services); Western Valleys Motor Services, and Lewis & James of Cross Keys. However, the new title, Western Welsh Omnibus Company, was used when they wrote to the Maesteg Council in July 1929, to complain about rival competitor F.J. John obstructing the Maesteg Bus Stand with 'out of service' buses. They also stated they were not prepared to make a joint timetable for the Maesteg-Bridgend service, but would provide frames showing their own timetables.

On 16th January 1930, Western Welsh OC, notified the Maesteg Licensing Committee, that they had decided to purchase the omnibus business of F.J. John, subject to the Council agreeing to the transfer of licences. The application was refused, but four weeks later the Licensing

Committee discussed that issue again, together with the long standing applications of Messrs Brewer, and D.J. Thomas, for licences on that same route between Maesteg and Bridgend. The Licensing Committee decided to grant all three operators licences to run a jointly operated service between Maesteg and Bridgend, with five conditions: [1] The application by Western Welsh for transfer of the licences formerly held by F.J. John, for Maesteg to Bridgend, is granted on condition that the company undertake to run a half hourly service, instead of a 20 minute service as present. [2] Due to congestion on the Maesteg to Caerau route, the application to transfer F.J. John's licence, was not granted. [3] D.J. Thomas, and Messrs Brewer were informed that the Council would be prepared to grant them these licences to run a service between Maesteg and Bridgend, making a 15 minute service with Western Welsh. [4] The operators on the Maesteg to Bridgend service were asked to agree to an interchange of tickets. [5] The licences to the new operators will be granted on condition they undertake to observe Trade Union rates of wages, and hours, for employees.

Western Welsh objected to these conditions because Penybont RDC (Bridgend), had granted a licence at their end without conditions. Four weeks later, the Maesteg Licensing Committee asked D.J. Thomas, and Messrs Brewer, whether they still desired to run a service between Maesteg and Bridgend, before they held a conference with Penybont RDC, and Bridgend UDC. Both operators confirmed their long standing desire, and the process began.

Maesteg UDC, gave notice on 6th May, 1930, that the talks with Penybont and Bridgend Councils were unsuccessful, and with the apparent desire of both authorities to virtually grant a monopoly to Western Welsh, representations would again be made with a view to obtaining licences for D.J. Thomas, and Messrs Brewer. In the event of their continued refusal, an appeal would be made with the Ministry of Transport to hold an inquiry.

Maesteg Council continued representing Messrs F.J. John, D.J. Thomas, and A.E. & F.R. Brewer at the Traffic Commissioners hearings, in support of their request for a licence to operate Maesteg to Bridgend (for further information, see notes of F.J. John, pages 261-5).

In the meantime, Maesteg UDC gave their Licensing Committee a new title. As from May 1930, it was known as the Omnibus & Hackney Carriage Committee, and at this point in time, activity became extremely busy, with operators clambering to gain extra services before the introduction of the new Road Traffic Act (1930). Besides, there were the usual characters running un-roadworthy, unlicensed, and dirty vehicles, on irregular services. However, it kept the Hackney Carriage Inspector really busy, with several prohibitions and prosecutions.

When timing issues worsened in September 1930, the Committee investigated the viability of time recorder clocks, to introduce a proper checking system, ensuring timetables were adhered to. They introduced a new set of rules and timetables for a trial period of 3 months, and stated that if it was unsuccessful, the Council would consider operating a Municipal service. The Clerk was then instructed to obtain prices for 20 seater, and larger omnibuses, and to report upon the powers of the Council to operate a Municipal Bus Service, but nothing became of it!

When omnibus licensing passed to the Ministry of Transport in April 1931, there were still nine omnibus operators, and ten Hackney (car) operators currently licensed with Maesteg UDC, all of which were operating stage carriage services.

AE & FR BREWER

BREWER'S MOTOR SERVICES LTD

The roots of this well renowned omnibus company can be traced back to the late 19th century, when the brothers, Albert Edward Brewer, and Frederick Rowland Brewer, were born to Ann (Annie), and Albert Harry Brewer. They were born at Blaenllechau, (near Ferndale), in the Rhondda Fach Valley, South Wales, on 10th May, 1895, and 26th May, 1898, respectively.

Their father, Albert Harry Brewer (born in Manchester, 1872), was a collier at one of the collieries in the Rhondda Fach Valley, but later in life, changed his vocation to work on the railway. His change of job brought the family to a smallholding at 5 Pontrhyd-y-Cyff Road, Llangonoyd (Llangynwyd), Maesteg, in 1910, where at the age of 15, Albert Edward Brewer was working as a 'Colliery Weigher', whilst his younger brother Fred, was still at school.

Fred left school a year later, to work at another local colliery, known as the Gellyhir Level, near Lletty Brongû, Llangonoyd.

However, the family moved on from Llangonoyd, to live at 45 Coegnant Road, Caerau, and by 1917, Fred was married, and living at 21 Hermon Road, Caerau. By 1918, the brothers started a dairy business known as 'Brynkwood Dairy', from 21 Hermon Road, with a milk round in the village of Llangonoyd (Llangynwyd). Fred Brewer stated that in the beginning, he worked regular night shifts at the colliery, and afterwards collected milk from Brynllywarch Farm, to sell on their milk round, which at first was worked by horse and cart. There were no milk bottles in those days, customers supplied their own jugs, and the milk was ladled out of large milk churns carried on the back of their cart. Milk was a halfpenny per Gill (quarter pint), in those far gone days.

After WW1 ended, Fred relinquished his job at the pit in order to concentrate on the dairy, and extended his back yard to accommodate extra dairy equipment. Eventually the brothers built up their sales to around 200 gallons of milk per day, covering the whole of the Llynfi Valley.

When they travelled down the valley to Llangynwyd in those early days, people were asking for lifts on their milk cart, so they started giving lifts for a couple of extra pennies, and soon realised there was potential there to run a passenger service. They then bought a second-hand, Scottish built, Arrol-Johnston motor lorry for their deliveries, which was also used to transport milk to the creamery when the 1919 rail strike stopped local farmers sending their milk by rail.

In due course, the Arrol-Johnston was replaced by a new Ford 'TT' lorry, registered L 9530, to Albert Brewer, of 45 Coegnant Road, in May 1921. Both Lorries were used to give lifts to local people, but the Ford was destroyed by fire just five months after delivery.

Nevertheless, in order to carry passengers legally, Albert Brewer received his first Hackney Carriage licence for the Ford lorry on 9th August, 1921, together with a drivers licence from the Maesteg Licensing Authority.

The main form of transport in the valley at this particular time was the railway, but there were as many as 20 taxi operators running some form of 'stage carriage service' between Maesteg and Caerau, many of them unlicensed. They appeared, and disappeared just as quickly.

The first omnibus purchased by A.E. & F.R. Brewer, arrived in February 1923. It was a new 20hp Maxwell, 14 seater, painted maroon and black, and built in Detroit, USA. This was registered NY 2484, and in the mornings, during their milk deliveries, it carried milk churns at the front, and passengers at the back. After mid-day, it operated the Maesteg (Town Hall) to Caerau service until 11.00 pm, driven by Fred Brewer, while his brother Albert took the fares. The 'free for all' service had no timetables, and Fred recalled 'we would take about 12 to 14 shillings between mid-day and 11.00 pm, with the fare at tuppence ha'penny (2½d)'.

The Maxwell was soon repainted maroon and yellow, and later repainted blue and white, which became their standard livery of the period.

Competition was *extremely* intense, with numerous incidents, but in July 1923, a 1919 Napier 25/30hp, 20 seat charabanc, registered L 5492, was purchased off Henry R. Evans, of 15 Talbot St, Maesteg. Evans abandoned his tours business, after Porthcawl UDC refused him licences to operate circular tours around Porthcawl, in conjunction with day excursions from Maesteg.

A month later, competitor South Wales Commercial Motors complained to the Licensing Committee of 'Piracy' on the Maesteg to Caerau route, and A & F Brewer were questioned about it. SWCM had been competing on the Maesteg to Caerau route since March 1921, as an extension of their Bridgend to Maesteg service, and were unhappy with the amount of competitors they had. On 4th October, 1923, however, SWCM reluctantly, offered their share of the Caerau route to A & F Brewer, which was approved by the Licensing Authority.

Above: A.E. & F.R. Brewer's first omnibus, a Maxwell 20 hp, 14 seater, registered **NY 2484**, which was purchased new in February 1923. The chassis was built in Detroit, USA, but the bodywork was built in the UK.   *(Courtesy Byron Gage).*

Above: The second omnibus acquired by A.E. & F.R. Brewer, was this 1919 Napier 25 hp charabanc, **L 5492**, with a 20 seat body built by its previous owner, H.R. Evans, of Maesteg. It was acquired from Evans when he ceased operating in July 1923, and remained with Brewer, painted blue and white, until July 1935. *(Courtesy Byron Gage).*

Above: In January 1924, this 'RAF' type Leyland 36/40 hp, **NY 4610**, with Leyland 'Edinburgh style' 30 seat body, arrived at their dairy in Hermon Street, Caerau. It had an unladen weight of 4 ton 19¾ cwt, and was painted into the company's blue & white livery. It's pictured here outside the Duffryn Hotel, in Coegnant Road, Caerau. *(Courtesy The Bus Archive/Roy Marshall).*

Above: A later view of the 'RAF' type Leyland, **NY 4610**, after it had been fitted with pneumatic tyres. The advantage of having pneumatic tyres was more than a softer ride, as the vehicle's speed limit was increased from 12 mph to 20 mph, besides, vehicles fitted with pneumatic tyres were entitled to cheaper road fund tax. This bus served the business well until its withdrawal in 1932. It was sold in February 1936, for continued use as a lorry, to W.H. Ford & Sons, of 9 Thomas Street, Swansea.
(Courtesy of The Bus Archive).

At this point in time, their Napier and Leyland buses were garaged near the Duffryn Hotel in Caerau. They bought their petrol each day in 2 gallon cans, costing one shilling and ten pence (1/10d). A very costly method, so in March 1931, they asked the local authority for permission to install a 500 gallon petrol tank in their back yard, at 17b Hermon Street, Caerau. Permission was granted.

By 1925, they employed part-time drivers to assist them on the bus route, as they were by then running three buses, and the milk round.

Another new competitor, Frederick James John, of Barnardo Street, Nantyffyllon, arrived on the scene in June 1925, after receiving his first Hackney Carriage licence from the Licensing Committee. After several attempts, he was granted a licence to challenge A & F Brewer, and all other competitors on the controversial Maesteg to Caerau route in December 1925. He was also granted a licence to run a joint service with SWCM, from Maesteg to Bridgend via Garth. Frederick John was the younger brother of William John, an established operator on the Maesteg to Caerau route, and a brother to Arthur Price John, who was also a car operator on the Maesteg to Caerau route. Further details of the controversial Frederick John, and his enterprise, can be found on pages 261-5.

The following year saw the 1926 General Strike in the UK, from 4th May, to 12th May, 1926. The strike, called by the General Council of the TUC, had been instigated by the mine owners' intention to reduce miners' wages, and increase their working hours. The strike was generally settled within nine days, but some miners struggled on until November before returning to work, defeated! It was a tough period for the Brewer brothers too, as they ran up a debt of £3,000 by helping the miners. They provided a bus to 'The Glee Party' from Maesteg, and drove it around West Wales, with the party singing to raise money for the 'soup kitchens'. Fred Brewer stated: 'My brother and I took it in turns. We would be away for six weeks at a time, and everyone would sleep in the bus, sending the money back home to buy food. We had a primus stove and cooked breakfast for the 23 people on board, buying our own food, and paying for the petrol as we toured around'.

After all that, the brothers concentrated solely on the bus company, and sold their milk round to clear their debt. However, the after effects of the General Strike, and the Recession which followed, continued for many more years.

In the meantime, A.E. & F.R. Brewer formed an association with C.K. Andrews Ltd., of Uplands Garage, Swansea, who held a franchise for 'Morris' vehicles, amongst other marques, for West Glamorganshire and East Carmarthenshire. There was an assortment of no less than eight Morris's in the Brewer's fleet by 1937, new and second-hand, some of which were bodied at C.K. Andrews' very comprehensive workshops. In addition to Morris, the company later bought Dennis buses through the C.K. Andrews' franchise, and at least one was bodied by C.K. Andrews.

In March 1928, Griffith Hughes, an established motor car operator, and competitor on the

Above: Morris Commercial chassis were not very popular amongst the omnibus owners of South Wales, but in 1927, Brewer's bought their first two buses of Morris manufacture, followed by many more. However, this Morris Commercial, 14 seat bus, is unidentified, but is probably **WN 3424**, fitted with bodywork built by C.K. Andrews, of Swansea. *(Courtesy Byron Gage)*.

Above: This 1927, Morris Commercial 'TX', 14 seater, registered **DE 5861**, originated from the fleet of J.R. Ford, Pembroke Dock, but arrived with Brewer's in December 1929. It was acquired from 'The Blue Bus Co', of Neath. *(Byron Gage collection).*

Caerau route, exchanged his only motor car, for a second-hand S.P.A. (**S**ociedad **P**iemontese **A**utomobili) bus, registered BX 5196. At the same time, the Council were preparing to charge bus and taxi proprietors a fee to use Maesteg Bus Station, as stated on page 16.

On 1st May, 1928, A & F Brewer asked the Licensing Authority for permission to run a new local circular bus service, from Maesteg (Town Hall), to Garth, via Llwydarth Road, but it was refused. They reapplied twice again in May, but were refused on the grounds that SWCM were already serving the lower road and the district of Garth, with four trips a day on their Bridgend service, which was jointly operated with Frederick John, of Nantyffyllon.

However, two weeks later, Fred John asked for a similar route through the district of Garth, terminating at the Cross Inn, Cwmfelin. That service was unfairly granted to him, and at the same Licensing Committee meeting, Fred was reprimanded for his unacceptable punctuality on the first journey each morning to Bridgend. Passengers were regularly late for work!

In revenge, Brewer's immediately applied for two more new licences; Maesteg to Bridgend, and Maesteg to Cwmfelin Square, or Llangynwyd School. After investigation, the Licensing Committee decided to grant Brewer's a circular service, via Castle Street, Bridgend Road, and Llwydarth Road, and vice-versa, for a period of three months, pending its sanction by Penybont RDC. Fourteen days later, A & F Brewer were asked to suspend putting that service into operation, as there was an objection from Penybont RDC Licensing Authority!

At the same time, the Great Western Railway Co. (Road Motor Services dept), asked for a licence to run buses between Bridgend and Caerau Railway Station, via Maesteg Bus Station. Their application was refused, due to the fact that Brewer's application for Maesteg to Bridgend was refused by Penybont RDC.

On 14th May, 1929, it was D.J. Thomas (Cream Line Services) turn to ask for a licence to run between Maesteg and Bridgend, and that was also deferred. At the same meeting, A.E. & F.R. Brewer asked for permission to run a 15 minute service from George Street, Caerau, to Maesteg, via Hermon Road, and Coegnant Road. This was granted to Brewer's, but fourteen days later, Fred John asked for a licence to run the same route, which was refused.

Fred John, was at the centre of every dispute involving Caerau route operators, and on 4th July, 1929, complained to the Licensing Committee of unfairness, regarding Brewer's receiving the above licence. However, the Committee discussed the issue, and as Brewer's were the *only* applicant at the time of issue, rightfully allowed the new route to continue.

Around the same time, complaints were made against A.E. & F.R. Brewer, and Frederick John, for allowing buses to stand on the highways at Hermon Road, and Picton Street, Caerau, respectively, for long periods both day and night. This matter was passed to the police, and within a short space of time, A.E. & F.R. Brewer acquired new garage premises at Caerau.

On 1st August, 1929, competitors South Wales Commercial Motors Ltd., together with the Great Western Railway Co. Ltd. (Road Motor Services), Western Valleys Motor Services Ltd., and Lewis & James, of Cross Keys, amalgamated to form a new company named Western Welsh Omnibus Services Ltd., (WWOC), which was based in Cardiff.

Western Welsh immediately made complaints to Maesteg UDC, regarding vehicle congestion at Maesteg Bus Station, and made a statement saying they would not include the services of 'authorised' joint operators on their timetables.

Above: This Morris 'Viceroy' touring coach, would have been a very modern addition to the fleet in its time, fitted with curtains.
(Byron Gage Collection).

> ### Before Making Selections
> consult
> ### Brewers' Motor Service
>
> B.M.S.
>
> TO SECRETARIES AND ORGANISERS.
>
> The Season for TRIPS AND TOURS is upon us once more. You will soon be thinking of making arrangements for your ANNUAL OUTING. May we help in giving practical advice in the important matter of arranging a comfortable and enjoyable trip? A secretary's work is made easier when he knows that reliable information can be had at request. B.M.S. have had many years' experience in the arranging of Tours and Trips, and feel naturally proud that they have in past years been favoured with the patronage of all kinds of Organisations in the district and further afield.
>
> May we help you in the arranging of your Next Trip? Inquiries and estimates are free, with no obligation whatsoever. Tell us what you wish to have done, and our experience is at your service. On the receipt of a postcard or 'phone message, our Mr. Brewer will call upon you and give all information.
>
> **B.M.S. stands for Beautiful Modern Saloons**

The matter of congestion at Maesteg Bus Station was already in hand with the local authority, who decided that the stand for Hackney Carriages (motor cars), be moved to the lower end of Church Street, allowing the Town Hall Bus Station to be available for buses *in service* only.

A month later in September 1929, motor car competitors David Hamer, and Fred Pratt, of Caerau, asked for permission to run 'extra omnibuses' on the Caerau to Maesteg route, whilst D.J. Thomas was again asking for a licence to run a bus service between Maesteg and Bridgend. All applications were temporarily deferred, together with the application made by Western Welsh, in January 1930, when they proposed to purchase Frederick John's complete business, subject to Council approval.

In February 1930, D.J. Thomas asked the Maesteg Licensing Committee for a meeting regarding his pending licence application for Maesteg to Bridgend. The Committee agreed to a meeting, and invited A & F Brewer also, as they were joint applicants for a Maesteg to Bridgend service. Also present was a representative from Western Welsh OC, who was still asking for the transfer of Frederick John's licences.

The Committee decided that due to congestion on the Maesteg to Caerau route, WWOC would only be granted transfer of Fred John's Maesteg to Bridgend licence, with a proviso that they adjust their timetable to accommodate D.J. Thomas, and Messrs Brewer on the route too, and agree to inter-available return tickets, with trade union rates of wages and hours for their employees.

This decision triggered off a lengthy dispute between Maesteg, Bridgend, and Penybont Councils, as Penybont RDC had allegedly granted the licence solely to WWOC, without consultation with Maesteg UDC, but two months later, Maesteg Licensing Committee relaxed their decision, allowing WWOC a half hourly service between Maesteg and Bridgend.

On 6th May, 1930, the Council's Hackney Carriage Inspector made a visit to Brewer's depot and carried out an examination on three Morris buses. Bus AX 8743 was satisfactory, whilst buses UT 694 and DE 5861 were defected, and after minor repairs, were later reinstated.

At the next Committee meeting on 6th May, 1930, it was decided that the continued refusal of Penybont and Bridgend Councils, to grant licences to D.J. Thomas, and Messrs Brewer, was bias, as it was the apparent desire of those Authorities to grant a monopoly to Western Welsh. It was then decided that discussions should be held again, and in event of their continued refusal, an appeal be made to the Ministry of Transport to hold an enquiry. However, the licence applications were again refused.

In the meantime, the newly formed Maesteg Council's 'Omnibus & Hackney Carriage Committee', withheld the transfer of Fred John's licences to Western Welsh OC.

Simultaneously, due to continued animosity, and irregular running on the Caerau service, the Council considered providing roadside time recording clocks, to inaugurate a proper checking system, and to ensure timetables were being fully observed. They also drew up a proposed timetable, reproduced below, giving all current operators a share of the service. The timetable

Maesteg & Caerau Bus Service
Via Picton Street & Tonna Road

LEAVE MAESTEG. THOMAS	W. JOHN	BREWER	HUGHES	PRATT	BREWER	THOMAS	F. JOHN	BREWER
8 30	8 40	8 50	9 0	9 10	9 20	9 30	9 40	9 50
10 0	10 10	10 20	10 30	10 40	10 50	11 0	11 10	11 20
11 30	11 40	11 50	12 0	12 10	12 20	12 30	12 40	12 50
1 0	1 10	1 20	1 30	1 40	1 50	2 0	2 10	2 20
2 30	2 40	2 50	3 0	3 10	3 20	3 30	3 40	3 50
4 0	4 10	4 20	4 30	4 40	4 50	5 0	5 10	5 20
5 30	5 40	5 50	6 0	6 10	6 20	6 30	6 40	6 50
7 0	7 10	7 20	7 30	7 40	7 50	8 0	8 10	8 20
8 30	8 40	8 50	9 0	9 10	9 20	9 30	9 40	9 50
10 0	10 10	10 20	10 30	10 40	10 50	11 0	11 10	11 20
LEAVE CAERAU.								
		8 20	8 30	8 40	8 50	9 0	9 10	9 20
9 30	9 40	9 50	10 0	10 10	10 20	10 30	10 40	10 50
11 0	11 10	11 20	11 30	11 40	11 50	12 0	12 10	12 20
12 30	12 40	12 50	1 0	1 10	1 20	1 30	1 40	1 50
2 0	2 10	2 20	2 30	2 40	2 50	3 0	3 10	3 20
3 30	3 40	3 50	4 0	4 10	4 20	4 30	4 40	4 50
5 0	5 10	5 20	5 30	5 40	5 50	6 0	6 10	6 20
6 30	6 40	6 50	7 0	7 10	7 20	7 30	7 40	7 50
8 0	8 10	8 20	8 30	8 40	8 50	9 0	9 10	9 20
9 30	9 40	9 50	10 0	10 10	10 20	10 30	10 40	10 50
11 0	11 10							

P.S.—On Fridays and Saturdays, a six minutes' service is run, commencing at 4.30 p.m. from Maesteg and Caerau.
Sunday Service starts at 1.20 p.m.

was approved by all Maesteg to Caerau operators, except Fred Pratt, William John, and his notorious brother, Frederick James John. Bus stops along the route were also set up and agreed upon by all, except the three rebels, Fred Pratt, William John, and Fred John.

However, it was reported that Fred John had failed to comply with the new timetables, and was 'defiant'. As a result, the Hackney Carriage Inspector was asked to inspect his omnibuses.

All this hassle, was in the interim period between the passing of the Road Traffic Act 1930, and its introduction in April 1931, a period when operators all over the country were scrambling to obtain extra licences and extra services.

At this particular point, Maesteg Council deferred all new applications, and in September 1930, reconsidered their previous intention of establishing a Municipal Bus Service.

Fred Pratt, D.J. Thomas, and Caradog James of Nantyffyllon, were just three Maesteg operators that tried to take advantage of the Licensing Committee, to run extra buses during weekends before the licensing rules changed, but they were refused.

By January 1931, there were still nineteen Hackney licenced operators running in Maesteg, albeit, eleven of which were car operators. Brewer's had the largest fleet, with seven licensed vehicles operating from a new address, 17b Hermon Rd, Caerau. The car operators inevitably disappeared throughout the 1930s, whilst Brewer's expanded into the coaching scene.

The next major item in the company's history was the introduction of the Road Traffic Act 1930. This Act of Parliament passed in August 1930, removed all aspects of passenger vehicle licensing from the local authorities, giving the Ministry of Transport's Traffic Commissioners full control of Public Service Vehicles, passenger services, and their licensing in Great Britain.

These Traffic Commissioners, with the power vested in them, brought about improved operating conditions, an adherence to timetables and stability of fares. All stage carriage and express service routes had to be licenced, and the granting of such licences, which had previously been under the jurisdiction of the local authorities, were then only obtainable through the Ministry of Transport's Traffic Commissioners. Licences to drive and conduct a public service vehicle also became the Traffic Commissioners responsibility. Under this new licensing system, all public service vehicle operators were issued with operator numbers, by which they were identified. Consequently, the number issued to Messrs A.E. & F.R. Brewer, was TGR 267.

After implementing the new Traffic Act fully, in April 1931, every omnibus operator had to re-apply to the new authority for renewal of each Road Service Licence held, and re-apply annually thereafter. Likewise, any changes to services, times, fares, or new routes, all had to be applied for, and the licences would only be granted when approved by the Traffic Commissioners. However, the first licences A.E. & F.R. Brewer applied for under the new Traffic Act in April 1931, was to renew the licences held by them during the past year on the following routes, in accordance to their published timetables, which were:-

TGR 267/1   **Caerau (Blaenllynfi Hotel)** to **Maesteg (Town Hall/Bus Station)**
             via: Tonna Road.

TGR 267/2 Caerau (Church) to **Maesteg (Town Hall/Bus Station).**
via: Hermon Road, and Coegnant Road.

TGR 267/1 and 267/2, were both granted on 8th July, 1931. TGR 267/1 was issued with the special conditions listed below, whilst TGR 267/2 was issued with the same conditions, except for condition 1 (the authorised route).

[1] *The authorised service shall be operated on the following route only: via Castle Street, High Street, Picton Street, Tonna Road, and Caerau Road.*
[2] *The standing places for this service shall be the Hackney Carriage stands at Caerau, Nantyffyllon, and Maesteg, which are at present being used by vehicles operating between Caerau and Maesteg.*
[3] *The licensee shall only be entitled to take up passengers at the said standing places at Caerau, Nantyffyllon, and Maesteg, respectively, and shall not be entitled to take up passengers at any other place.*
[4] *The licensee shall immediately after setting down passengers, take his place in rotation at one of the said standing places, and vehicles on the stand shall at all times leave in order of rotation.*
[5] *Not more than six vehicles shall be allowed to stand at the same time at any of the said standing places, and if upon arrival at any of the said standing places, the licensee finds that there are already standing at such standing places, the authorised number of vehicles the licensee shall proceed to one of the other standing places.*
[6] *The fares to be charged on the said route shall be as follows:-*

Maesteg (Town Hall Square) to Stand at Caerau.	2½d.
Maesteg (Town Hall Square) to Stand at Nantyffyllon	1½d.
Stand at Caerau to Stand at Maesteg	2½d.
Stand at Caerau to Stand at Nantyffyllon	1½d.
Stand at Nantyffyllon to Stand at Maesteg	1½d.
Stand at Nantyffyllon to Stand at Caerau.	1½d.

[7] *The licensee in operating the authorised service, shall observe and conform to all statutory and other legal observations, and provisions, applying thereto, or to vehicles used on the service, and in particular, shall not permit any such vehicle to be driven at a speed which is dangerous to the public, and shall not race with other vehicles used on the same route.*
[8] *Not more than one vehicle shall be used by the licensee in operating this service, and that vehicle shall be of the type set out by the licensee in his application for this licence or a similar type.*
[9] *The licensee shall at all times observe and carry out the instructions of the Inspector of Police in charge at Maesteg, and shall observe and perform all directions and instructions issued by the Maesteg UDC, and in the event of any disagreement as to such instructions and directions, the matter in dispute shall be referred to the Traffic Commissioners for the South Wales Traffic Area.*
[10] *The licensee shall observe and perform all the terms and conditions of an agreement in writing dated the 15th day of October, 1931, and signed by him/her.*

On 17th June, 1931, the following 'new' licence was asked for:-

TGR 267/3   To run a group of **Excursions & Tours**, all within the SWTA, starting from **Caerau**, **Nantyffyllon**, and **Maesteg**. *Tours to run from Easter to September inclusive. Maximum number of vehicles to be used on this group of tours in any one day is two.*

This licence application was heard at a public inquiry held at Bridgend County Court, on 8th July, 1931, together with TGR 267/1 and 267/2. All three were granted, and on the same day, they submitted another two 'new' licence applications:-

TGR 267/4   **Excursions & Tours**, starting from **Abergwynfi (Great Western Railway Hotel)**, including Glyncorrwg, and Cymmer. *Tours run throughout the year. The licence was granted 16/10/1931, to start from* **Abergwynfi** *only.*

TGR 267/5   **Maesteg (Bus Station)** to **Bridgend (Bus Station)**, via Tondu.

The application TGR 267/5 above, had been an ongoing issue between Brewer's, WWOC, and the joint Licensing Committees of Maesteg, Bridgend, and Penybont, for over 3 years, as mentioned earlier in the story. Ultimately, A & F Brewer were refused the licence.

In the meantime, joint 'omnibus' operators of the Maesteg to Caerau service, A & F Brewer, D.J. Thomas, Griff Hughes, F.J. John, Wm John, and Fred Pratt, finally signed the joint timetable agreement in August 1931, and faithfully agreed to observe the rules at all times.

By May 1933, licence TGR 267/2 received a modification: 'With liberty to extend the service as far as George Street, Caerau', and in September 1947, it was modified again with an extension beyond George Street, to serve Brynheulog, a new housing estate at Caerau.

Above: This unidentified Dennis Lancet II, is thought to be **WN 6788**, which was bodied by C.K. Andrews, Swansea, or **WN 7598**, bodied by Dennis Bros. Both were supplied new to Brewer's, by C.K. Andrews, Swansea, in 1934.   *(John Jones collection).*

Above: This post war line up of vehicles outside Brewer's depot in Caerau, consists of (*left to right*), Dennis Lancet II, **WN 6788**, bodied by C.K. Andrews of Swansea, and retro-fitted with an AEC 7.7 diesel engine; Mulliner bodied Bedford OB, **JTG 622**; and pre-war Duple bodied AEC 'Regal', **ENY 712**, by then fitted with 35 bus seats. *(Copyright The Bus Archive / Roy Marshall).*

The next licence application, submitted on 13th June, 1934, TGR 267/6, was again a rather controversial one, asking to provide a 'new' stage carriage service between Maesteg (Bus Station) and Neath (Victoria Gardens). The application is described below:

267/6—**Brewers Motor Services**, of Caerau Garages, Caerau, for a road service licence to provide a new service of stage carriages between Maesteg (Bus Station) and Neath (Victoria Gardens) via Caerau, Cymmer, Duffryn Rhondda, Cynonville, Pontrhydyfen, and Cimla. The service is to be run all the year round. The frequency of the service will be : Daily, leave Maesteg 7.10 a.m. and every 2 hours until 9.10 p.m. ; leave Neath 8.10 a.m. and every 2 hours until 10.10 p.m. Additional journeys, Fridays and Saturdays : Leave Maesteg 1.40, 3.40, 5.40, 7.40, and 9.40 p.m. ; leave Neath 2.40, 4.40, 6.40, 8.40, and 10.40 p.m. Sundays : Leave Maesteg 1.10 p.m. and every 2 hours until 9.10 p.m. ; leave Neath 2.10 p.m. and every 2 hours until 10.10 p.m.

Fare table :—

	Neath	Cimla	Cefnaeson	Farmers	Efail C.	Efail F.	Pontrhydyfen	Oakwood	Cynon	Duffryn	Cymmer	Caerau	Maesteg
Neath	—	3d.	8d.	10d.	10d.	1/-	1/-	1/2	1/6	1/8	1/10	2/2	2/3
Cimla	2d.	—	—	—	7d.	9d.	9d.	11d.	1/3	1/5	1/7	1/11	2/1
Cefnaeson	5d.	2d.	—	—	—	—	—	—	—	—	—	—	—
Farmers	6d.	3d.	1d.	—	—	—	—	—	—	—	—	—	—
Efail C.	7d.	4d.	2d.	1d.	—	—	—	8d.	9d.	1/-	1/4	1/6	
Efail F.	8d.	5d.	3d.	2d.	1d.	—	—	—	—	—	—	—	—
Pontrhydyfen	9d.	6d.	4d.	3d.	2d.	1d.	—	6d.	8d.	10d.	1/2	1/4	
Oakwood	10d.	7d.	5d.	4d.	3d.	2d.	1d.	—	5d.	6d.	8d.	1/-	1/2
Cynon	1/-	9d.	7d.	6d.	5d.	4d.	3d.	3d.	—	—	6d.	10d.	1/-
Duffryn	1/1	10d.	8d.	7d.	6d.	5d.	4d.	4d.	1d.	—	4d.	8d.	10d.
Cymmer	1/3	1/-	10d.	9d.	8d.	7d.	6d.	6d.	4d.	3d.	—	4d.	6d.
Caerau	1/6	1/3	1/1	1/-	11d.	10d.	9d.	9d.	7d.	6d.	3d.	—	—
Maesteg	1/8	1/5	1/3	1/2	1/1	1/-	11d.	11d.	9d.	8d.	5d.	—	—

Return fares in bold type.

Cheap evening fares : Cynon-Maesteg 9d., Duffryn-Maesteg 8d.

The application TGR 267/6 was supported by Maesteg UDC, but the objectors were numerous:- Western Welsh OC; South Wales Transport Co; Blue Bird Services, Skewen; Neath Omnibus Co; and the Great Western Railway Co. The first public hearing regarding it, was held at Neath County Police Court, on 11th October, 1934, but was adjourned several times. The ongoing case must have been a record, as the licence was not finally refused until three and a half years later, in January 1938.

In November 1933, local Llangynwyd operator, David Thomas, asked for a stage carriage service licence between Cwmfelin (Full Moon), and Caerau (School Road), via Maesteg Hospital. Thomas' application was successfully objected to by A & F Brewer, WWOC, and South Wales Transport.

On 23rd January, 1935, WWOC re-applied for Fred John's licences, TGR 584/1, his share of the joint service between Maesteg Bus Station, and Caerau (Blaenllynfi Hotel), and TGR 584/3 E & T's starting from Caerau. (These two licences were finally refused on 19th January, 1938).

267/1—**Brewer's Motor Services (A. E. and F. R. Brewer** T/A), Caerau.
343/1—**Griffith Hughes**, Blaenllynfi Hotel, Caerau.
354/1—**William John**, 17, St. Michael's Road, Maesteg.
432/1—**David John Thomas (Cream Line Services)**, 47, Neath Road, Maesteg.
584/1—**Frederick James John**, 65, Picton Street, Nantyffyllon.
1862/1—**Fred Pratt**, Riverside Cottage, Castle Street, Maesteg, for modification of the road service licences in respect of the services of stage carriages between Maesteg (Bus Station) and Caerau (Blaenllynfi Hotel) via Castle Street, High Street, Picton Street, Tonna Road, and Caerau Road ; and
267/2—**Brewer's Motor Services (A. E. and F. R. Brewer** T/A), Caerau, for modification of the road service licence in respect of the service of stage carriages between Caerau (Church) and Maesteg via Hermon Road and Coegnant Road.

To introduce the following revised time table :—

Caerau—Maesteg :—

Operator	A.E. & F.R. Brewer	A.E. & F.R. Brewer	A.E. & F.R. Brewer	Griffith Hughes	A.E. & F.R. Brewer	Fred Pratt	A.E. & F.R. Brewer	A.E. & F.R. Brewer	A.E. & F.R. Brewer	D.J. Thomas	A.E. & F.R. Brewer	F.J. John	A.E. & F.R. Brewer	A.E. & F.R. Brewer	A.E. & F.R. Brewer	D.J. Thomas	A.E. & F.R. Brewer	W. John
	a.m.	a.m.	noon.	a.m.	a.m.	a.m.	a.m.	a.m.	a.m.	a.m.	a.m.	p.m.	a.m.	a.m.	a.m.	a.m.	a.m.	a.m.
Caerau depart ..	10 0	8 15	..	8 30	10 6	8 36	8 42	..	8 54	9 0	9 6	..	9 18	9 30	9 36	9 42	..	9 54
	..	..	..	10 18	..	10 30	10 36	10 42	..	10 54	11 0	11 6	..	11 18	..	11 30	11 36	11 42
	..	11 54	12 0	12 6	..	12 18	..	12 30	12 36	12 42	..	12 54	1 0	1 6	..	1 18	..	1 30
	p.m.	p.m.		p.m.	p.m.	p.m.		p.m.	p.m.	p.m.		p.m.	p.m.	p.m.		p.m.	p.m.	p.m.
	1 36	1 42	..	1 54	2 0	2 6	..	2 18	..	2 30	2 36	2 42	..	2 54	3 0	3 6	..	3 18
	..	3 30	3 36	3 42	..	3 54	4 0	4 6	..	4 18	..	4 30	4 36	4 42	..	4 54	5 0	5 6
	..	5 18	..	5 30	5 36	5 42	..	5 54	6 0	6 6	..	6 18	..	6 30	6 36	6 42	..	6 54
	7 0	7 6	..	7 18	..	7 30	7 36	7 42	..	7 54	8 0	8 6	..	8 18	..	8 30	8 36	8 42
	..	8 54	9 0	9 6	..	9 18	..	9 30	9 36	9 42	..	9 54	10 0	10 6	..	10 18	..	10 30
	10 36	10 42	..	..	..	10 12	..	..	..	..	..	10 45	..	..	..	11 5	..	..

Operator	A.E. & F.R. Brewer	A.E. & F.R. Brewer	A.E. & F.R. Brewer	Griffith Hughes	A.E. & F.R. Brewer	Fred Pratt	A.E. & F.R. Brewer	A.E. & F.R. Brewer	A.E. & F.R. Brewer	D.J. Thomas	A.E. & F.R. Brewer	F.J. John	A.E. & F.R. Brewer	A.E. & F.R. Brewer	A.E. & F.R. Brewer	D.J. Thomas	A.E. & F.R. Brewer	W. John
	a.m.	a.m.	p.m.	a.m.	a.m.	a.m.	a.m.	a.m.	a.m.	a.m.	a.m.	p.m.	a.m.	a.m.	a.m.	a.m.	a.m.	a.m.
Maesteg arrive ..	..	8 27	..	8 42	8 48	8 54	..	9 6	9 12	9 18	..	9 30	..	9 42	9 48	9 54	..	10 6
	10 12	10 18	..	10 30	..	10 42	10 48	10 54	..	11 6	11 12	11 18	..	11 30	..	11 42	11 48	11 54
	p.m.	p.m.		p.m.		p.m.	p.m.	p.m.		p.m.	p.m.	p.m.		p.m.		p.m.	p.m.	p.m.
	1 48	12 6	12 12	12 18	2 12	12 30	..	12 42	12 48	12 54	..	1 6	1 12	1 18	..	1 30	..	1 42
	..	1 54	..	2 6	2 12	2 18	..	2 30	..	2 42	2 48	2 54	..	3 6	3 12	3 18	..	3 30
	..	3 42	3 48	3 54	..	4 6	4 12	4 18	..	4 30	..	4 42	4 48	4 54	..	5 6	5 12	5 18
	..	5 30	..	5 42	5 48	5 54	..	6 6	6 12	6 18	..	6 30	..	6 42	6 48	6 54	..	7 6
	7 12	7 18	..	7 30	..	7 42	7 48	7 54	..	8 6	8 12	8 18	..	8 30	..	8 42	8 48	8 54
	..	9 6	9 12	9 18	..	9 30	..	9 42	9 48	9 54	..	10 6	10 12	10 18	..	10 30	..	10 42
	10 48	10 54	..	..	..	10 24	..	..	..	..	..	10 52(Nantyffylon)	..	..	..	11 17	..	..

*—Via Hermon Road and Coegnant Road.

From 4.30 p.m. on Fridays and Saturdays buses will run at 6 minute intervals via Caerau Road and Tonna Road. The Sunday service begins at 1.30 p.m.

Above: In March 1937, the six joint operators of the Caerau to Maesteg service, asked to modify the timetable to a frequency of up to a six minute interval, as shown above. Their request was granted on 17th March, 1937.

As already mentioned, Western Welsh had been trying to absorb Frederick John's business since January 1930, and on 6th February, 1935, re-applied for his third licence, TGR 584/2, Maesteg to Bridgend. This was a service jointly operated between F.J. John and WWOC, and after a hearing held on 20th February, 1935, the licence was finally granted in May 1935, and incorporated into WWOC's Bridgend to Maesteg service, TGR 441/29.

Five months later in October 1935, Brewer's, together with WWOC, and the Great Western Railway Co., successfully opposed another competitor's application. It was the application of David Elias Owen, of 71 Jersey Road, Blaengwynfi, for an Excursions & Tours licence, starting from Blaengwynfi.

On 31st March, 1937, two of the joint operators on the Caerau service, Griffith Hughes, and D.J. Thomas (Cream Line Services), applied for permission to introduce inter-available weekly tickets on their services only. The tickets were a choice of a 12 tripper (12 single journeys) 1/6, or a weekly ticket with an unlimited number of journeys for 2/6. Brewers successfully objected to their request, as the conditions of their licence stated inter-availability of return tickets between all six joint operators. Their application was refused on 15th September, 1937.

At this point in time, A & F Brewer were extremely unfortunate. First of all, there was a fire on 30th September, 1937, where they lost a Studebaker, 20 seat coach, built on an American goods vehicle chassis, and fitted with a petrol engine.

Eight months later, in May 1938, they lost another six buses and coaches in a fire that destroyed their Duffryn garage.

The vehicles lost in that garage fire were a new Dennis Lancet II, registered BTX 599; a Gilford Hera, registered WG 2315; a Morris Commercial 'TX', registered WN 3424; an unidentified Dennis coach; a Morris 'Director'; and a Morris 'Viceroy'.

Following the fire, the company hired buses from other operators, in order to keep the wheels turning, and are reputed to have bought six replacement vehicles from Praill's Motors Ltd., the dealers at Hereford.

However, only five replacement vehicles are recorded, suggesting that the sixth damaged vehicle was either not replaced, or was repaired.

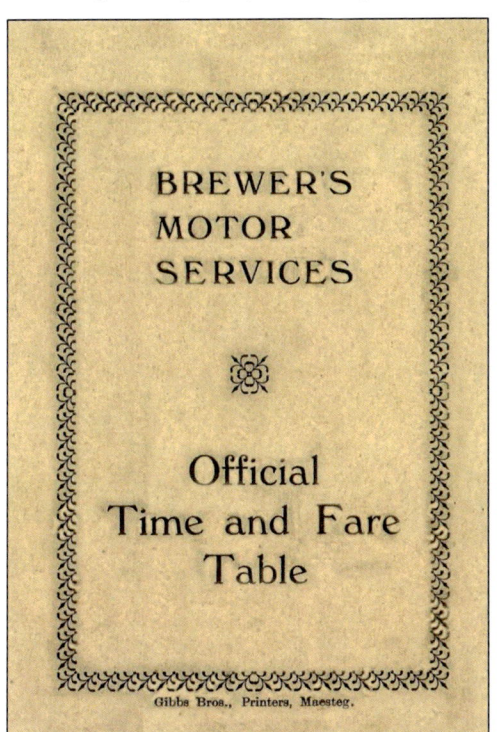

Brewer's timetable and fare table.   *(Courtesy Byron Gage).*

Afterwards, all operations moved from their fire damaged garage near the Duffryn Hotel, in Coegnant Road, to the site of the old Caerau Laundry, at the top of Blaencaerau Road, Caerau, where new garages were built.

Above: ENY 712 was an AEC Regal O662, with Duple C37F coachwork, acquired new in June 1939. It was a replacement for one of the fire damaged vehicles lost in May 1938, and later in its working life was downgraded to DP35F, with the fitting of bus seats. It's seen here in this view at the depot, sometime before withdrawal in May 1959. *(Copyright The Bus Archive/Roy Marshall).*

World War 2 was declared on 3rd September, 1939, and within a few days the company were compelled to introduce emergency timetables on their services, in order to conserve fuel when fuel rationing began on 16th September. Services were reduced to a very basic frequency – merely maintaining services to accommodate workers. Licences to operate Excursions & Tours were suspended, in order to conserve fuel and rubber, as were the licences for Express Carriage services three years later. During the war years, licences to provide extra services, or any modification to existing services, had to be applied for as usual, but were only authorised by the Ministry of Defence (Ministry of War Transport), and referred to as Defence Permits.

In addition to this, War Department Officials toured all bus and coach operators in Britain during July 1940, requisitioning buses and coaches for military use, usually taking the operators newest buses and coaches. In Brewers Motor Services' case, two Duple bodied Dennis Lancet II coaches were commandeered, and returned after the hostilities were over.

It appears that no less than eight Defence Permits were issued to Brewers Motor Services, by the regional Transport Commissioner, to operate services of special need during the hostilities. Records of these services have not been kept – maybe for security reasons, but were known to be numbered TGR 267/7 to 267/14. Only four of those licences have been traced, and are listed opposite.

TGR 267/7	**Caerau** to **Maesteg (Ewenny Road Factory Site)**.	
	Workmen's stage carriage service.	
TGR 267/8	**Maesteg** to **Coegnant Colliery (Caerau)**. *Workmen's stage carriage.*	
	via: Station Street, Castle Street, and Coegnant Road.	
	Previous licence granted to H.J. Uphill, Caerau (TGR 1222/3).	
TGR 267/11	**Maesteg (Bus Station)** to **Garth**. *Stage carriage service.*	
	via: Castle Street, and Bridgend Road.	
	Previous licence granted to Cream Line (Maesteg) Ltd.	
	(TGR 3427/2).	
TGR 267/13	**Maesteg (Bus Station)** to **Llangynwyd Church**. *Stage carriage service.*	
	via: Commercial Street, Llwydarth Road, and Cross Inn.	

There is a possibility that the missing numbers were issued to operate the Caerau – Maesteg services of competitors William John; Fred Pratt; Frederick John; Griffith Hughes; and Cream Line Services. Those five jointly operated services were absorbed by Brewer's under MoWT direction, in order to conserve fuel, and were eventually incorporated into Brewer's service.

Fred Pratt, and William John's services were first to be absorbed in 1940, followed by Frederick John in July 1943, with Griffith Hughes following in 1945. Last of the competitors on that route, D.J. Thomas (Cream Line [Maesteg] Ltd), surrendered his share of the service in June 1945, but continued operating a workmen's service alongside his haulage business.

D.J. Thomas retained his other licences, and bought two new Bedford OB coaches in 1947, but his licence renewal for a workers service to the Margam Carbide Works, was refused in July 1947. He then made a deal with his sister-in-law, Martha Thomas, the proprietor of Llynfi Motor Services, who purchased his last two remaining coaches, and the E & T licence, before he sadly passed away on 11th April 1948.

Returning to June 1943, Brewer's received their first wartime vehicle, a Guy Arab II, which had been authorised by the Ministry of War Transport. The perception of a double deck vehicle during times of austerity were incredible, but the Traffic Commissioner decided that roads around the Caerau area were unsuitable, and refused authority for operation. Brewer's retained its registration, FNY 420, and sold the bus to 'United Welsh Services' of Swansea, in September 1943, who reregistered it DWN 370.

This is the only view available of Brewer's 1934 Albion 'Victor' **AWA 486**, acquired in January 1941.   *(Courtesy B. Gage).*

Above: The company received no less than eight of these wartime, Bedford OWBs, all of which were bodied by Duple. They gave excellent service of between eight and twenty-one years, five being retro-fitted with Perkins 'P6' diesel engines. Numerically the last one purchased (at £810), was **FNY 895,** in February 1945. This was one of the five, retro-fitted with a Perkins P6 engine, and saw service until January 1966, working colliery services in its final years. *(Copyright The Bus Archive / Roy Marshall).*

Above: Maesteg Bus Station is the backdrop for this view of **FTG 479**, an AEC 'Regal' 0662, with Harrington B36F bodywork, which was the second of a long line of AECs in the Brewer's fleet. It arrived new in April 1946, and gave faithful service until mid-1960. Following its sale, it was converted into a farm lorry by September 1961. *(John Jones collection).*

Immediately after the hostilities were over, competitors Western Welsh applied for a new local service in Maesteg. Their application for a 7 day service, TGR 441/394, dated 14th August, 1946, was to run a circular stage carriage service, from Maesteg Bus Station, to the Maesteg Housing Estate, via Garn Road, Station Road, and the Housing Estate, returning via Neath Road, to the Bus Station. It was granted on 6th November, 1946.

In addition to Brewer's annual licence renewals on 19th March, 1947, they made one 'new' licence application:-

TGR 267/15   **Abergwynfi** to **Bridgend Trading Estate**.   *Workmen's stage carriage.*
via: Cymmer, Caerau, Maesteg and Aberkenfig.
Weekly fares: Abergwynfi & Cymmer, 12/8d, Caerau & Nantyffyllon, 8/8d.

It was granted on 28th April, 1947, for **Caerau** to **Bridgend Trading Estate**, with one special condition:
[1] Not to pick up passengers after leaving Iron Bridge, Maesteg, and on return journeys, not to drop off passengers before Iron Bridge, Maesteg.

Note: This licence was modified 16th April, 1952, diverting one vehicle via Brynmenin Factory Site, (Hunt Partners Ltd), instead of Aberkenfig. Changed to Express Carriage 11th June 1952.

One licence modification asked for on 3rd September, 1947, was to extend service TGR 267/8, to include Caerau Colliery. The modification was granted on 12th November, 1947.

Above: A splendid view of this suposedly rebodied AEC 'Regal III', **GTX 162**, pictured in Maesteg Bus Station, working a service to Caerau via Coegnant Road. **GTX 162**, was one of a pair new to the company in August 1947, with Duple 'A', C35F coachwork. It was withdrawn in July 1955, and in June 1959, it was rebuilt by Neath Coachworks, to B37F layout, whilst its twin, GTX 163, was withdrawn in August 1959. This was finally withdrawn in July 1968.   *(Copyright The Bus Archive / Roy Marshall).*

Above: Another view of the AEC 'Regal III' **GTX 162**, which was rebuilt by Neath Coachworks of Cilfrew, Neath, in 1959. The lines of its cab and front roof dome reveal its origins as a Duple 'A' body, which point out a rebuilt body. *(John Jones collection).*

Above: 'Brewers on tour'. Pictured here are **GTX 363**, a 1947 AEC 'Regal', with Harrington C33F coachwork, and a pair of identical Duple 'Vista' C29F bodied Bedford OBs, **HTG 528** dating from July 1948, and **GTG 438** dating from May 1947. The list price of a Bedford OB with Duple 'Vista' coachwork in 1948, was £1,325-10-0. They were the backbone of numerous fleets in Britain, large and small, from eary post-war days, until well into the 1960s. *(Courtesy of Byron Gage).*

Above: The sixth AEC 'Regal' purchased by Brewer's was this '0662' type, **HTG 129**, fitted with Harrington C33F coachwork. This one arrived in May 1948, and was pictured here on lay-over at the Coach Park, Barry Island, near Cardiff, working an excursion to the famous seaside resort in the 1950s. This particular coach was withdrawn in 1961.   *(John Jones collection).*

Right: Another view of the AEC 'Regal' '0662 type', **GTX 363**, which had splendid Harrington C33F coach-work, complete with rear 'Dorsal Fin'.
This coach was new to Brewer's in September 1947, and was withdrawn without trace, in 1961.
(Byron Gage collection).

Having 'seen off' all their competitors on the Caerau to Maesteg route, the company decided in February 1948, to withdraw the special workmen's weekly tickets issued on that service, which created a great deal of animosity with the travelling public.

The Maesteg Council intervened, and asked Western Welsh to introduce a bus service to Caerau, stating that the Caerau Miners Lodge Committee had already passed a resolution to that effect. They pointed out that Brewer's were taking advantage of their position, and there was much dissatisfaction over it, as passengers were now having to pay the full rate each day.

Brewer's promised to restore the workers' weekly tickets, but failed to honour their promises, so the Council met again to discuss the issue. The matter was discussed, together with an issue regarding would be passengers finding it impossible to be accommodated onto buses at intermediate stops between Caerau and Maesteg, on inward journeys to Maesteg. The Caerau Miners Lodge again asked the Council to apply to Western Welsh to extend their Bridgend – Maesteg service to reach Caerau, but their request was declined due to the licensing laws.

The worker's weekly tickets however, were not reinstated!

The following short period stage carriage service licence was issued in July 1948:-

TGR 267/Sp/1   **Caerau** to **Bridgend**, via Maesteg.   *31/7/1948 to 7/8/1948 only.*
On the occasion of the National Eisteddfod held at Bridgend.

Above: Tilling Stevens chassis were quite popular amongst South Wales operators, but the history of this particular TSM D60A7 is not very definitive. Glamorganshire registered **ANY 166**, in April 1935, it was new to D.O. Jones, t/a Jones Bros, West Street Garage, Gorseinon. D.O. Jones passed away in 1936, and his widow licensed the business for a year, but transferred it to Ivor John Summers, of the same address, in September 1937. It arrived with Brewer's *by July 1948*, probably long before, via the War Department. However, it is seen here with Brewer's at an unknown location, carrying its original Plaxton C32F body. It received a new Longford body, built to C33F layout, in 1949, which is pictured opposite.   *(John Jones collection).*

Above: This view of the 1935 Tilling Stevens D60A7, **ANY 166**, was taken at Maesteg Bus Station, sometime after it was rebodied by Longford Coachworks, to C33F layout in 1949. Not a good investment really, as it was withdrawn in December 1953, with no further trace, probably scrapped.
(D.A. Jones / LTBPS).

Above: The ubiquitous Bedford OB. 12,693 Bedford OB chassis were built between 1945 and 1951, besides an additional 73 produced before the outbreak of war in 1939. They could be found on every road in Britain, and were operated by most operators, large and small. **JNY 273**, seen here at Maesteg, was bodied by Mulliner, to Duple design, with B31F layout. It was new to Brewer's in April 1949, and sold to a private Cardiff owner in 1961, for caravan conversion, but the project was abandoned, and the vehicle was dumped in a field near Cardiff, still complete as a bus.
(John Jones collection).

Above: Seen here at Maesteg Bus Station, awaiting passengers for an excursion to the seaside resort of Porthcawl, is **JNY 770**, an immacultely presented, AEC 'Regal III', with the attractive lines of Harrington C33F coachwork. It was one of seven Harrington bodied Regals in the fleet, and arrived in June 1949, giving excellent service until July 1963. It's quite possible that the Bedford OWB alongside, is standing by to duplicate the excursion, in the event of an overload. *(Copyright The Bus Archive/Roy Marshall).*

Above: A one off in the fleet was this Maudslay 'Marathon III', **JTG 34**, fitted with Burlingham C33F coachwork. This was also new to Brewer's in June 1949, and was withdrawn in February 1963. *(Copyright The Bus Archive / Peter Yeoman).*

Above: JTG 854 was another AEC 'Regal III' to join the fleet in 1949, but this was fitted with 35 seat Duple 'A' coachwork. It's seen here, en route for the 'Collier's Paradise', Porthcawl. *(John Jones collection).*

Above: This is another view of the the Maudslay 'Marathon III', **JTG 34**, pictured opposite. Its chassis was basically an AEC Regal III. It was merely badge engineering, after Maudslay were absorbed by AEC. *(Copyright The Bus Archive / Roy Marshall).*

Above: Another splendid view of an immaculate Harrington bodied AEC 'Regal III', **JTG 901**. This was one of three Regals delivered to the company in March 1950, ready for the new coaching season, but unlike its sisters, this one's livery scheme is different. With respect, it had cream front mudguards when new. *(Copyright The Bus Archive / Roy Marshall).*

Above: Harrington's delightful coachwork was also carried on AEC 'Regal III', **JTX 152**, pictured here. The rear dorsal fin, fitted as standard to this style of coachwork, was a credit to the craftsmanship delivered by the famous Hove coachbulders.
(John Jones collection).

Above: Numerically last of the 1950 'Regal IIIs' received by the company, was **JTX 153**, seen on the left of ths view. It's accompanied here by AEC 'Regal III', **JTG 901**, delivered in the same month, March 1950, and AEC 'Regal' **HTG 129**, delivered in May 1948. All three were bodied by Thomas Harrington Coachworks, Hove, East Sussex. *(Copyright Byron Gage).*

Above: **JTX 358**, on the left of this view, was the penultimate 'new' Bedford OB purchased by Brewer's in March 1950, and carried Mulliner B31F bodywork. It is seen here in 1960, after sale to Porthcawl Recreations Ltd, 'Coney Beach' Porthcawl, for staff transport, to the Coney Beach Amusement Park. It's accompanied here by Porthcawl Recreations' Duple bodied Bedford OWB, **VTX 644**, which was a former 'Royal Navy' vehicle. *(Copyright unknown. John Jones collection).*

In the period from 1948-51, there were no new licence applications, but in March 1950, the following short period licence was issued, and became an annual request:-

TGR 267/Sp/3 **Maesteg (Bus Station)** to **Maesteg (Cemetery)**.
The service is to run on Saturday and Sunday, 1st and 2nd April, 1950, only. Half hourly service on both days.   Fare 3d single.

A year later, in March 1951, the request for a short period licence was repeated:-

TGR 267/Sp/4 **Maesteg (Bus Station)** to **Maesteg (Cemetery)**,
via: Castle Street, and Cemetery Road, *17th and 18th March, 1951, only.*

Returning to 1947, plans were drawn up for a new Steelworks to be built at Margam, Port Talbot. Planning was granted, and the new Steelworks, known as Abbey Works, was built in phases, and formally opened by its owners, 'The Steel Company of Wales Ltd.' on 17th July, 1951. When it became fully operational in 1953, it became the largest steel producing complex in Europe.

In the meantime, the Brewer family saw a huge potential there to expand their service network. Creating a very bitter dispute, in an already restrained relationship with neighbouring Llynfi Motor Services, they submitted the following licence application on 5th December, 1951:-

TGR 267/16 **Caerau & Nantyffyllon** to **Port Talbot (Abbey Works)**,
via: Maesteg, Bryn, and Taibach.
Workmen's stage carriage service.
Monday to Friday, 4 x return journeys daily, Saturdays, 1 x journey.

Within a few days, Llynfi Motor Services reciprocated, and submitted an application to modify their existing Maesteg (Town Hall), to Port Talbot (Abbey Works) service, to start from Caerau (Square), instead of Maesteg (Town Hall).

Both operators lodged objections against each other's applications, and a hearing was held at the Crown Court, of Swansea, Guildhall, on Monday 28th January, 1952, where Brewer's licence application was refused, and Llynfi's licence modification was granted.

However, their bitterness continued indefinitely, and in fact, Brewer's submitted an objection against Llynfi's request for a revision of timetable on the Caerau to Abbey Works route, six weeks later, on 5th March, 1952.

This was purely bitterness, as Llynfi's service did not interfere with any of Brewers' services.

Additionally, Brewer's increased their early morning journeys from Caerau to Maesteg by five, in order to stop Llynfi picking up prospective passengers on that section of route. That figure was reduced to four extra journeys per day four weeks later.

In April 1952, another annual short period licence was issued as follows:-

TGR 267/Sp/5 **Maesteg (Bus Station)** to **Maesteg (Cemetery)**,
via: Castle Street and Cemetery Road, *5th and 6th April, 1952, only.*

Above: In post war times, Brewer's had a penchant for the AEC chassis, and their 1951 delivery included **KTG 764**, pictured here. Its 30ft long body was built locally by Longford Coachworks, to B40F layout.   *(Copyright The Bus Archive / Roy Marshall)*.

Above: **KTX 741** was the last AEC 'Regal III' purchased by the company, and arrived in May 1951, fitted with this fully fronted, FC37F, Longford body. It was withdrawn in May 1965, and sold without trace.   *(Copyright The Bus Archive / Roy Marshall)*.

Above: The third vehicle delivered in May 1951, was **KTX 742**, a very early Bedford SB, with Duple 'Vega' coachwork, unusually fitted with 33 bus seats. Seen here on Commercial Street, Maesteg, it was later retrofitted with a Perkins P6 diesel engine, and ran until February 1966. After withdrawal, it was sold for further service, to A.G. Reed, Bridgend. *(Copyright A.J. Douglas).*

Above: The company's first underfloor engined vehicle, was **LTX 170**, an AEC 'Regal IV' with B44F bodywork, built by the famous Charles H. Roe coachworks in Leeds. It was delivered in April 1952, and ran until July 1967. *(Copyright John Bennett).*

Above: The second AEC 'Regal IV' delivered to Brewer's, was **LTX 470**, in May 1952, fitted with Duple 'Ambassador' C41C coachwork. It is pictured here at Cardiff Civic Centre, and was withdrawn from service in July 1972. *(John Jones' collection).*

Above: **MNY 335** was the last AEC 'Regal IV' delivered to the company in December 1952. This particular one was also bodied by Roe Coachworks, to B44F layout, and became an exhibit on the Maudslay Stand, of the 1952 Commercial Motor Show, where it carried a 'Maudslay' badge. 'Maudslay' were taken over by AEC in 1948, and afterwards, the only vehicles assembed at Maudslays Coventry plant were 100% AEC. Although, the name was retained until 1950, there were some badge engineered Maudslays produced afterwards, basically to give AEC extra stand space at Motor Shows. *(John Jones' collection).*

In the period from March 1953, to December 1953, the following licences were asked for:-

TGR 267/Sp/6   **Maesteg (Bus Station)** to **Maesteg (Cemetery)**,
via: Castle Street, and Cemetery Road.   *Stage Carriage.*
Special short period licence issued for 28th and 29th March, 1953, only.

Stage carriage licence asked for on 22nd July, 1953:-

TGR 267/17   **Caerau** to **Bridgend Trading Estate**,
via: Nantyffyllon, Maesteg, Llangynwyd, Tondu, Aberkenfig & Bridgend.
For the conveyance of workpeople employed at the Avon Tyre Co. Ltd., The Trading Estate, Bridgend.   *3 x shifts per working day.*
Fares between Maesteg, and Angelton House (Penyfai), to the Bridgend Trading Estate, to be the same fares as authorised to WWOC, on their service between Maesteg and Bridgend Trading Estate, (TGR 441/385).
This application was WITHDRAWN on 16th September, 1953.

On 22nd July, 1953, applications to *vary conditions* of licences were asked for:-

TGR 267/3   **Excursions & Tours** starting from Caerau, Nantyffyllon, and Maesteg.
The modifications were: Excursions to Cardiff, Newport, and Swansea, shall only be operated for theatrical performances, sporting events, and other special events, and in addition, on 12 occasions a year for general purposes such as shopping. Max number of vehicles on any one day on the group to be 20. Max number of vehicles on any one day on any one tour to be 7.

TGR 267/4   **Excursions & Tours** starting from Abergwynfi, Glyncorrwg and Cymmer.
The modifications asked for were the same as TGR 267/3 above.

Both applications were objected to by Llynfi Motor Services, and the Traffic Commissioner decided NOT to vary the conditions attached to these licences, on 16th September, 1953.

However, three months later, Brewer's applied to take over three of the four workmen's stage carriage service licences held by David Thomas, Llangynwyd, which are recorded as:-

TGR 267/18   **Llangynwyd** to **Cwmdu Colliery,**
via: Cwmfelin, Llwydarth Road, and Garth.
(Previous licence granted to D. Thomas, Llangynwyd, TGR 1069/1).

TGR 267/19   **Maesteg (Llwydarth Road Post Office)** to **Cwmdu Colliery**,
via: Bethania St, Ewenny Rd, Park Site, Talbot St, Castle St, Bridgend Rd, and Heol Faen. *(Previous licence granted to D. Thomas, TGR 1069/8).*

TGR 267/20   **Maesteg** to **Bridgend Trading Estate**,
via: Llangynwyd, Coytrahen, Tondu, Aberkenfig, Sarn, and Penyfai.
(Previous licence granted to D. Thomas, Llangynwyd, TGR 1069/11).

TGR 267/18, 19, and 20, were all granted on 3rd February, 1954, but in the meantime, three special short period licences were issued, in order to continue running those services:-

TGR 267/Sp/7   **Llangynwyd** to **Cwmdu Colliery.**   Period 7/12/1953 to 30/1/1954.

TGR 267/Sp/8   **Maesteg** to **Cwmdu Colliery**.   Period 7/12/1953 to 30/1/1954.

TGR 267/Sp/9   **Maesteg** to **Bridgend Trading Estate**. Period 7/12/1953 to 30/1/1954.

Above: A fine pair of Leyland PSUC1/1 'Tiger Cubs' at Maesteg Bus Station, with identical Weymann 'Hermes' B44F bodywork. On the right is Brewer's **OTG 600**, new in July 1954, working a 'local hop' to Llangynwyd Church, whilst Western Welsh **HUH 24**, new in October 1953, is working another 'local hop' to the Maesteg Housing Estate.   *(Courtesy The Bus Archive/Roy Marshall).*

Above: Another vehicle with Weymann 'Hermes' body was **OTG 601**, but this was built on an AEC 'Reliance' chassis. It arrived in July 1954, and was the first of a long line of AEC 'Reliances' in the fleet, giving the company 20 years service before its withdrawal in 1974. It was photographed here at Maesteg Bus Station, en route to Caerau.   *(Courtesy The Bus Archive / Roy Marshall).*

Above: Also purchased in July 1954, along with the Leyland 'Tiger Cub' and AEC 'Reliance' pictured on the previous page, was a pair of Duple (Midland) B40F bodied Bedford SBOs. One of the pair, **OTG 547**, is seen here en route for Llangynwyd Church, with Western Welsh **HUH 24** (1024), parked alongside, also destined for Llangynwyd. In the backdrop is WWOC, GUH 430, and United Wesh, Bristol MW, WCY 701. *(Courtesy The Bus Archive / Roy Marshall).*

Above: The second Bedford SBO delivered to Brewer's in July 1954, was registered **OTX 697**, and is seen here on layover at the depot yard in Caerau. This also had Duple 'Midland' B40F bodywork. *(Courtesy The Bus Archive / Peter Yeomans).*

In April 1954, the following short period stage carriage service licence was asked for:-

TGR 267/Sp/10   **Maesteg (Bus Station)** to **Maesteg (Cemetery)**.
Period of operation 10th & 11th April, 1954, only.

An identical short period licence was asked for a year later in March 1955, together with a new stage carriage licence, on 27th April, 1955:-

TGR 267/Sp/11   **Maesteg (Bus Station)** to **Maesteg (Cemetery)**.
Period of operation 2nd & 3rd April, 1955, only.

TGR 267/21   **Caerau (Square)** to **Maesteg (Catholic Church)**.   *Sundays only.*
via: Nantyffyllon (Bee-Hive), and Maesteg (Garn Road). *2 x journeys in each direction, and other journeys for festivals and special services as required. The service had previously been authorised on TGR 267/1.*
This application was granted on 6th July, 1955.

On 8th June, 1955, the following two Express Carriage services were asked for:-

TGR 267/22   **Caerau** to **Blackpool**, via: Hirwaun, Brecon, Leominster, and Shrewsbury. Returning via Shrewsbury, and Brecon.
Picking up at Caerau Square, Nantyffyllon (Beehive Hotel), Maesteg (Town Hall), and any other safe point in the Maesteg UDC area. To be operated during the Miners' holiday period in this area, and during the period of the Illuminations. Only to be operated for pre-booked parties.
Fares: 30/- per head for 3 days, 32/6 per head for 4 days, 35/- per head for 5 days, 40/- per head for 8 days. Children: 3 years to under 14 years, two-thirds of adult fares.   Objector: British Railways.
Granted 3rd August, 1955, *with added conditions: [1] No journeys to operate on 23/9/1955, or on 1st & 15th October 1955. [2] Not more than two vehicles shall be used on each journey, except on 16/7/1955, when three may be used.*

TGR 267/23   **Abergwynfi** to **Blackpool**, via: Hirwaun, Brecon, Leominster, and Shrewsbury. Returning via Shrewsbury and Brecon.
Picking up at Abergwynfi (Great Western Hotel), Glyncorrwg (Glyncorrwg Hotel), Cymmer (Avondale Hotel), and any other safe point in the Glyncorrwg RDC area. Conditions and fares: same as TGR 267/22 above. Objector: British Railways. Granted 3rd August, 1955.

Concurrently, the following short period Express Carriage licences were issued:-

TGR 267/Sp/14   **Abergwynfi** to **Worcester**, via: Monmouth, Ross, and Great Malvern. Return via Gloucester and Chepstow.
To be operated for the Three Counties Show at Worcester, on 14th, 15th, 16th June, 1955, only.   Proposed Fare: 14/-

TGR 267/Sp/13   **Abergwynfi** to **Haverfordwest**, via: Neath, Carmarthen, and St Clears. Return same route. *To be operated for the Royal Welsh Show at Haverfordwest, on 20th, 21st, 22nd July, 1955.   Proposed fare 10/6.*

TGR 267/Sp/12 **Abergwynfi** to **Abergavenny**, via: Cardiff and Newport.
To be operated for the Abergavenny Show, on 1st September, 1955.
Proposed fare: 8/-

Above: Having received their first AEC 'Reliance' a year earlier, Brewer's decided to purchase their first AEC 'Reliance' coach, which was delivered in May 1955, as **RTG 501**. This vehicle was fitted with splendid Duple 'Britannia' C41F coachwork, and is seen here at Maesteg Bus Station. It was replaced with a new 'Reliance' in 1972. *(Courtesy The Bus Archive / Roy Marshall).*

P.V.O.A. OFFICE-HOLDERS

Mr. Brewer appointed national chairman

MR. ALBERT EDWARD BREWER, of Brewer's Motor Services Ltd., Caerau, near Bridgend, Glam, has been elected chairman of the national council of the Passenger Vehicle Operators Association. Mr. Brewer has for some years past been chairman of the South Wales area of the P.V.O.A. and has served for a considerable time as a vice-chairman of the Association's national council. He has succeeded Mr. F. Broomfield, secretary of Barton Transport Ltd., who held the post for two years.

Reappointments as vice-chairmen of the national council are: Mr. F. J. Speight, George Ewer and Co. Ltd.; Mr. H. W. B. Richards, Salopia Saloon Coaches Ltd.; and Mr. T. Hoyle, of T. Hoyle and Son, Halifax.

A new appointment as vice-chairman is that of Mr. A. Bolton, of Ribblesdale Coachways Ltd., Blackburn. Mr. S. D. Oddy, of Surrey Motors Ltd., is reappointed as hon. treasurer. Mr. John M. Birch, managing director of Birch Bros. Ltd., remains as chairman of the P.V.O.A. national executive and finance committee.

Mr. A. E. Brewer.

P.V.O.A. area chairman are: EAST MIDLAND, Mr. L. W. Evans, of East Kirkby; NORTHERN, Mr. W. Emmerson, O.K. Motor Services, Bishop Auckland; NORTH-WESTERN, Mr. F. Brazendale, of Sale; SCOTTISH, Mr. W. Dodds, James Dodds and Sons Ltd.; SOUTH WALES, Mr. Brewer; WESTERN, Mr. Walter Feltham, G. Feltham and Sons Ltd.; WEST MIDLAND, Mr. Richards; YORKSHIRE, Mr. Hoyle; and LONDON AND HOME COUNTIES, Mr. S. H. Waters, United Service Transport Co. Ltd.

Above: Mr Albert Edward Brewer received the position of National Chairman of the Passenger Vehicle Operators Association, in May 1956.

Above: In post-war years, Brewer's Motor Services made multiple vehicle purchases annually, but for four consecutive years 1955 – 1958, they bought just one new vehicle each year. In July 1956, they received delivery of **TTX 536**, this AEC 'Reliance' MU3RV, with Weymann 'Hermes' B44F bodywork, which is seen here on Blaencaerau Road, Caerau, en route to Maesteg. The Brewer's bus depot is just visible in the backdrop. **TTX 536** was withdrawn, and used for spares in 1971.
(Copyright The Bus Archive / Roy Marshall).

Besides the annual renewal of Road Service Licences, the only licences applied for between 1956 and 1962, were short period licences listed below:-

TGR 267/Sp/15	**Maesteg (Bus Stn.)** to **Maesteg (Cemetery)**.	
	via: Castle Street, and Cemetery Road. *24th & 25th March, 1956, only.*	
TGR 267/Sp/16	**Maesteg (Bus Stn.)** to **Maesteg (Cemetery)**.	
	via: Castle Street, and Cemetery Road. *13th & 14th April, 1957, only.*	
TGR 267/Sp/17	**Maesteg (Bus Stn.)** to **Maesteg (Cemetery)**.	
	via: Castle Street, and Cemetery Road. *29th & 30th March, 1958, only.*	
TGR 267/Sp/18	**Maesteg (Bus Stn.)** to **Maesteg (Cemetery)**.	
	via: Castle Street, and Cemetery Road. *9th & 10th April, 1960, only.*	
TGR 267/Sp/19	**Maesteg (Bus Stn.)** to **Maesteg (Cemetery)**.	
	via: Castle Street, and Cemetery Road. *25th & 26th March 1961, only.*	

It will be noted, that this annually operated service was not applied for in 1959.

Above: Another Weymann 'Hermes' bodied AEC 'Reliance' MU3RV, **VTX 88**, arrived brand new in June 1957. This particular 'Reliance' was pictured at Aberavon Beach Car Park, circa 1962/3, working a private hire to the one time 'Seaside Resort'. To the left of the picture is Brewer's Roe bodied AEC Regal IV, MNY 335. *(Copyright The Bus Archive / Roy Marshall).*

Above: YNY 247 delivered in May 1958, was, another AEC 'Reliance' MU3RV, fitted with synchromesh gearbox, vacuum brakes, and the lightweight Weymann 'Hermes' B44F bodywork. Pictured here at the depot yard, on 16th May, 1976, this 'Reliance' gave the company 'Yeoman' service. It was withdrawn after 20 years service, in May 1978, and was afterwards retained as a towing vehicle. However, it was finally broken up by May 1982. *(Copyright John Jones).*

Above: It was quite a surprise in April 1959, to see this Albion 'Nimbus' NS3N, **897 BTG**, entering the Brewer's fleet. This was bodied by Willowbrook to B31F layout, and after 17 years service, it passed to G.M. Jones, Morriston.   *(Copyright unknown).*

Above: Another change of chassis manufacturer from the customary AEC in June 1959, was this Leyland 'Tiger Cub' PSUC1/2, **887 CTG**, fitted with Duple 'Britannia' C41C coachwork. It was captured here at Sandy Bay, in the 'Seaside Resort' of Porthcawl, accompanied by an earlier Duple 'Britannia' bodied AEC 'Reliance', RTG 501.   *(Copyright The Bus Archive / Roy Marshall).*

Above: Looking a little battered in this view, is **212 FNY**, another AEC 'Reliance' with Weymann B45F bodywork. This one was delivered in April 1960, and is seen here on lay-over near the depot in Caerau. *(Copyright Byron Gage).*

Above: Strangely, **801 HTX** had a prang on the same panel too! This Weymann B45F bodied AEC 'Reliance' was photographed near Llangynwyd Church, on 2nd August, 1980. This vehicle also gave 'Yeoman' service. It was new in November 1960, and was taken out of service September 1983, passing to a preservationist at Barry a month later. Its whereabouts are now unknown, but it is still listed on DVLA website. *(Copyright John Jones).*

More short period licences for Excursions & Tours in 1961, are shown below:-

TGR 267/Sp/20 **Excursions & Tours** starting from Caerau.
To Berkley Castle, and Slimbridge (day), *30/7/1961 to 13/8/1961*.
To Cheddar (day), *8/8/1961*.
To Cheltenham & Bourton-on-the-Water (day), *30/7/1961 to 13/8/1961*.
All tours to run during the Miners' Holidays only.

TGR 267/Sp/21 **Excursions & Tours** starting from Abergwynfi (Great Western Hotel).
Tours, as listed above on TGR 267/Sp/20.

In 1962, the usual annual short period licence was asked for to Maesteg Cemetery:-

TGR 267/Sp/22 Maesteg (Bus Station) to Maesteg (Cemetery).
Period: Saturday 14/4/1962, and Palm Sunday, 15/4/1962.

Furthermore, one new Express Carriage licence was asked for on 25th April, 1962:-

TGR 267/24 **Cymmer** to **Newport (Llanwern Steelworks)**, via: A4063 to Bridgend, and A48 to Newport & Llanwern.
Times; 5.30 am start Cymmer, arrive Llanwern, 7.25 am.
Only personnel employed by Messrs J.W. Morris & Son, Electrical Engineers, Bridgend Trading Estate, to be carried on this service.
Licence granted 20th June, 1962, and surrendered 13th February, 1963.

Above: Pictured outside Brewer's Motor Services' depot in Blaencaerau Road, Caerau, when new, is this attractive Plaxton 'Embassy' C41F bodied AEC 'Reliance' 2MU3RV, registered **98 KTG**. This was delivered in May 1961, and served the company well until 1975. Sadly, it ended its days as a 'site hut' at Stormy Down, circa 1979. *(Copyright The Bus Archive / Roy Marshall).*

Above: Pictured here at Maesteg Bus Station, on 19th January, 1980, about to depart for Llangynwyd Church, is **605 MNY**, another AEC 'Reliance' 2MU3RV, but this time fitted with Weymann B45F bodywork. This vehicle entered service in October 1961, and again, gave over 20 years service. A tribute to the engineering staff and drivers employed by Brewer's. *(Copyright John Jones).*

Above: **277 PNY** was another AEC 'Reliance', but the 36ft version designated 4MU3RA, fitted with Plaxton 'Embassy' C51F coachwork. It was one of only two 36 ft 'Embassy' bodies built with extreme front entrance, in May 1962, and was received in all over cream livery, from Arlington Motors' dealer stock, in June 1962. It was licenced the following month. *(John Jones collection).*

Above: Another vehicle with Plaxton 'Embassy' coachwork was **557 PTX**, a Bedford SB8, delivered in June 1962. This Bedford was withdrawn in July 1975, and had passed to Abercarn RFC, by February 1976, for further use. Just visible in this view, taken on 17th December, 1972, is the rear end of Weymann bodied AEC 'Reliance', 605 MNY, seen opposite.   *(Copyright John Jones).*

Above: A splendid view of the company's first 36 ft. long saloon bus, taken at Coney Beach, Porthcawl, on 25th July, 1976. This AEC 'Reliance' 4MU3RA, registered **278 TNY**, had Weymann B53F bodywork, and was new to the company in April 1963. After 25 years' service, it passed to United Welsh Holdings 'Helproute', with the Brewer's business.   *(Copyright John Jones).*

Above: Seen here at Maesteg on 5th June, 1976, is **433 UNY**, a 36 ft. long (11 metre), Leyland 'Leopard' PSU3/3R, with BET style Marshall 'Camagna' B59F bodywork, featuring 3+2 seating. This was new in July 1963, and passed to Kenfig Motors, at nearby Kenfig Hill, in February 1979, for further service. *(Copyright John Jones).*

Above: 873 WNY was a Bedford SB5, fitted with Bedford 330 cu. inch diesel engine, and Plaxton 'Embassy III' C41F coachwork. It joined the fleet in December 1963, and is seen here at Maesteg on 4th August, 1971. Withdrawn in July 1975, it found a new home with D.D. Jones, of Pandy Mill, near Meidrim, Carmarthenshire, where it worked until April 1980. *(Copyright John Jones).*

The only licences applied for between April 1962, and October 1965, were the following short period licences:-

TGR 267/Sp/23 **Maesteg (Bus Station)** to **Maesteg Cemetery.**
To operate on Saturday, 6th April, and Palm Sunday, 7th April, 1963.

TGR 267/Sp/24 **Maesteg (Bus Station)** to **Maesteg (Cemetery)**.
To operate on Saturday, 21st March, and Palm Sunday, 22nd March, 1964.

TGR 267/Sp/25 **Maesteg (Bus Station)** to **Maesteg (Cemetery)**.
To operate on Saturday, 10th April, and Palm Sunday, 11th April, 1965.

At this point in time, Albert Edward & Frederick Rowland Brewer had been trading for some 45 years as a private unregistered company. With the business continually expanding, they decided that the time had come when it was essential to register the business as an Incorporated Company, in order to safeguard themselves, and the family, in the event of a crisis, and to satisfy the Inland Revenue Inspector.

After lengthy discussions, the family decided to register the business on 16th December, 1963, as **'A.E. & F.R. Brewer Limited'** (trading as Brewers Motor Services), Caerau Garages, Caerau, Bridgend.

The business was incorporated with company number 00784742, and the directors were listed as Albert Edward Brewer, and Frederick Rowland Brewer.

However, for reasons unknown, the management failed to notify the Traffic Commissioners of their change of title to an incorporated status (Limited Company), until January 1974, an unbelievable ten years later.

Surprisingly, the company retained their original operator reference number, which was not normal practice after a change of entity on a licence. More details on page 76.

On 17th November, 1965, the company finally decided to apply for a permanent stage carriage licence, to operate their special 'annual' service to Maesteg Cemetery.

The application read as follows:-

TGR 267/25 **Maesteg (Bus Station)** to **Maesteg (Cemetery)**,
via: Castle Street, and Cemetery Road.
Every 30 minutes, 10.10am to 6.10pm, on Saturdays prior to Palm Sunday only, and on Palm Sundays, leave Maesteg (Bus Station), every 30 minutes, from 1.30pm to 5.30pm.

The licence was granted as applied for, on 26th January, 1966.

TGR 267/15 Was surrendered on 9th February, 1966.

<u>Above:</u> Lightweight Bedford chassis featured regularly in the Brewer's fleet, and this Bedford VAL14, **ANY 135B**, arrived in May 1964, fitted with Plaxton 'VAL' C52F coachwork. It left the fleet in March 1982, passing to Jones Motors, Login, Carmarthenshire. The Bedford J2SZ2 alongside, ABX 521B, with Plaxton 'Embassy' C20F coachwork, was owned by Long's of Abercrave. It had been acquired in January 1966, from Lynne James, Pontyates, who took delivery of it in August 1964.   *(Copyright John Jones).*

<u>Above:</u> In July 1964, Brewer's bought two of these Bristol SC4LK buses from Eastern National O.C, Norwich. This particular one, registered **9572 F**, with Eastern Coachworks B35F body, was new in December 1957. The SC4LKs were reputed to be underpowered, but economical with their 3.8 litre, 4 cylinder Gardner 4LK engines, coupled to a David Brown 5 speed, constant mesh gearbox, and Bedford axle. It was also stated that they were very noisey and uncomfortable vehicles to travel in. However, Eastern National and United Counties regarded them as unsuitable, and quickly disposed of them. Brewer's withdrew both in June 1970, and eventually sold this one in 1973, for a moble home conversion.   *(Copyright The Bus Archive / Roy Marshall).*

Above: **608 JPU** was the second, and last Bristol SC4LK acquired by the company in July 1964. This was also withdrawn in June 1970, and was sold for further use to a non PSV owner, 'Bethlehem Church', at Cefn Cribwr, near Bridgend, by November 1972.
(Copyright of the late John Wiltshire).

Above: In February 1965, the company took delivery of another AEC 'Reliance' 4MU3RA, **DTG 676C**, but this time fitted with Willowbrook DP49F coachwork, built to Duple (Midland) design. This vehicle was still operational 23 years later, when the business fell into the hands of United Welsh Holdings' subsidiary, 'Helproute', in January 1988.
(Copyright The Bus Archive / Roy Marshall).

Above: Brewer's acquired two former Western Welsh, 1954 Leyland 'Tiger Cubs', JBO 56 and HUH 41, in 1966. Pictured here at Caerau, is **JBO 56**, a 'Tiger Cub' PSUC1/1, with Weymann 'Hermes' B44F bodywork, which entered service in February 1966. It passed to Andrew Scott, a contractor, at Port Talbot, by December 1972. *(Copyright The Bus Archive / Roy Marshall).*

Above: Former Western Welsh (1041) **HUH 41**, a 1954 Leyland 'Tiger Cub' PSUC1/1, with Weymann 'Hermes' B44F bodywork, was the second WWOC vehicle acquired. It entered service in March 1966, and was withdrawn in 1971. *(Copyright unknown).*

Above: **LNY 586D** was a Bedford VAM14, delivered in August 1966, fitted with the popular Leyland 400 diesel engine, and Duple 'Viscount' C45F coachwork. It was photographed here at the depot yard, on 15th July, 1973, and passed to Morris Travel, of Pencoed, Bridgend, in May 1977. *(Copyright John Jones).*

Above: Bedford was again management's choice of chassis for the 1967 tour season. This Bedford VAL14, **NTG 410E**, with a Leyland engine, was delivered in May 1967, and passed to Jones Motors, Login, Carmarthenshire, in 1982. *(Copyright unknown).*

Above: This Bedford VAL70, **SNY 818F**, with Duple 'Viceroy' C52F coachwork, was delivered in May 1968. The VAL70s were fitted with larger Bedford 466 cu. in. (7.64 litre), diesel engines. Not being very popular, all three VALs, **SNY 818F**, **NTG 410E** and **ANY 135B**, were withdrawn and sold to Jones Motors, of Login, Carmarthenshire, for spares, in 1982. *(Copyright John Jones).*

An interesting development occurred in January 1968, when the Minister of Transport announced details of the Road Traffic Act 1968. The Act, which was implemented by Transport Minister Richard Marsh, gave stage carriage bus operators financial grants of 25% towards the purchase of 'new' service buses, provided the vehicle complied with certain requirements of the Ministry of Transport, including, for example, an extreme front entrance doorway under driver supervision, and suitable for one-person operation.

The intention of the grant scheme was to encourage operators to modernise their fleets, and to make buses more competitive in terms of comfort, with private cars. The scheme applied initially only to buses used primarily on stage carriage services. But in 1970, when the grant was increased to 50%, it was agreed that coaches could also qualify for a grant, if used to sufficient extent on such bus services, providing the coach bodies were built with minor essential modifications, such as 'jack knife entrance doors', destination display, and other features which complied with the bus grant specification.

Conditions attached to the 'New Bus Grant', stated that qualifying operators would have to refund the grant if they sold the vehicle, or ceased to use it for stage service within five years of its delivery.

The scheme, which came into being on 1st September, 1968, and ended in March 1984, was a blessing to operators like Brewer's Motor Services, who used the scheme to update their fleet. In addition to the bus grant, a provision was made to increase the fuel duty rebate (introduced in 1965), from 50% to 100%. This was from 10d to 1/7d per gallon rebate, paid to operators of rural bus services, from 1st January, 1969, combined with the introduction of 'Rural Bus Grants', subsidising un-remunerative rural bus services.

At this point in time, the company were running a total of 29 vehicles, 13 AEC, 8 Bedford, 5 Leyland, 2 Bristol, and 1 Albion.

However, the first 'grant aided' vehicle ordered by the company was delivered in August 1969, to full grant specification, as WNY 453H. It was another AEC Reliance, but this time fitted with a Plaxton 'Derwent' body, and is pictured below.

Above: **WNY 453H** was an AEC 'Reliance' 6MU4R, fitted with the AH505 engine, and Plaxton 'Derwent' B47F bodywork. It was the first vehicle the company purchased with aid from the 'New Bus Grant', and entered service in August 1969. This view was taken at the depot yard when the vehicle was on a short lay-over, 15th July, 1973.   *(Copyright John Jones).*

Returning to June 1968, the long established business of Haydn James Uphill, at Caerau (dating from 1920), together with three elderly vehicles were absorbed. One of Uphill's Bedford OB's was operated for a short period, whilst his only stage carriage service licence (workmen), listed below, was applied for on 26th June, 1968:-

TGR 267/26   **Caerau** to **Cwmdu** (**St John's Colliery**).
             via: Nantyffyllon and Maesteg. *3 x shifts per day, when Colliery is working. Previous licence granted to H.J. Uphill (TGR 1222/1). Granted 28/9/1968.*

In the meantime, the following short period licence was issued, in order for Brewers to continue running the service:-

TGR 267/Sp/26   **Caerau** to **Cwmdu** (**St John's Colliery**).
                Period: 1/7/1968 to 24/8/1968.

Above: There's a good load visible aboard this AEC 'Reliance' **WNY 453H**, as it heads down the Llynfi Valley from Caerau, to Maesteg Bus Station. **WNY 453H**, fitted with the 505 engine, was the first vehicle the company purchased with assistance from the Government's 'New Bus Grant' scheme, in August 1969. It was scrapped in 1983. *(Copyright The Bus Archive / Roy Marshall).*

Above: The second 'Grant Aided' vehicle, **WTX 334H**, was a Leyland 'Tiger Cub' PSUC1/12, with Willowbrook DP45F bodywork, which arrived in October 1969. Pictured at the depot on 20th August, 1986, converted to B45F specification, it had a lengthy working life, passing to United Welsh Holdings' subsidiary, 'Helproute Ltd', in January 1988. The Helproute title, was formally changed to A.E. & F.R. Brewer Ltd., in May 1988, with no connection to the Brewer family whatsoever. *(Copyright John Jones).*

Above: The chassis of this 1959 AEC 'Reliance' 2MU3RV, **TWN 557**, was acquired in November 1968, from BET owned, Neath & Cardiff Express, Briton Ferry. The vehicle had been involved in a very serious accident, and its original Park Royal body had been scrapped before arrival. The chassis was rebodied by Willowbrook, in October 1969, giving Brewer's fifteen years service, before passing to Blue Bus Services, Rugeley, Staffs, in March 1985, for further use. *(Copyright The Bus Archive / Roy Marshall).*

Above: In November 1970, the company took delivery of their first Ford public service vehicle. It was a Ford R192, registered **BTG 577J**, another 'Grant aided' vehicle, fitted with Willowbrook B45F bodywork, built to full grant specification. The Ford 330 cu. in. 6 cylinder diesel engine was capable of 115 bhp, and was coupled to a 5 speed synchromesh gearbox. Seen here at Sophia Gardens, Cardiff, during the 'Miners Gala' day, 14th June, 1975, it gave the company 14 years service before disposal to Joe Sykes, the Carlton (South Yorkshire), scrap dealer, in December 1984. Purely speculation - but after its metal components were recycled and melted down in the furnaces, it could well have been transformed into a 'Ferrari'. *(Copyright John Jones).*

Above: In December 1970, management returned to the heavyweight chassis, and bought two more AEC 'Reliances', with 505 engines. Pictured here is the first to arrive, **BTG 737J**, with Plaxton 'Panorama Elite II', C51F coachwork. This was not built to grant specification, and passed with the business to 'Helproute Ltd', in January 1988. *(Copyright The Bus Archive / Roy Marshall).*

Above: BTX 973J was the second AEC 'Reliance' to arrive in December 1970. However, this one was built to full grant specification, with Plaxton 'Derwent' B55F bodywork, and is seen here at Caerau, on 17th December, 1972, with a man made 'Colliery waste tip' in the backdrop (since removed). *(Copyright John Jones).*

Above: Seen here at Maesteg Bus Station on 19th January, 1980, en route for Caerau, via Coegnant Rd., is **DTG 297J**. This was another new AEC 'Reliance', and was delivered in July 1971, with Willowbrook B45F bodywork. *(Copyright John Jones).*

By early 1969, the Brewer's fleet consisted of 29 vehicles, mainly heavyweights. The fleet was made up of thirteen AEC; eight Bedford; five Leyland; two Bristol; and one Albion. Competitors, Llynfi Motor Services, were quite a way ahead of Brewer's at this time, as they were operating 37 vehicles, but in subsequent years the Llynfi fleet was more than halved, to 17 vehicles, whereas Brewer's reached their peak in June 1987, with 34 vehicles.

Decimalisation of British currency was introduced on 15th February, 1971, which in turn brought about the amendment of fares on all routes. This meant rounding off fares to the nearest penny or half penny, without having a fare increase.

In July 1972, a local competitor, Idris Benjamin Jones, of 22 Griffiths Terrace, Caerau, submitted an application on TGR 5322/1, for an Express Carriage service from Blaengwynfi Square, to the Louis Edwards Factory, at Maesteg, via Cymmer, Caerau and Nantyffyllon. As the proposed service was 'encroaching' upon Brewer's long standing service between Caerau and Maesteg, and that of South Wales Transport between Cymmer and Maesteg, both operators successfully objected to the application, and Mr Jones withdrew his application on 27th September, 1972.

On a new application number, Mr Jones later successfully gained a licence, TGR 5478/3, to operate an Express Carriage service between Blaengwynfi, and Maesteg (Revlon Factory).

In June 1973, Brewer's asked for a modification to their licence TGR 267/20, to extend the service to start from Abergwynfi (Great Western Hotel), via Glyncorrwg (Glyncorrwg Hotel), Cymmer (Avondale Hotel), and Croeserw Housing Site, Cymmer.

The modification was granted on 1st August, 1973.

Above: Pictured here near Brewer's garage in Caerau, on 19th March, 1978, with Cymmer (Mountain) Road visible in the backdrop, is another new AEC 'Reliance', **KNY 968L**. New in August 1972, to C51F layout, it was one of only fourteen 'Reliances' built with grant specification Willowbrook 'Expressway 002' bodies, and acquired with aid from the 'New Bus Grant'. *(John Jones).*

Above: LNY 589L, was a Bedford YRQ, with Duple 'Viceroy Express' C45F coachwork, delivered to Brewer's in August 1972. It was another 'Grant Aided' vehicle, and was photographed at the depot on 8th April, 1973. *(Copyright John Jones).*

Above: **LTX 591L** was new in November 1972, and is seen here on 16th June, 1974, at the same location as KNY 968L opposite, but facing in the opposite direction. It was another AEC 'Reliance' 6MU4R, with almost identical Willowbrook 'Expressway 002' coachwork, and an exhibit of the 1972 Commercial Motor Show. The difference was, **LTX 591L** had a 10 metre chassis and body, and only 45 seats, but somehow its style gave the impression of 'dual purpose' rather than a coach. *(Copyright John Jones).*

Above: Seen here approaching Maesteg on 24th February, 1974, is yet another AEC 'Reliance' 6MU4R, **NKG 176M**. Brewer's had a penchant for the AEC chassis. This was delivered in August 1973, fitted with the AH505 engine, and Willowbrook bodywork, built to B53F layout, and passed to 'United Welsh Holdings', with the business, in January 1988. *(Copyright John Jones).*

Above: Plaxton 'Panorama Elite III' Express coachwork was fitted to this AEC 'Reliance' 6U3ZR, **PTX 620M**, which was bought with aid from the 'New Bus Grant' in August 1973. It was photographed here at Coedely Colliery, Tonyrefail, on 7th February, 1984, by this time, reseated from 51 to 53 seats, and repainted into the new style of livery. This vehicle also passed to United Welsh Holdings with the business, in January 1988.
(Copyright John Jones).

Taking into consideration that the company was incorporated in December 1963, management had inevitably neglected their duty to notify the Traffic Commissioner of that change until January 1974 – ten years later, when they asked for transfer of licences, TGR 267/1, 2, 3, 4, 8, 11, 13, 18, 19, 20, 21, 22, 23, 25, 26, to the new entity, **A.E. & F.R. Brewer Limited**. All those licences were renewed in April 1974, surprisingly, without a change of operator number.

However, circumstances were not very well in May 1974. Albert Brewer contacted Western Welsh OC, stating that 'he was in considerable difficulty with the Pay Board, coupled with the increasing complexity of Local Authority negotiations, staff shortages etc., it had brought him to the point where he may consider selling'.

Talks took place at National Bus Company level, where it was decided that a takeover of Brewer's was not desired, due to the fact that the existing stage carriage fares were exceedingly low, well below NBC, coupled with Brewer's rates of pay, which were so low, they felt that a takeover would immediately receive a demand for parity of wages and conditions, which would put them in extreme difficulty, having to raise fares and Private Hire rates in line with WWOC rates. Ultimately, negotiations ended.

Two months earlier, in March 1974, local competitor Lewis & Jacob, of Maesteg, changed their title to Avon Garage (Glamorgan) Ltd., Llwydarth Road, Maesteg, and two months later, surrendered that licences, to continue under the original Lewis & Jacob licence.

Above: The only vehicle purchased in 1974, was this AEC 'Reliance' 6U3ZR, **GKG 257N**, in November, with six speed synchromesh gearbox, and Duple 'Dominant I' coachwork. This was not built to the 'New Bus Grant' specification, so would have cost full price. It's seen here at the depot on 16th May, 1976, in a new style of livery. *(Copyright John Jones).*

Above: In January 1975, **GNY 913N**, a third Willowbrook 'Expressway 002' bodied coach arrived, but this was built on a Bedford YRT chassis, to C51F 'Grant Specification'. It appeared as a Willowbrook demonstrator, at the 1974 Commercial Motor Show, and is seen here at King Edward VII Avenue, Cardiff, on 14th June, 1975. *(Copyright John Jones).*

Above: Two more Bedfords arrived in July 1975, and numerically first was **JHB 532N**, a YRQ with Duple 'Dominant Express' C45F coachwork. It's seen here at Church Street, Maesteg, on 29th May, 1986, entering the bus station. *(Copyright John Jones).*

Above: The second Bedford to arrive in July 1975, was **JHB 533N**, a YRT with Duple 'Dominant Express' C53F coachwork, which is seen here at North Beach Car Park, Tenby, on 25th August, 1975. This was another vehicle that passed into the hands of United Welsh Holdings subsidiary, 'Helproute Ltd', the new owners of Brewer's, in January 1988. *(Copyright John Jones).*

Above: A surprise purchase in October 1975, was that of four Cardiff Corporation, 1968 AEC 'Swifts', MBO 516/518/521/523F, with corresponding fleet numbers. Pictured here at Maesteg Bus Station, en route for Caerau, is **MBO 516F**, which entered service in December 1975, and passed to K & P John, Llanharry, Bridgend, in March 1983, where it worked for a further three years.
(Copyright The Bus Archive / Roy Marshall).

Above: Another former Cardiff Corporation AEC 'Swift' MP2R, was **MBO 518F**, which is seen here in Caerau, on 4th August, 1979. This also entered service in December 1975, and passed to K & P John, Llanharry, in March 1983. These 'Swifts' had unusual style dual entrance Alexander bodies, with step entrances, and seated 47, with 18 standees. They were fitted with AEC AH505 engines, that were said to be 'underpowered', and 'tended to overheat'. *(Copyright of the late John Wiltshire).*

Above: Numerically the last Alexander 'W' bodied AEC 'Swift' acquired from Cardiff, was **MBO 523F**, which is seen here outside the depot. It was also the last 'Swift' to be licensed by Brewer's in May 1976, and was sold to Joe Sykes, the Carlton dealer, in December 1984, who passed it on to an unknown non-PSV owner in the Cardiff area, by October 1985. *(Copyright Kevin Lane).*

The feud between Brewer's and Llynfi MS, was rekindled when Brewer's asked for another new stage carriage service between Caerau and Maesteg on 3rd December 1975:

TGR 267/27   **Caerau (Blaenllynfi Hotel)** to **Maesteg** (Bus Station).
               via: Tonna Road, Heol-Ty-Gwyn, and Neath Road.
               Mon to Sat. 4 x return journeys daily.

Llynfi Motor Services immediately responded with an objection to their application, which in turn prevented the issue of the following short term licence to operate the service:

TGR 267/Sp/27   **Caerau (Blaenllynfi Hotel)** to Maesteg (**Bus Station**): **Refused.**

However, after a public inquiry, the full term licence was granted on 7th April, 1976, with two conditions: [1] No passengers to be picked up between the Pentyla / Heol-Ty-Gwyn junction, and Maesteg Bus Station, on the inward journey, nor set down between those points on the outward journey. [2] The minimum fare charged between Heol-Ty-Gwyn and Maesteg Bus Station, to be not less than the fare authorised to Llynfi MS, between the same locations.

Brewer's then asked to extend the starting point of TGR 267/1 from Blaenllynfi Hotel, Caerau, to the new Blaencaerau Housing Estate. That was granted on 26th January, 1977, and on 1st December, 1976, they unsuccessfully objected to an Excursions & Tours licence application from competitors, Wilkins Coaches (Cymmer) Ltd.

At this point in time, Brewer's had 14 school contracts, all the National Coal Board Colliery contracts in the Maesteg area, besides works contracts to Bridgend, with a fleet of 32 vehicles.

Above: This AEC 'Reliance' 6U3ZR, with AH760 engine, **MWO 296P**, was purchased new in June 1976, fitted with Plaxton 'Supreme' C53F coachwork, to standard coach specification. However, it may have been on lease, as it was exchanged 10 months later, for a new 'Grant Aided' Reliance, with Supreme II coachwork (OUT 631R, pictured below). *(Copyright Byron Gage).*

Above: This AEC 'Reliance' 6U3ZR, registered **OUT 631R**, was delivered in April 1977, to replace AEC 'Reliance' MWO 296P (pictured above), delivered 10 months earlier. It had the AH691 power unit, coupled to 'Monocontrol' transmission (semi automatic), and was first licensed in May 1977. It passed to 'Helproute Ltd', the new owners of Brewer's MS, in January 1988, and quickly passed to C.A. Warren, Neath. It then passed to R.M. Gower, Burry Port, in August 1990, where it received the cherrished registration, SIB 1304. This view was taken on 11th September, 1977, at Caerau. *(Copyright John Jones).*

Above: **WJF 378S** was another 6U3ZR AEC 'Reliance', new in May 1978, to 'New Bus Grant' specification. Fitted with Duple 'Dominant II' C53F coachwork, it passed to Eynon's, Trimsaran, in June 1984, and Davies Bros (Pencader) Ltd., in 1988. One can not go by looks, as it was an absolute beast to drive, with wandering steering, and brakes that tended to fade. I drove it regularly 1990-6, and was glad to see the back of it in Feb.1997, when it was sold for preservation – later scrapped. *(Copyright John Jones).*

Above: The last new AEC purchased by the company was **YNY 459T**, in January 1979, another 'Reliance' 6U3ZR, with grant specification Duple 'Dominant II' coachwork. It was part exchanged for a Caetano 'Algarve' bodied DAF immediately upon expiry of the five year rule regarding 'Bus Grant' vehicles. It is seen here at Caerau, on 18th November, 1979, and passed to C.A. Warren, (Bluebird of Neath), in 1984. *(Copyright John Jones).*

In November 1977, the company were granted permission to amend the destination point of TGR 267/20, to read Bridgend Trading Estate, and Waterton Industrial Estate.

A year later, in November 1978, they asked to revise the route of TGR 267/11, which operated to Turberville Housing Site, Garth, to include Crown Road, Chestnut Grove Housing Site and Cemetery Road. Permission was granted on 27th December, 1978, and in July 1979, permission was granted to delete 'Caerau Colliery' from licence number TGR 267/8.

In the meantime, the new Tory Government embarked upon a programme of deregulation, and privatisation of bus services, and brought into being 'The Road Traffic Act 1980'. This Act which came into effect on 1st October, 1980, allowed Express Carriage Services over 30 miles in distance, to be freed from licensing regulations, and Excursions & Tours would not require licensing at all. Additionally, the restriction of advertising Excursions & Tours, were lifted. The Act also abolished the licensing of bus conductors, and brought about the new 'coloured' operator licence discs. At the same time, operator licence numbers were changed from TGR xxx prefix, to PG xxx prefix (in the SWTA), with other traffic areas following suit with their own appropriate Traffic Area letters. The Transport Minister, Mr Norman Fowler, also announced that the 'New Bus Grant' scheme would cease by 31st March, 1984.

On 1st October, 1980, another new stage carriage licence was asked for:

PG 267/28   **Maesteg (Bus Station)** to **Llangynwyd (Heol-y-Bryn)**.
Mon to Sat, hourly, 9.15 to 17.15.

Objections were received from South Wales Transport and National Welsh (Western Welsh), and after a public hearing, the licence was granted, with the 17.15 journey deleted.

Amendments to service PG 267/20 were asked for in December 1980: [1] to withdraw the condition referring to 'employees only to be carried on this service'. [2] to amend condition so that it reads: The holder of the licence shall not set down passengers on the outward journey, except at the Bridgend/Waterton Estate, and no passengers will be picked up except on the Bridgend/Waterton Estate on the return. This amendment was granted on 18th February, 1981.

On 29th October, 1980, South Wales Transport and National Welsh OC, applied [1] to amend clause 2, of schedule 1, on their joint service between Bridgend (Bus Stn.) and Neath (Victoria Gardens), to read 'No passengers shall be conveyed for purely local journeys which both start and terminate within the Maesteg and Caerau section of the route'. [2] Amend the fare table in consequence of item 1. The amendment was granted to both operators in February 1981.

Further stage carriage services applied for by Brewer's in November 1981, were:-

PG 267/29   **Caerau** to **Beddau (Cwm Colliery)**, via: A4063 Aberkenfig; M4 to junction 34; A4119 and A473 to Beddau. *4 x journeys per working day, Mon to Sat. Only employees of Cwm Colliery to be carried.*

PG 267/30   **Caerau** to **Coedely Colliery**, via: Aberkenfig, M4 to Junction 34; A4119 to Coedely. *4 x journeys per working day. Same conditions as above.*

Both licences were granted on 3rd February, 1982, but in the meantime, short period licences PG 267/Sp/28 & 29 respectively, were issued to run the services from 30/11/81 to 29/5/82.

Above: From 1979, until the demise of the family business in January 1988, vehicle intake was mainly secondhand. This Willowbrook B45F bodied AEC 'Reliance' 2MU3RA, **ANY 433B**, dating from 1964, was one of three former Gelligaer UDC vehicles, acquired from Rhymney Valley District Council, in August 1979. *(Copyright The Bus Archive / Roy Marshall).*

Above: Another Rhymney Valley DC, AEC 'Reliance' 2MU3RA acquired by the company was **LTG 734D**. This had also been new to Gelligaer UDC, as B42D, but its Willowbrook bodywork was converted to B45F by Gelligaer. It's seen here at Heol-y-Cyw, near Bridgend, on 9th April, 1983, after sale to Martin & Billett, Pontycymmer, in January 1983. It then passed to R.M. Appleton, Bridgend (ABC Services), in April 1985, with Martin's business (by such time, he was operating on his own from Tonna). However, Appleton had ceased operating by September 1987, with no further trace of this vehicle. *(Copyright John Jones).*

Above: Last of the trio of former Gelligaer UDC vehicles, acquired via Rhymney Valley DC, in August 1979, was **RTG 221M**, a 1973 Bedford YRT, with Duple 'Dominant I Express', C53F coachwork. It is seen here on 19th January, 1980, and passed to 'Helproute Ltd', a company formed to absorb Brewer's Motor Services in 1988. *(Copyright John Jones).*

Above: With closure of AEC's factory imminant in 1979, Brewer's turned their choice of chassis manufacturer to Leyland Motors, and purchased this 'Leopard' PSU3F/5R, **CEP 117V**, with Plaxton 'Supreme IV Express' coachwork in December 1979. It's seen here at the depot on 19th January, 1980, and passed to 'Helproute Ltd' with the business in 1988. *(Copyright John Jones).*

Above: This former Merthyr Tydfil (152), Leyland 'Leopard' PSU4/2R, **DHB 152F**, was one of four East Lancs bodied 'Leopards' taken into stock from Merthyr. This one arrived in May 1980, and is seen making a right turn from Castle Street, Maesteg, into Talbot Street, on 19th July, 1980. It was sold in August 1986, to Capitol Coaches, Cwmbran, for spares. *(Copyright John Jones).*

Above: Seen here in Cardiff, on 5th December, 1981, is **ECY 278V**, a Plaxton 'Supreme IV Express' bodied Bedford YMT, bought with the 'New Bus Grant' in June 1980. This was sold in January 1986, to Owens of Yateley, Hants. *(Copyright John Jones).*

Above: DHB 156F, was another former Merthyr Tydfil (156), Leyland 'Leopard' PSU4/2R, with East Lancs B42D bodywork, which arrived in September 1980. Licensed in December 1980, it is seen here at Caerau on 5th June, 1981, and was used as a towing vehicle by September 1985, and scrapped in 1987. *(Copyright John Jones).*

Above: Pictured here at the depot on 5th June, 1981, is another former Merthyr 'Leopard' **EHB 265G.** This was a longer vehicle, type PSU3A/2R, with East Lancs B51F body, and was sold locally to K & P John, Llanharry, in June 1986. *(Copyright John Jones).*

<u>Above</u>: **GTH 536W**, delivered in March 1981, was another Leyland 'Leopard' PSU3F/5R, identical to the delivery of 1979, with Plaxton 'Supreme IV Express' C53F coachwork. It is seen here at Cardiff, on 6th February, 1982.   *(Copyright John Jones)*.

<u>Above</u>: **NNY 510E** was an AEC 'Reliance' 6MU4R, with Willowbrook body, new to Pontypridd UDC (97), in June 1967. After overturning in 1969, it was rebuilt with a new Willowbrook B45F body. Brewer's acquired it from the renamed local authority, Taff-Ely Borough Council (97), in May 1981, and is seen here at Castle Street, Maesteg, on 1st June, 1982.   *(Copyright John Jones)*.

Above: The last Merthyr Tydfil Transport 'Leopard' acquired by the company was **EHB 264G**, in July 1981, which is seen here at Castle Street, Maesteg on 1st June, 1982. This 1968, East Lancs B51F bodied vehicle, at 20 years old, passed to the United Welsh Holdings Ltd., subsidiary, 'Helproute' in January 1988, with the Brewer's undertaking. *(Copyright John Jones).*

Above: Pictured here at Carmarthen Bus Station (*before its major redevelopment of 1997-8*), is Brewer's Leyland 'Leopard' PSU3F/5R, **MEP 969X**, fitted with grant specification Duple 'Dominant IV Express' C53F coachwork. This coach and MEP 970X pictured overleaf, were the last two grant aided vehicles acquired by Brewer's, and were delivered in March and April 1982 respectively. MEP 969X and its unidentified partner behind would have been visitors to the ancient county town, on a Wednesday, Carmarthen's Market Day, where one could buy anything from a Cow, to a loaf of bread. *(Copyright The Bus Archive / R. Marshall).*

Above: Seen here on King Edward VII Avenue, Cardiff, participating in the Cardiff bus rally, 27th June, 1982, is the company's first Dennis 'Lancet', **MEP 970X**. Fitted with B53F Wadham Stringer 'Vanguard II' bodywork, it was new to Brewer's in April 1982, and passed to United Welsh Holdings subsidiary, 'Helproute' with the Brewer's business, in January 1988. *(Copyright John Jones).*

Above: As we know, Brewer's had a preference for the AEC chassis, and pictured here is the very last of that marque purchased by the company, in September 1982. **OYU 573R**, was a 1977 AEC 'Reliance' 6U3ZR, with standard Duple 'Dominant II' C55F coachwork, acquired from National Travel (South East), London. Seen here at Caerau on 29th January, 1987, it passed to United Welsh Holdings subsidiary, 'Helproute', with the Brewer's undertaking, in January 1988. *(Copyright John Jones).*

Above: This Leyland 'Leopard' PSU5C/4R, **XDG 215S**, 'went around the block a few times'. It was new to National Travel (South West), f/n 215, in March 1978, passed to South Wales Transport, in April 1981, to the dealer Kirkby, in November 1982, to Cavalier, Hounslow, December 1982, to Brewer's, May 1983, to United Welsh Holdings subsidiary 'Helproute', in January 1988, and to Cwmavon RFC afterwards. This view was taken at Barry, on 11th October, 1983. *(Copyright John Jones).*

Above: **UPD 269X** was a Dennis 'Lancet', with Wadham Stringer 'Vanguard II' B45F bodywork, and a former demonstrator for the manufacturers, Hestair-Dennis of Guildford. Acquired in May 1983, it is seen here on 10th September, 1983, outside the former Nantyffyllon Workmen's Institute, making a right turn from Heol Tywith, into Bangor Street. *(Copyright John Jones).*

Above: Pictured here at the Coaching Symposium, held at the National Exhibition Centre (NEC), Birmingham, on 19th February, 1984, is Brewer's first DAF, **A644 WCY**. It was a MB200 model, fitted with Caetano 'Algarve' C48FT coachwork, built by Salvadore Caetano Coachworks, in Oporto, Portugal. This was the first Caetano 'Algarve' delivered to a South Wales operator, and passed with the business to United Welsh Holdings subsidiary, 'Helproute', t/a AE & FR Brewer Ltd., in 1988. *(Copyright John Jones).*

Above: Photographed outside Brynllynfi Hotel, Caerau, upon delivery, with the dealer's poster still in the window, is **A504 WTH**, the company's second DAF MB200, fitted with Caetano 'Algarve' coachwork. This coach arrived at a very difficult time, March 1984. It was the beginning of the year long 'Miners Strike', resulting in huge losses of revenue. *(Copyright Byron Gage).*

Above: The third DAF MB200 acquired by Brewer's, **C950 GTH**, arrived in January 1986. This one however, was fitted with LAG 'Galaxy' C53FT coachwork, and was photographed on Taff Embankment, Cardiff, in 1989. *(Copyright John Jones).*

Delivery of two new DAF coaches in February and March 1984, introduced a pleasant new style of livery to the fleet. They were delivered just ahead of the devastating one year long 'Miner's Strike', 6th March, 1984, to 3rd March, 1985, which affected the lives of more or less everyone living and working in coal mining communities. The strike had a 'knock-on' effect to local businesses like Brewer's, who suffered huge losses of revenue.

During these lean times, South Wales Transport, and National Welsh Omnibus Co, withdrew their jointly operated service between Maesteg Bus Station, and Park Estate, on 1st September, 1984.

Brewer's received a short period licence to take-over that service from the following day:

PG 267/Sp/30   **Maesteg (Bus Stn)** to **Maesteg (Park Estate)**. *Period 2/9/1984 - 1/3/1985.*

At the same time, the full term licence was asked for:-

PG 267/31   **Maesteg (Bus Stn)** to **Maesteg (Park Estate)** circular route,
via: Garn Road, Brynllywarch, and Neath Road.   *Granted 19/12/1984.*

The company surrendered licence PG 267/8, Coegnant / Caerau Colliery, on 2nd January, 1985, but in consideration, those collieries, had been closed since 1981, and 1979, respectively!

After the Miner's Strike ended, another local competitor, M.T. Hart of Maesteg, who had absorbed the Maesteg business of Lewis & Jacob in 1980, asked for two new licences to serve Blaenant/Treforgan Collieries, in the Neath Valley, and Ffaldu/Garw Colliery in the Garw Valley. Both licences were granted in November, 1985, but Ffaldu/Garw immediately closed.

The next major item in the company's history was deregulation, which was brought about by the Road Traffic Act 1985, introduced by the Conservative Government. The Act, scheduled to be implemented on 26th October, 1986, was basically the transfer of bus service operation from public bodies to private companies, as legislated by the Act. It abolished Road Service Licensing and allowed the introduction of competition on local bus services for the first time since 1931. To operate a service, all an accredited operator was required to do was to provide 56 days' notice to the Traffic Commissioner, of their intention to commence, cease, or alter operation on a route.

Having said that, the transition into deregulation actually began on 6th January, 1986, with various provisions of the Act coming into force on that day:-

[1] The term 'Stage Carriage Service' changed to 'local service'.

[2] The term 'Express Carriage' was abolished.

[3] Requirement to notify 'Express Services' abolished.

[4] Licensing of 'Stage Carriage Services' abolished - changed to 'local service registration'.

From 1st March, 1986, the layout of 'Local Service Registration' (previously Stage Carriage licensing), changed to a different format. The following registrations are in accordance with paragraph 10, of schedule 6, to the 1985 Transport Act, and lists all the 'Local Services' Brewer's registered with the Traffic Commissioners, on 1st March, 1986:

PG/0718/267 **Caerau Park Estate** to **Garth (Maiden Street)**,
via: Tonna Road, Maesteg Bus Station, Bridgend Road, Chestnut Grove, Turberville Estate, and Hermon Road. *Mon-Sat, excluding Wed. afternoon. 9 x return journeys, hourly from 8.45am. Local service. Single deck 36-55.*

PG/0719/267 **Caerau (Blaenllynfi Hotel)** to **Maesteg (Ewenny Road Factory Site)**,
via: Tonna Road, Maesteg Bus Station, and Castle Street,
Mon-Fri (unless otherwise specified). 2 x return journeys daily, with 1 x extra journey on Thursdays. Local service. Single deck 36-55.

PG/0720/267 **Caerau Park Estate** to **Llangynwyd (Heol-y-Bryn)**,
via: Hermon Road, Maesteg Bus Station, Garth, Cwmfelin, Llangynwyd, Heol-y-Bryn, and Heol-Ty-Gwyn. *Mon-Sat (excluding Wed. afternoon). 9 x return journeys, hourly from 8.55am. Local service. Not B/H. S/d 36-55.*

PG/0721/267 **Caerau (Caerau Garages)** to **Lady Windsor Colliery (Ynysybwl)**,
via: Caerau, Nantyffyllon, Maesteg, Llangynwyd, Coytrahen, Tondu, Aberkenfig, & Pontypridd. *National Coal Board service, limited stops. Mon-Sat, in accordance to NCB shift requirements. Single deck 36-55.*

PG/0722/267 **Croeserw Housing Estate** to **Bridgend Trading Estate**,
via: Croeserw, Caerau, Nantyffyllon, Maesteg, Garth, Llangynwyd, Aberkenfig, Mill Lane, and Bridgend. *Mon-Sat, 1 x return journey daily, with 1 x extra journey on Fridays.   Single deck 36-55.*

PG/0723/267 **Caerau (Brynllynfi Hotel)** to **Waterton Industrial Estate (Bridgend)**,
via: Nantyffyllon, Maesteg, Garth, Llangynwyd, Coytrahen, Tondu, Aberkenfig, Bridgend, and Litchard. *Mon - Sat, 1 x return journey daily, 2 x inward journey's on Fridays. Local service. S/deck 36-55.*

PG/0724/267 **Caerau** to **Abernant Colliery, (Cwmgorse)**,
via: Nantyffyllon, Maesteg, Llangynwyd, Croeserw Housing Estate, Abergwynfi, Cymmer, Cwmavon, Velindre, Sandfields, and Port Talbot. *Mon - Fri, in accordance with NCB Shift requirements. Limited Stops. Local service. S/deck 36-55.*

PG/0725/267 **Maesteg (Bus Station)** to **Llangynwyd Church & Village**,
via: Talbot St, Commercial St, Llwydarth Road, and Llangynwyd Road. *Palm Saturday only, 14 x half hourly return journeys commencing 10.15am. Local service. S/deck 36-55.*

PG/0726/267 **Blaencaerau Housing Estate/Blaenllynfi Hotel** to **Maesteg (Park Estate)**,
via: Caerau Park Estate, Tonna Road, and Hermon Road. *Mon - Sat, excluding Wednesday afternoon. 9 x outward, 10 x inward, hourly journeys, commencing 9.00am. Local service. S/deck 36-55.*

PG/0727/267 **Caerau & Heol-y-Bryn, Llangynwyd** to **Betws Colliery (Ammanford)**,
via: Llangynwyd, Cwmfelin, Maesteg, Nantyffyllon, Caerau, Cymmer, Dyffryn Rhondda, Cwmavon, Port Talbot, Baglan, and Briton Ferry. *Mon – Sat, in accordance to NCB shift requirements. Limited stops. Local Service. S/deck 36-55.*

PG/0728/267 **Maesteg (Bus Station)** to **Maesteg (Cemetery)**, via: Crown Road, *Only on Palm Saturday. 15 x half hourly return journeys from 10.00am. Local service. S/deck 36-55.*

PG/0729/267 **Caerau (Caerau Garages)** to **Coedely Colliery (Tonyrefail)**,
via: Nantyffyllon, Parc Estate, Maesteg, Coytrahen, Tondu, Aberkenfig, and Talbot Green. *Mon – Fri, in accordance with NCB shift requirements. Limited stops. Local service. S/deck 36-55.*

PG/0730/267 **Abergwynfi** to **Swansea**, via: Glyncorrwg, Cymmer, Croeserw Housing Estate, Caerau, Nantyffyllon, and Maesteg. *Wednesdays only, 1 x return journey daily, from first Wed. in November, to the Wed. of the last complete week before Christmas. Local service. Limited stops. S/deck 36-55.*

PG/0731/267 **Croeserw Housing Estate** to **Porthcawl**,
via: Cymmer, Caerau, Nantyffyllon, Maesteg, Garth, and Llangynwyd. *Sundays only, 1 x return journey from Spring B/H Sunday, to the Sunday before August B/H Monday. Local service. Limited Stop. S/deck 36-55.*

PG/0732/267 **Caerau (Caerau Garages)** to **Cwm Colliery (Beddau)**,
via: Maesteg, Aberkenfig, Cross Inn, and Beddau. *Local Service. Mon-Fri, in accordance with NCB shift requirements. S/deck 36-55.*

Above: After the 1984/5 'Miners Strike', Colliery closures accelerated. Consequently, British Coal (formerly National Coal Board), transferred employees to work at collieries further afield, resulting in new contracts, and extra vehicles being deployed. Brewer's bought their first midibuses for that work, such as this 1979 Ford 'A0609', **YNY 71T**, with unusual Moseley 'Faro III' C25F coachwork. It arrived in April 1986, from Len Hopkins Coaches, of nearby Ogmore Vale, and is seen at Barry on 29th May, 1986.
(Copyright John Jones).

Above: In early 1987, the company purchased this pair of Bristol LHS6L's with Eastern Coachworks 7ft 6 inch wide, DP27F bodies, from Nottingham City Transport (735/731). Registered **JUG 352N**, and **MUA 45P** respectively, they are pictured here together at Maesteg, and were new to West Yorkshire as 36/45. They entered service with Brewer's, in April and March 1987, respectively. Both vehicles passed to United Welsh Holdings in January 1988, and several owners later, MUA 45P is now in preservation, with the Merseyside Transport Trust, in the livery of a previous owner, Merseyside PTE. *(Copyright Byron Gage).*

Above: Another view of the much travelled Leyland O.401 engined Bristol LHS6L, **JUG 352N**, which had been new in 1975 to West Yorkshire Road Car Co. It was acquired in April 1987, from Nottingham CT (735), and had worked for Merseyside PTE in the interim period after leaving West Yorkshire. This view was taken on 24th August, 1987, at Maesteg. *(Copyright John Jones).*

Above: D186 PWN was an integrally built MCW 'Metrorider' MF150/7, fitted with 25 coach seats, and was new to the company in June 1987. It's seen here on lay-over at Caerau Garages, on 24th August ,1987, and was sadly the ultimate vehicle purchased by the family partnership. The 'family undertaking' of A.E. & F.R. Brewer Ltd. passed to 'Helproute Ltd'., t/a A.E. & F.R. Brewer Ltd., a subsidiary of United Welsh Holdings Ltd., on 9th January, 1988, ending a fine story of enterprise and achivement.

(Copyright John Jones).

A year later, in March, 1987, five more local services were registered:

PG/5394/267   **Maesteg (Bus Station) to Llangynwyd Church & Village.**
To introduce a new route and timetable. Commencing on 5th April, 1987.

PG/5395/267   **Maesteg (Bus Stn) to Maesteg (Hospital).** *Commencing 5th April, 1987.*

PG/5396/267   **Maesteg (Bus Stn) to Garth (Maiden St), or Llangynwyd (Heol-y-Bryn).**
Commencing 5th April, 1987.

PG/5397/267   **Maesteg (Bus Station) to Maesteg (Parc Estate).**
Commencing 5th April, 1987.

PG/5398/267   **Caerau Parc or Blaencaerau to Maesteg (Bus Station).**
Commencing 5th April, 1987.

On 22nd April, 1987, the company asked for an increase of vehicle allocation by two single-deck vehicles on their operator licence, PG 267/SI. The Transport Manager was named as Vernon Brewer, and their request was granted as applied for, on 9th September, 1987.

A short while later, it was the desire of director, Mrs Linda M. Watts (F.R. Brewer's daughter), to sell the business. It was offered to Daryll Davies, of 'D' Coaches, Swansea, but in the meantime, the management team of United Welsh Holdings Ltd., the newly privatised South Wales Transport Co., heard of its availability, and outbid Daryll Davies.

Above: On 8th January, 1988, the staff of Brewer's Motor Services were crudely informed of the company's sudden demise, when this notice appeared in the office window. The business had been bought by United Welsh Holdings Ltd., the holding company of South Wales Transport, who formed a subsidiary, 'Helproute Ltd', to absorb the Brewer's undertaking. **NB:** United Welsh Services Ltd., was not in existance until 11/11/1988, and United Welsh Coaches was incorporated January 1989. *(Copyright T.S. Powell).*

THE 'NEW' A.E. & F.R. BREWER Ltd. UNDERTAKING

On 23rd November, 1987, **United Welsh Holdings Ltd.,** the holding company of the newly privatised **South Wales Transport Co.,** incorporated a new subsidiary, **'Helproute Ltd.'** (Incorporation N° 02197238), in order to absorb the Brewer's Motor Services undertaking.

The new company, 'Helproute Ltd', (t/a: A.E. & F.R. Brewer), of Heol Gwyrosydd, Penlan, Swansea, SA5 7BN (address of the parent company, and South Wales Transport), took control of the Brewer's undertaking, on 9th January, 1988, with 'D' Coaches of Swansea, former Transport Manager, D.B. Fowles 'jumping ship' to run the new company, as General Manager.

The new company had given the Traffic Commissioners the requested 56 days' notice of their intention to commence operating the former Brewer's services, and the Brewer family gave 56 days' notice of cancellation of all their Road Service Licences, as from 9th January, 1988. The cancelled licences were: PG/0718/267 to PG/0732/267 and PG/5394/267 to PG/5398/267. Their operator licence, PG 267/SI, was surrendered in April 1988.

All members of staff transferred to the new company under the Transfer of Undertakings (Protection of Employment) Regulations. Thirty-four vehicles were transferred with the business, along with all services, works contracts, school contracts and garage premises.

Returning to January 1988, the newly formed company, Helproute Ltd., (t/a: A.E. & F.R. Brewer), applied for an operator licence, for 35 single-deck vehicles, to operate from the former Brewer's Motor Services Ltd., operating centre, known as Caerau Garages, Caerau, Maesteg. The Transport Manager was registered as Alan David Kreppel, a director and partner of the newly privatised South Wales Transport Co (SWT), Incorporation N° 00133884.

The Helproute Ltd., 'O' licence, PG/6385/SI was granted as applied for, on 23rd March, 1988.

In the meantime, six additional local services were registered to start from 29th April, 1988, and with effect from 5th May, 1988, the company name, Helproute Ltd., was legally changed to **A.E. & F.R. Brewer Ltd.,** with the Secretary of State's approval, retaining the 'Helproute' incorporation number, 02197238, and legal address.

Two months later, in July 1988, the parent company, United Welsh Holdings Ltd., surprisingly purchased Brewer's long term rivals, **Llynfi Motor Services,** Maesteg, and merged that business into the Brewer's undertaking. All members of Llynfi staff transferred to Brewer's under the Transfer of Undertakings (Protection of Employment) regulations, except management. All licences, services, contracts, and seventeen vehicles, were taken over on Sunday, 10th July, 1988. The garage premises and yard at Maesteg, were used on a temporary basis, but were not acquired. The Llynfi garage at Maesteg Road, Bryn, was not acquired, but Llynfi's office/Travel Agent's shop at 28A Talbot St, Maesteg, was retained under the trading name of **Travelwise (Wales) Ltd.,** another subsidiary company of United Welsh Holdings.

Travelwise (Wales) Ltd., had been incorporated two months earlier, on 9th May, 1988, with Incorporation N° 02253955, from the same address as the parent company, Heol Gwyrosydd, Penlan, Swansea.

In the light of all this activity, another subsidiary company, **United Welsh Services Ltd.,** was incorporated on 11th November, 1988, and registered with company Nº 02108485.

However, on 30th November, 1988, David Beverly Fowles was added as Transport Manager on the A.E. & F.R. Brewer Ltd., licence (PG 6385/SI), in addition to Alan David Kreppel.

Simultaneously, the parent company applied for another new operator licence ('O' licence), in the name of **'Setprime Ltd', t/a: United Welsh Coaches,** Heol Gwyrosydd, Penlan, Swansea. Their operating centre was registered at 21 Alexander Road, Gorseinon, Swansea (formerly the premises of D. Bassett & Sons (Gorseinon) Ltd; Red & White Services; and BTC owned United Welsh Services Ltd., and latterly, South Wales Transport). A licence was granted for 35 single deck vehicles at Gorseinon, on 25th January, 1989, with the Transport Managers again registered as A.D. Kreppel, and D.B. Fowles.

On 17th December, 1988, Setprime Ltd., acquired the Swansea based operations of Jeffrey David Cleverly (Capitol Group), Cwmbran, together with five Volvo coaches, FTH 993-7W. This acquisition, was actually the tail end of the former Morris Brothers business, at Upper Bank, Swansea, which became the basis of a new coaching unit, **'United Welsh Coaches'**, set up at the *former* United Welsh Services Ltd. depot, in Gorseinon. It was formed with the intention of wiping out all the smaller coach companies in the surrounding area.

The operator licence Setprime Ltd., was granted in early January 1989, and by 25th January, the Setprime Ltd. title was officially changed to **'United Welsh Coaches Ltd'**.

Above: This 1981 Mercedes-Benz L307D, **MBB 404X** (75), with a Reeve Burgess 12 seat PSV conversion, was acquired in April 1989 from the dealer, Yeates of Loughborough, having previously operated in the large fleet of Cyril Evans, Senghenydd, near Caerphilly, Mid-Glamorgan. *(Author's collection).*

Above: The new company re-registered this 1982 Duple 'Dominant IV', bodied Leyland 'Leopard' from *MEP 969X* to **YBK 132**, a registration donated by a former Llynfi MS, Leyland 'Leopard'. It later received f/n 155, and registration NTH 156X. *(John Jones).*

Above: This former Brewer's Motor Services, DAF SB2300, *B697 VCX*, with Plaxton 'Paramount 3200' body, received cherished registration **556 DHO**, off a former Brewer's MS, Plaxton 'Supreme' bodied Bedford YMT, in March 1988.   *(Author's collection).*

Above: 948 RJO (159), was another Leyland 'Leopard' from the original Brewer's fleet (*GTH 536W*). This vehicle was later transferred to the United Welsh Coaches fleet, where it was re-registered JTH 44W, in August 1992. *(Author's collection).*

Above: There was a huge influx of secondhand vehicles after the absorption of Brewer's and Llynfi, to allegedly replace elderly, and non standard marques. **KUB 669V** was a 1979 Leyland 'Leopard' PSU3E/4R, with Plaxton 'Supreme IV' body, and was one of seven Leopards acquired from West Yorkshire RCC (2585), in 1988. It was later re-registered 278 TNY.

(Copyright Byron Gage).

Above: A terrific amount of re-registering of vehicles was carried out within the United Welsh Holdings group, and in some instances, a change of registration would sometimes take place four or five times. This Leyland 'Leopard' **278 TNY** (152), was originally registered *KUB 669V*, pictured opposite. It was later re-registered, ETH 68V. *(Copyright Byron Gage).*

Above: This Bedford YNT, **B930 AAX**, with Plaxton 'Paramount 3200' coachwork, was one of a pair the parent company hired from J.D. Cleverly, Cwmbran, in May 1989, due to vehicle shortage. These Bedfords ran in Capitol Coaches livery (a livery Cleverly adopted from the take over of Morris Bros, Swansea), and were licensed to Brewer's associate fleet, United Welsh Coaches Ltd. *(Copyright Byron Gage).*

Above: UTF 723M, was another Leyland 'Leopard' PSU3B/4R, with Duple 'Dominant I' C49F coachwork, which was acquired from Ribble MS. It was photographed here at Cardiff, not Carmarthen which is displayed on its destination blind. On the other hand perhaps the driver had dislexia. *(Author's Collection).*

Above: Another former Ribble Motor Services vehicle, was this Leyland engined Bristol RESL6L, **LRN 328J** (328), with Marshall B43F bodywork, which was acquired in May 1988. Built in 1971, it saw a total of 21 years service. *(Author's collection).*

Above: Maesteg had their fair share of minibuses running around during the minibus era of the 1980s and 1990s. This Mercedes-Benz L608D, with Robin Hood, B20F conversion, **C210 HTH** (210), is seen here at the Caerau depot, carrying local branding appropriate to the area, 'Llynfi Mini'. It was transferred from the associate company, SWT, in 1988. *(Copyright Byron Gage).*

Above: F606 AWN (606), was a 1988 Mercedes-Benz 709D, with Reeve-Burgess B25F bodywork, and also carried the 'Llynfi Mini' branding. The minibuses allocated to Maesteg were used to pioneer new routes within the community. *(Author's collection).*

Above: Pictured here at Tyndal St, Cardiff, working a 'Private Hire' is **C213 PNJ** (78), a 1985, Mercedes-Benz L608D, with an Alexander DP20F, PSV conversion. It was one of three L608D's acquired from Brighton & Hove, in July 1990. *(Vernon Morgan).*

Above: With the absorption of Brewer's Motor Services, and Llynfi Motor Services, in 1988, the parent company acquired numerous non-standard vehicles, AEC, Bedford, and Dennis marques, which were quickly replaced by Leylands from within the group, and elsewhere. **RWN 477S** (477), seen here at Talbot Square, Maesteg, on 11th June, 1988, was a Duple 'Dominant I' bodied Leyland 'Leopard' transferred from the SWT fleet, and repainted into Brewer's livery. *(Copyright John Jones).*

Above: Seven of these Duple 425 'Integrals' were acquired brand new by United Welsh Holdings between 1986-9. **F100 CEP** (B137), seen here at Caerau, was delivered to Brewer's in 1989, fitted with 54 seats and toilet. It was later reseated, and transferred to the United Welsh Coaches fleet, later moving to the SWT fleet, for the 'Cardiff Shuttle' 100 route. *(Author's collection)*.

In February 1990, United Welsh Holdings sold their three principle companies, South Wales Transport; A.E. & F.R. Brewer Ltd; and United Welsh Coaches Ltd., to **Badgerline Holdings PLC.,** Weston-Super-Mare. Badgerline Holdings, had already acquired other former NBC companies in the Midlands, South-West of England, and Essex, retaining the individual company identities, together with the individual operator licences and legal addresses.

A month later in March 1990, there was a change of Transport Managers at the Brewer's operating centre, when Graham G. Davies and W.E. Harris were authorised, instead of Allan D. Kreppel and D.B. Fowles. Concurrently, there was a huge amount of service changes, and new services were registered throughout the area. The services operated are not included in this story, to allow extra space for photographs of the extremely diverse fleet operated.

However, on 1st June, 1990, A.E. & F.R. Brewer Ltd., absorbed the business of a local competitor, D.H. Stolzenberg (DLJ Private Hire), Maesteg, along with thirteen vehicles.

It will be noted that D.H. Stolzenberg had previously sold a PSV business in March 1972, to Llynfi Motor Services, without conditions, and restarted a new business five years later. However, after sale of this second business to Brewer's in June 1990, he restarted another PSV business just four months later, in October 1990, but on this occasion, the business was cunningly registered as a partnership between J.V. Gilbert, and Maureen Stolzenberg. Mr Stolzenberg used his wife's name as a business partner, and joint licence holder, on licence Nº PG 6606/SN. The new company, J.V. Gilbert & M. Stolzenberg, t/a Llynfi Coaches, once again competed against Brewer's services. However, when Mr Gilbert retired in June 1995, the partnership became D.H. & M. Stolzenberg, trading as Llynfi Coaches.

1991 saw Badgerline absorb the Skillplace Training concern from United Welsh Holdings, and in April 1991, Graham Davies relinquished his position of Transport Manager at the Caerau Garage. From July 1991, A.D. Kreppel and D.B. Fowles, returned as TMs, alongside W.E. Harris, at the company's newly registered operating centre, Plot 4, Heol-Ty-Gwyn Industrial Estate, Maesteg. Brewer's had outgrown their Caerau depot, due to expansion.

However, extra business was acquired in the Bridgend area after the collapse of privatised National Welsh OC, in January 1992, and in August 1992, the company's legal address changed once again, to Acacia Avenue, Sandfields Estate, Port Talbot, SA12 7DW, due to reorganisation of the Badgerline group. This former South Wales Transport depot, (originally Thomas Bros), at Port Talbot, became Brewer's head office, and principal operating centre. The reorganisation involved transferring control of SWT's Port Talbot depot, and United Welsh Coaches' Gorseinon depot, to A.E. & F.R. Brewer Ltd., and at the same time, United Welsh Coaches' vehicle licences were surrendered in exchange for Brewer's licences.

This transformation brought about a huge increase to vehicle authorisation on the Brewer's 'O' licence, PG 6385/SI. On 16th September, 1992, their licence authorisation was increased from 35 single deck vehicles, to 10 minibus, 100 single deck, and 14 double deck vehicles. At the same time, additional operating centres were authorised at Acacia Avenue, Port Talbot; Morris Travel, Litchard Industrial Estate, Bridgend; Heol-Ty-Gwyn Industrial Estate, Maesteg; and at Alexandra Road, Gorseinon. There were no changes to Transport Managers.

Above: This former Hants & Dorset, 1976 Leyland National, **PJT 255R**, was a 10351A/1R model, fitted with 41 seats, and arrived at Brewer's from Eastern National OC (1500), in April 1992. It is seen here at Maesteg in November 1992. *(Copyright Byron Gage).*

Above: Shortly after United Welsh Holdings acquired the Brewer's business, there was an influx of second-hand vehicles from all over the country. This particular Leyland National 11351A/1R with B49F layout, **MAR 796P** (B687), arrived from Eastern National OC (1774), and had passed to the new, Rhondda Transport by 1992. *(Author's collection).*

Above: The parent company, United Welsh Holdings, incorporated several new companies after acquiring South Wales Transport, in May 1987. Skillplace Training Ltd., was incorporated on 20th November, 1987, and was set up as a subsidiary company to provide training services to the Bus & Coach industry. However, after a difficult financial year, 1996-7, that company ceased trading. This 1973, former London Country (BL16), Bristol LHS6L, **SPK 116M**, with Eastern Coachworks B35F bodywork, was just one of several training vehicles owned by the sister company. Skillplace acquired this from North Mymms Coaches, Potters Bar, Hertfordshire, having previously operated for four years, with Silcox Motor Coach Co., at Pembroke Dock, f/n 116. *(Copyright Vernon Morgan).*

Above: In December 1991, there was an influx of nine second-hand Leyland Nationals, and **XEU 859T** (711) above, was one of them. This was a 10351B/1R (series B) model, new to Bristol Omnibus (711), in July 1979, and arrived via Badgerline, Bristol. It was one of the first vehicles to carry the new Brewer's livery of Poppy Red, and White, in January 1992. *(Author's collection).*

Above: NWS 904R (715), was a Leyland National 11351A/2R, 49 seater, new to Bristol (1457), in March 1977. It arrived at Brewer's in December 1991, and is seen here in Caerau, soon afterwards, working a schools service. *(Author's collection).*

Above: In February 1992, Brewer's received a batch of six Ford Transit minibuses, from the new mother company, Badgerline, in order to inaugurate new services around Bridgend after National Welsh's demise. **B440 WTC** (4440), a Dormobile B16F bodied Ford Transit, is seen here leaving the Market Street terminus, Bridgend, for Pencoed, on 21st February, 1992. *(Byron Gage)*.

Above: Another former Badgerline vehicle was this Dormobile bodied Ford Transit, **C479 BFB** (4479), which is seen here at Bridgend Town Centre, about to depart for the Bridgend suburb of Bettws, on 17th February, 1992. Close behind is another former Badgerline, Dormobile bodied Ford Transit, **C401 AHT** (4401), heading for another suburb of Bridgend, Brackla, with both vehicles displaying signs on their windscreens stating, 'On Hire To Brewers'. *(Copyright Byron Gage)*.

Above: **HHJ 379Y** (183, previously 379), was a 1983 Leyland Tiger, with Alexander 'TE' C53F coachwork. New to Eastern National OC, it was one of three acquired from Badgerline subsidiary, Thamesway, in February 1991, followed by another three later that year from the same source. They eventually passed into the fleet of South Wales Transport.   *(Author's collection).*

Above: Acqired in July 1990, was **C200 PCD** (276, previously 76), another former Brighton & Hove Mercedes-Benz L608D, with a 20 seat PSV conversion by Alexander, which is seen here at Maesteg depot on 1st July, 1993. Brewer's ran several of these van derived minibuses, some of which were transferred from the associate fleet, South Wales Transport.   *(Copyright Byron Gage).*

Above: Port Talbot Bus Station is the backdrop for this view of Eastern Coachworks C53F bodied, Leyland 'Leopard' PSU5E/4R, **ANA 94Y** (163). It was one of three (ANA 92-4Y), acquired in April 1992, from Eastern National (1310), and was new in December 1982, to National Travel (North West). It was one of the last dozen 'PSU5 Leopard' chassis built. *(Author's collection).*

Above: 'United Welsh Coaches' vehicles, were all licensed to Brewer's, from September 1992. Seen here at Trimsaran, on 13th July, 1994, is UWC, **YBK132** (139), an integrally built Leyland 'Royal Tiger Doyen', which was new to Badgerline, Bristol (2400), as *D400 GHT*, in 1986. Its cherished registration was cascaded down from a Llynfi Motor Services 'Leopard'. *(Vernon Morgan).*

Above: As mentioned on page 112, fifteen of these Mercedes-Benz L608D minibuses with Robin Hood PSV conversions were transferred from the associate company, South Wales Transport, between May 1992, and January 1993. **C209 HTH** (209), is seen here working a Bridgend local service to Cefn Glas, on 29th March, 1993. *(Copyright Byron Gage).*

Above: Former Eastern National (3108), via Thamesway (3108), Bristol VRT, **UAR 598W** (598), seen here at Cardiff Bus Station, was one of the first deckers licensed to the Brewer fleet, in September 1992. It was one of eleven VRTs transferred to Brewer's, from the fleets of United Welsh Coaches, and South Wales Transport. 598 was previously United Welsh (U598). *(V. Morgan).*

Above: In September 1992, Brewer's acquired five integrally built Leyland 'Lynx' 51 seat buses. Three were brand new, with 'personalised' registration marks, K10-12 BMS, whilst the other two were former Volvo-Leyland demonstrators. Pictured here at Wyndham Street, Bridgend, working its regular route, 232 to Cymmer, is former demonstrator, **J916 WVC** (508), which was new in January 1992, and fitted with a Volvo engine. *(Author's collection).*

Above: Numerically the second former Volvo-Leyland demonstrator acquired by Brewer's in September 1992, was Volvo engined, **J375 WWK** (509), which was also captured on Wyndham Street, Bridgend, working a slightly different service to Cymmer. Some of the '232' journeys were extended to reach the villages of Abercregan, Glyncorrwg, and Blaengwynfi, from 25th April, 1993. Those particular journeys were renumbered 236. *(Author's collection).*

Above: In October 1992, three brand new Leyland 'Lynx' 51 seater buses, with 'personalised' registration marks **K10-12 BMS** arrived to compliment the two former 'Lynx' demonstrators pictured on the previous page. All three were powered with Cummins engines, and were reseated to 47. **K11 BMS** (511), is seen here at the Maesteg depot on 1st July, 1993. *(Copyright Byron Gage).*

Above: This Dennis 'Javelin' 12SDA, **K9 BMS** (170), with Plaxton 'Premiere 320' coachwork, was one of a pair delivered to Brewer's, in June 1993, for the 'United Welsh Coaches' fleet. They were followed by three more identical Javelins, L6/8/14 BMS, a year later. K9 BMS was sold in 1998. Note the personalised registration mark, BMS: 'Brewer's Motor Service'. *(Byron Gage).*

Above: Former South Wales Transport, **BEP 981V** (981), a Bristol VRT/SL3/501, with Eastern Coachworks H43/31F bodywork, was one of the second batch of VRTs cascaded down to Brewer's in October 1993. It is seen here entering Port Talbot Bus Station, working a local town service. *(Author's collection).*

Above: Not all Brewer's vehicles received fleet livery, as seen in this view of **BEP 982V** (982). This Bristol VRT, and its stablemate 959 to the rear, were received from SWT in October, and January 1993, respectively, whilst 971 on the right, arrived in September 1992, and were all still carrying SWT livery when photographed in Gorseinon depot, on 16th October, 1994. *(Vernon Morgan).*

Above: Brewer's first 'new' Mercedes-Benz midi-buses, K401-410 BAX (401-410), arrived in March 1993. **K404 BAX** (404), seen here at Wyndham Street, Bridgend, on 24th September, 1994, was one of the ten 811D's, fitted with Plaxton 'Beaver' B31F bodies, and is about to depart on service 62, to North Cornelly, via Laleston, Cefn Cribwr, Kenfig Hill, & Pyle. *(Copyright Byron Gage).*

Above: Former Badgerline Leyland 'Tiger' TRCTL11/3R, **B221 WEU** (166), fitted with Duple 'Laser 2' C47FT coachwork, was photographed here at Manor Park, Tenby, on 2nd July, 1994, working a private charter. Only two Duple 'Laser' coaches were ever operated by Brewer, and both were cascaded down from the parent company of the time, Badgerline. *(Copyright Vernon Morgan).*

On 20th January, 1993, A.E. & F.R. Brewer Ltd., applied for renewal of their 'O' licence, PG 6385/SI, asking for an increase of authorisation to 104 single deck, and 20 double deck vehicles, with Transport Manager's given as Mark Burnley Howarth, and Alun Phillips.

Operating Centres were registered as:-

[1] Bus Garage, Acacia Avenue, Port Talbot, 35 s/d and 13 d/d.

[2] The Bus Garage, Alexandra Rd, Gorseinon, 30 s/d and 7 d/d.

[3] Heol-Ty-Gwyn Industrial Estate, Maesteg, 22 s/d.

[4] Compound, 5 North Road, Bridgend Industrial Estate, 17 s/d.

The licence was granted as applied for, on 17th March, 1993, but a variation was issued on 11th May, 1994, when Transport Manager, M.B. Howarth was replaced by Phil Collier.

On 19th September, 1993, three local services of Broadwest Ltd., Ogmore Vale, were absorbed, and the local services of K.C. Viles, Brynna, Pontyclun, were absorbed on 31st July, 1995.

As the local service network expanded, so did the fleet of licensed vehicles. On 6th July, 1994, the company were granted another increase to their vehicle authorisation, from 104 single deck, and 20 double deck vehicles, to 110 single deck, and 20 double deck vehicles.

Above: G841 PNW (506), was an 'Unique' integrally built, Van-Hool A600, 52 seat bus, built as a demonstrator for Van-Hool, in March 1990. Originally registered G680 TKE, it passed to Rhodes, of Yeadon, West Yorkshire, where it received cherished registration, A6 RLR. It afterwards became G841 PNW, and passed with Rhodes business to Yorkshire Rider (Badgerline Group), who transferred it to the Brewer's fleet on loan initally. Its seen here at Brewer's Port Talbot depot, on 30th May, 1994, still in Rhodes' livery, and driven here by Derek Simons, the principal driving instructor at Skillplace Ltd. *(Copyright Byron Gage).*

Above: G261 LUG (507), was a Leyland 'Lynx' that was new in November 1989, to Rhodes, Yeadon, West Yorkshire. It was acquired by Brewer's, together with the Van-Hool, G841 PNW, from Yorkshire Rider, after they absorbed Rhodes' business. It's seen here entering Swansea Bus Station, working the X3 service from Maesteg, on New Years Eve, 1994. This vehicle was fitted with a Cummins engine, and was transferred in mid-1996 to Western National OC. *(Copyright Vernon Morgan).*

Above: In June 1994, Brewer's received their first batch of eight Dennis 'Darts', L601-8 FKG (601-8). They were 9.8 metre, Plaxton 'Pointer' B40F models, and numerically the first one, **L601 FKG** (601) is seen here on 19th June, 1994. *(Byron Gage).*

Above: Another Leyland National 11351A, transferred from the South Wales Transport fleet, in January 1994, was **AWN 812V** (812), which is seen here at Maesteg depot on 11th August, 1994. *(Copyright Byron Gage).*

In April 1995, the parent company, Badgerline Holdings PLC, announced that they had agreed terms with an Aberdeen based bus group, Grampian Regional Transport PLC, (GRT), for a merger, creating a brand new company named **First Bus PLC.**

The merger went ahead on 16th June, 1995, following clearance by the Monopolies & Mergers Commission, and the English, and Scottish Courts. First Bus PLC., a Scottish registered company, became the second largest bus group in the UK, with a fleet of 5,600 vehicles, (4,000 of which were contributed by Badgerline). Moir Lockhead of GRT, became the chief executive, and Trevor Smallwood of Badgerline, became executive chairman of the group, which had 20 subsidiaries. All vehicles received 'First Bus' logo stickers in their rear windows from mid-June, replacing the familiar 'Badger' logo. The SWT; Brewer's; and United Welsh Coaches trading names continued to be used, along with the SWT and Brewer's 'O' licences.

Despite all this activity, the United Welsh Coaches depot at Gorseinon, changed its status to an outstation in March 1995, and was completely vacated in June 1996. Their intention of wiping out all the smaller coach companies in the Swansea area must have failed.

September 1995, saw the arrival of ten more new 9.8 metre Dennis 'Darts' with Plaxton 'Pointer' DP40F bodywork, registered N609-618 MHB (609-618), and on 1st October, 1995, Brewer's acquired the local services and contracts previously operated by Golden Coaches, of Llantwit Major. At the same time, the coaching unit of Cardiff City Transport Services Ltd., 'Cardiff Bus', together with their 'Vale Busline' operations were acquired. Acquiring this coaching unit brought into stock former Cardiff Leyland 'Tigers', B905/6 DHB (179/180), with Duple 'Caribbean' coachwork, along with a Scania K112CRB, registered 972 SYD, originally *E701 NNH* (196), fitted with Jonckheere coachwork. The fourth vehicle acquired, was a Scania K113CRB, registered F907 DHB (197), fitted with Plaxton 'Paramount 3500' coachwork.

Further expansion took place on 20th October, 1996, when Brewer's absorbed the six local services of **John Williams, Porthcawl**, and his subsidiary, **Porthcawl Omnibus Company**.

No vehicles or premises were acquired when Mr Williams slimmed down his business, but four of his vehicles were hired on a temporary basis, to cover a vehicle shortage at Brewer's. John Williams continued to operate school contracts and private hire until September 2001, when he finally retired from the industry.

Above: This former Merthyr Tydfil, Leyland 'Leopard' PSU4F/2R, **JUH 230W**, with Duple 'Dominant II' B47F bodywork, was one of four vehicles borrowed off John Williams, Porthcawl, to cover a vehicle shortage after Brewer's had acquired his local services, in October, 1996. This view was taken on 6th November, 1996, when it carried Brewer's fleet number (704). The sign on the windscreen read: '540 Bowens Arms to Dwr-y-Felin Lower', which was a Brewer's school service. *(Copyright Byron Gage).*

All this activity led to another increase in vehicle authorisation. On 22nd November, 1995, the company were granted an increase from 110 s/d, & 20 d/d, to 130 s/d, & 20 d/d vehicles, and to use 25 Tumulus Way, Llandow Trading Estate, South-Glamorgan, as an additional operating centre.

On 10th October, 1996, the new parent company, First Bus PLC, registered another new company, in the name of **'Quayshelfco 573 Limited'**, with incorporation Nº 03261587. This was a 'Shelf Company' – literally a ready-made company name, bought 'off the shelf'.

Retaining the same incorporation number, 03261587, the 'Shelf Company' name was quickly changed to **First Bus (South) Ltd**, on 18th November, 1996, which was the new controlling company for First Bus operations in South Wales, and Southern England.

Above: E203 PWY (451), was acquired from Quickstep Travel, Leeds, in January 1996, and is seen here at Albert Row, Swansea, working the 224 service to Margam, on 12th July, 1996. It was one of two Optare 'Star Rider' DP29F bodied, Mercedes-Benz 811D's received in 1996, and sold 1998. The remarks of one driver, 'they were horrible things to drive'. *(Vernon Morgan.)*

Above: D520 FAE (227), was one of five former Bristol Cityline, Dormobile bodied Mercedes-Benz L608D, acquired in October 1995. It is seen here in Porthcawl, working former Porthcawl Omnibus local service 65, on 21st October, 1996. *(Byron Gage.)*

Above: The company acquired the coaching unit of 'Cardiff Bus' on 1st October, 1995, together with their four coaches, two Leyland 'Tigers', B905/6 DHB, and two Scania's, 972 SYD/F907 DHB. All four were used, but Leyland, B906 DHB, and both Scania's were quickly sold. Leyland 'Tiger' TRCTL11/3RZ, **B905 DHB** (179), with Duple 'Caribbean' C51FT coachwork, seen here on 21st February, 1997, was the only one of the quartet to be retained, and received United Welsh Coaches livery. *(Byron Gage).*

Above: F546 EJA (419), was a Mercedes-Benz 709D, with bodywork built by Potteries Motor Transport (PMT), to DP25F layout. New to Walls of Wigan, Lancs, in August 1988, it arrived via Quickstep Travel, Leeds, in January 1996. *(Copyright Byron Gage).*

Above: A quartet of Leyland 'Tigers' were received from Rider, York, in March 1996, and seen here at Port Talbot on 23rd May,1996, is numerically the first one, **EWW 945Y** (162), a 1983 Leyland TRCTL11/3R, with Plaxton 'Paramount 3200' C53F coachwork. It was being prepared for the 471 School service, Pontrhydyfen, to Dyffryn Upper & Lower Schools. *(Byron Gage).*

Above: Seen here at the old Cardiff bus interchange, is **A658 KUM** (164), a former Rider, York, 1983 Leyland 'Tiger' TRBTL11/2R, with Duple 'Dominant' DP47F body, working the X5 service to Llantwit Major, in the Vale of Glamorgan. *(V.Morgan).*

Above: This 21 seat Wadham Stringer bodied Mercedes-Benz 709D, **J901 MAF** (429), arrived in March 1996, from Western National. It was new in November 1991, to Ede, of Par, Cornwall, with cherished registration, *J6 EDE*. *(Copyright Byron Gage).*

Above: In September 1996, three rebodied Leyland 'Leopards' arrived from Rider, York. The chassis of this PSU3D/4R, was new to Shamrock & Rambler, Bournemouth, as *REL 402R*, in February 1977, carrying Willowbrook '003' C47F coachwork. It was rebodied in April 1987, with this Plaxton 'Derwent II' B55F (later B51F) body, and reregistered **CSU 244.** *(Copyright Byron Gage).*

Above: VDH 244S (703), was another rebodied 'Leopard' acquired from Rider, York (a subsidiary of Yorkshire Rider), in Sept. 1996. It was a PSU3E/4R type Leopard, new to National Travel (West), in August 1977, with Willowbrook '003' coachwork. After its sale in 1985, a dealer had it rebodied with this new Duple 'Dominant' B51F body. It's seen here leaving Brewer's Port Talbot depot on 6th November, 1996, to work the 542 service, New Road, to Dwr-y-Felin Lower School. *(Copyright Byron Gage).*

Above: BVP 778V (706), was one of four PSU3E/4R type 'Leopards' (JUM 532V, BVP 776/8/81V), acquired from Potteries MT, in November 1996. They oused the four hired vehicles from John Williams (Porthcawl Omnibus Co). BVP 778V had Plaxton 'Supreme' C49F coachwork, and was new to Midland Red (778), in January 1980. It was photographed here at Port Talbot depot, on lay-over between school duties, on 6th December, 1996. *(Copyright Vernon Morgan).*

Above: Acquired from Yorkshire Rider (1400), in October 1996, as E218 WWW (previously *YR 3939*), was this Volvo B10M-61, with Jonckheere 'Deauville' C30FT coachwork. It carried Yorkshire Rider's 'Jet Rider' livery, and was re-registered with Brewer's *favourite* cherished registration mark, **300 CUH** (f/n 199), in November 1996. Its previous registration mark, E218 WWW, was interchanged with the doner of 300 CUH – a Duple 425, originally registered *E207 BOD* (140). *(Copyright unknown).*

Above: In December 1996, Brewer's took delivery of their last three step entrance 9.8m Dennis 'Darts', P619-621 PDW, which were allocated to Bridgend. Carrying Plaxton 'Pointer' bodywork, **P620 VDW** (620), is seen on 25th January, 1997. *(Byron Gage).*

Above: Seen here exiting the new Bridgend Bus Station, on 7th July, 1997, is **F721 FDV** (432), one of eight Mercedes-Benz 709Ds, with Reeve-Burgess DP25F bodies, acquired from First Bus subsidiary, Provincial, of Fareham, Hants, in November 1996. It was one of a large number of 709s that were new to Devon General, in November 1988. **F721 FDV** was photographed working service 45, from Bridgend to Talbot Green, via Bryncethin, Heol-y-Cyw, and Pencoed. *(Vernon Morgan).*

The United Welsh Holdings Ltd., subsidiary, trading as Skillplace Training Ltd., ceased trading on 31st March, 1997, and became dormant. The company had experienced a difficult year's trading, when its major customer undertook to do its own driver training internally. All remaining trade, and the assets of the Skillplace Training undertaking, were transferred to The South Wales Transport Co. Ltd.

In the light of all this, the senior management of A.E. & F.R. Brewer Ltd., were summons to attend a Public Inquiry with the Traffic Commissioners in July 1997, regarding maintenance issues. The notice read:-

Notice of Public Inquiry to be held on 1st August, 1997, at 1-6 St Andrews Place, Cardiff. The Traffic Commissioner will consider exercising his powers under Section 17 of the Public Passenger Vehicles Act 1981, to suspend, revoke, curtail or vary, any conditions attached to the licence (PG 6385/SI), held by A.E. & F.R. Brewer Ltd., The Bus Garage, Acacia Avenue, Sandfields Estate, Port Talbot. SA12 7DW.

The result of this inquiry, held on 1st August, 1997, was a 'warning' to the management, as to their future conduct, regarding maintenance of vehicles.

The company assured the Traffic Commissioner that they would fulfil several undertakings regarding maintenance of their vehicles.

Above: This Leyland 'Tiger' TRCTL11/3RH, with Plaxton 'Paramount 3200' C53F coachwork, **F615 XWY** (132), was one of four (F615/7/8/20 XWY), received from Yorkshire Rider, in 1996/7. This one arrived in the livery of 'Bradford Traveller' in June 1997, and is seen here leaving the old Cardiff Bus Station, at Wood Street, working the busy X2 to Porthcawl. *(Copyright Andrew Jarosz).*

Above: Another former Yorkshire Rider, Leyland 'Tiger' TRCTL11/3ARZA, with Plaxton 'Paramount 3200' C53F coachwork, was **NIL 2450** (180), previously *F618 XWY*. The management of Brewer's had a penchant for cherished registrations, with some marks being repeatedly used. This view was taken at Swansea (Quadrant) Bus Station, on 23rd July, 1998. *(Vernon Morgan).*

Above: H782 GTA (444), was a Mercedes-Benz 811D, with Carlyle DP29F body, new in June 1991, to Red Admiral, Portsmouth. Red Admiral was a joint venture between Badgerline, and Southampton Citybus, to compete against Portsmouth Corporation. Badgerline sold their share of Red Admiral to Southampton Citybus, who eventually bought Portsmouth CT. After a series of mergers, First Hampshire & Dorset acquired 'Peoples Provincial', who owned this former Red Admiral vehicle and ten others, passing them down the line to Brewer's, in June 1997, where it operated in this 'Provincial' livery. *(Copyright Byron Gage).*

Above: In January 1998, three Plaxton 'Verdi' B49F bodied, Dennis 'Lance' 11SDA buses arrived from Midland Red (West), L218-220 AAB (f/n 550-2). They were later renumbered 826-8, as shown here on **L218 AAB** (826). *(Copyright unknown).*

Above: There was a large influx of double deck vehicles for School, and College duties, in 1997/8. A variety of Bristol VRT; Leyland Atlantean; and MCW Metrobuses, arrived during that period, and seen here in this special livery adopted for the University of Wales Institute, Cardiff contract, is Northern Counties bodied Leyland 'Atlantean', **ANA 644Y** (953). This was acquired in September 1997, from Stagecoach Manchester, its origins being that of Greater Manchester PTE. *(Copyright Byron Gage).*

At the end of the financial year 31st March, 1998, a new company **First Cymru Buses Ltd**., was formed, to discard the separate trading names of South Wales Transport, A.E. & F.R. Brewer, and United Welsh Coaches.

On the same date, South Wales Transport acquired the entire share capital of its fellow subsidiary, A.E. & F. R. Brewer Ltd.

Brewer's local service licences were all cancelled from 31st March, 1998. They were all absorbed by The South Wales Transport Co. Ltd., the following day, 1st April, 1998. The A.F. & F.R. Brewer Ltd., operator licence was surrendered accordingly.

The fleet name 'First Cymru' was applied to all vehicles by May 1998, but the legal lettering and 'O' licences temporarily remained as The South Wales Transport Co. Ltd.

The legal lettering was finally changed to 'First Cymru Buses Ltd., on 28th March, 1999, and a new operator licence was issued in the name of First Cymru Buses Ltd., on 31st May, 1999.

Therefore, this would be the official date of The South Wales Transport Company's demise.

However, it is interesting to note that the 'O' licence number issued to First Cymru Buses Ltd., on 31st May, 1999, was PG 421 (renumbered PG 0000421 in 2002). This number was continuity of the licence number issued to The South Wales Transport Co. Ltd., <u>in April 1931</u>.

BREWERS MOTOR SERVICES – VEHICLE DETAILS

Reg Number	Chassis make & type	Chassis number	Body make & type	Seating	Date new	Remarks / Additional Information Previous owner	Date acquired	Date withdrawn
	Arrol-Johnson		Lorry		c1912	Ex unknown owner.		
L 9530	Ford 'TT' 20hp	4527230	Lorry		5/1921	New. (Livery Green).	5/1921	10/1921
NY 2484	Maxwell 20hp (30cwt)	22027		B14F	2/1923	New. (Livery Maroon/Black, to Maroon/Yellow, to Blue/White)	2/1923	1931
L 5492	Napier 25hp uw: 2t 11c 3qr	2911N	Built by original owner, Henry Evans, Maesteg.	Ch20	10/1919	Ex H.R. Evans, 15 Talbot St., Maesteg. (Livery Blue/White).	7/1923	7/1935
NY 4610	Leyland 36-40hp RAF type	20153	Leyland	30 to B32R	1/1924	New to Brewer's, at Brynkwood Dairy, Caerau. uw: 4t 19c 3qr. (Livery, Blue/White).	1/1924	1932
BO 2378	Sociedad Piemontese Automobili (SPA)				1919-20	Ex A.H. Morse. Cardiff.	by 4/1926	?
L 8708	AEC 'YD' 45hp	15162	Dodson (probably)	31	1/1921	Ex D. Bassett & Co, Gorseinon, Swansea. New to Gower Vanguard. (Livery, Blue/White).	12/1926	4/1928
BO 1844	Traffic 20-25hp (Goods vehicle chassis)		Worrell. Cardiff.		1917	Ex J. Worrell, City Road, Cardiff.	by 3/1928	12/1929
UH 313	Sociedad Piemontese Automobili (SPA)			B20F	?	Ex Gough's Motor Services. Mountain Ash, Glam.	12/1928	after 1935
BX 4384	Leyland A11 30-32hp (2½ ton chassis)		Leyland (later rebodied by C.K. Andrews, Swansea).	B20R	4/1924	Ex Llanelly Express Motor Service, Llanelly, via Jones Bros (Brynteg), Upper Tumble, Llanelly.	12/1928	after 1935
UT 694	Morris T	12983		B14	4/1927	Ex G.E. Hamblin. Groby, Leicestershire.	10/1929	?
AX 8743	Morris				1926	Ex Fisher & Huckson. Penhow, Monmouthshire	by 12/1929	?
DE 5861	Morris Commercial 'TX'			B14F	4/1927	Ex J.R. Ford. Pembroke. via: Blue Bus Co (G.C. Williams), Neath, Glam.	by 12/1929	12/1934
WN 3424	Morris Commercial			B14	11/1930	New Possibly lost in a fire.	11/1930	5/1938
RU 9716	Studebaker	3250477	C.K. Andrews. Swansea?	C20	1929	Ex South Wales Express. Cardiff. Destroyed in fire 30/9/37.	c1931-2	30/9/1937
WN 4046	Morris Commercial 'TX'		C.K. Andrews. Swansea.	B14R	1931	?? Destroyed in fire 5/38.		5/1938
	Morris Commercial 'Viceroy'		C.K. Andrews. Swansea. or Llewellyn's. Swansea.	C24R		Destroyed in fire 5/38.		5/1938
?	Morris Commercial 'Director'			20		New? Destroyed in fire 5/38.		5/1938

Reg	Type	Chassis no	Body	Body type	New	History	Date	Withdrawn
WN 6788	Dennis 'Lancet' fitted AEC 7.7 engine	170665	C.K. Andrews. Swansea.	B32F to B35F?	5/1934	New	5/1934	1/1960
WN 7598	Dennis 'Lancet'			B–F	1934	New? Destroyed in fire 5/38.	1934	5/1938
WN 8329	Dennis 'Ace' 30hp	200365	C.K. Andrews. Swansea.	B20F	6/1935	New	6/1935	1946
WN 9952	Dennis 'Ace'	200490	C.K. Andrews. Swansea.	B20F	5/1936	New (Supplied by C.K. Andrews). (Livery, Blue/White).	5/1936	12/1949 or 3/1951
WN 1684	Dennis 'E'	17603	South Wales Transport	B32R	2/1929	Ex South Wales Transport. Swansea.	by 6/1936	?
WG 2315	Gilford 'Hera' L176S (Leyland Tiger engine)	12193	Wycombe	C32F	6/1934	Ex Alexander 755, or Western SMT. Destroyed in fire 5/38.	1937	5/1938
BTX 599	Dennis 'Lancet II' uw 6t 2cwt	175172		B32	3/1937	New (Livery, Blue). Destroyed in fire 5/38.	3/1937	5/1938
TG 273	Dennis 'Dart' uw 3t 10cwt	75726		B20R	7/1930	Ex Dawkins Bros. Neath Abbey. Glam. (Livery, Blue/White).	3/1938	12/1939
CTX 865	Dennis 'Lancet II'	175329	Duple	C35	3/1938	New Exhibited at 1938 Commercial Motor Show.	3/1938	7/1940
DNY 140	Dennis 'Lancet II'	175504	Duple	C35	4/1938	New	4/1938	7/1940
DNY 148	Leyland 'Cub' SKP2	8322	Harrington	B26	3/1938	New	3/1938	12/1950
WN 853	Dennis 'E'	17413	South Wales Transport	B32R	5/1928	Ex South Wales Transport. Swansea.	1938	8/1948
DTG 77	Bedford WTB series II	1110	Duple	C26F	1/1938	New	1/1938	9-10/1952
CS 1498	Commer 'Centaur' B3	63006	Watson (Lowestoft).	B20F	3/1935	Ex Blane. Kilmarnock, East Ayrshire. via: Pralls (dealer), Hereford.	6/1939	by 1950
ENY 712	AEC 'Regal'	06623354	Duple	C37F to DP35F	6/1939	New	6/1939	5/1959
ATG 491	Thornycroft 'Handy' AE/FB4/1 (LWB)	25367	Thurgood	B20F	3/1936	Ex D.J. Thomas (Cream Line), Maesteg.	9/1939	10/1942
WG 1177	Leyland 'Cub' KP3 Normal Control.	589	Alexander Motors, Edinburgh.	C20F to B26F	6/1932	Ex Pitlochry Motor Co. Perthshire.	9/1939	3/1951
UH 7201	Thornycroft A2 long	18695	Hall Lewis	B20F	12/1929	Ex Western Welsh O.C.	5/1940	by 1948
AWA 486	Albion 'Victor' PK115	25001E	Cowieson	C26R	6/34	Ex Bailey Sheffield.	1/1941	2/1948
TH 9189	Dennis Arrow Minor	255024 or 255041	?	26	9/1937	Ex John Evans & Sons, Bancffosfelin, Carms. (This was new to David Grant Evans, Llanelly).	4/1941	1948

Reg	Chassis	Body	Seating	New	Notes	In service	Withdrawn
TX 4264	Leyland 'Lion' PLSC3	46270	Leyland	B31R	10/1927	Ex Willmore Bus Co, Neath. via South Wales Transport, and latterly, H. Bird, Neath.	6/1942	12/1952
FNY 420	Guy 'Arab II'	FD26101	Duple 'Utility'	H30/26R	6/1943	New **Note**: Not operated, see disposals list.	6/1943 not operated	9/1943
FNY 405	Bedford OWB – Perkins P6 engine fitted by 1952	14967	Duple 'Utility'	B32F to B30F	7/1943	New	8/1943	10/1957
FNY 406	Bedford OWB – Perkins P6 engine fitted by 1952	15115	Duple 'Utility'	B32F to B30F	8/1943	New	8/1943	1/1955
TG 8764	Thornycroft 'Handy' FB4 24hp	24907	?	B20F	12/1934	Ex F.J. John, Nantyffyllon, Maesteg. Acquired with F.J. Johns' share of the service.	1/7/1943	1/1944
FNY 420	Bedford OWB Perkins P6 engine fitted.	17710	Duple 'Utility'	B32F to B30F	4/1944	New	4/1944	11/1952
FNY 731	Bedford OWB	20514	Duple 'Utility'	B32F to B30F	6/1944	New	6/1944	11/1952
FNY 732	Bedford OWB	20604	Duple 'Utility'	B32F to B28F/B30F	6/1944	New	6/1944	6/1958
FNY 889	Bedford OWB Perkins P6 engine fitted	23344	Duple 'Utility'	B32F to B30F	11/1944	New	11/1944	1/1953
FNY 894	Bedford OWB	23321	Duple 'Utility'	B32F to B30F	1/1945	New	1/1945	12/1952
FNY 895	Bedford OWB Perkins P6 engine fitted	23528	Duple 'Utility'	B32F	2/1945	New	2/1945	11/1967
VJ 1252	Dennis 'G'	70456		14	10/1928	Ex Griffith Hughes, Caerau. Acquired with Hughes' share of the service.	1945 not operated	
CTG 251	Thornycroft 'Dainty' CF/FB4/1	26568	Thurgood	B20F	7/1937	Ex D.J. Thomas (Cream Line), Maesteg. Acq. with Cream Line's share of the service.	by 6/1945	3/1951
FTG 479	AEC 'Regal'	06624183	Harrington	B36F to B34F	4/1946	New	4/1946	5/1960 or 6/1960
GNY 509	Bedford OB	40511	Duple 'Vista'	C29F	3/1947	New	3/1947	5/1952
GTG 438	Bedford OB	48045	Duple 'Vista'	C29F	5/1947	New	5/1947	5/1952
GTX 162	AEC 'Regal III'	0962136	Duple 'A' rebuilt 6/1959, by Neath Coachworks.	C35F to B37F	8/1947	New	8/1947	7/1968
GTX 163	AEC 'Regal III'	0962137	Duple 'A'	C35F	8/1947	New	8/1947	8/1959
GTX 363	AEC 'Regal'	06625652	Harrington	C33F	9/1947	New	9/1947	5/1961
HTG 129	AEC 'Regal'	06625653	Harrington	C33F	5/1948	New	5/1948	4/1961

Reg	Chassis	Serial	Body	Seating	New	Notes	Acquired	Disposed
HTG 528	Bedford OB	79253	Duple 'Vista'	C29F	7/1948	New	7/1948	5/1952
ANY 166	Tilling Stevens D60A7	9130	Plaxton - Original body, rebodied Longford (1949)	C32F C33F	4/1935	Ex Ivor John Summers, Gorseinon, Swansea. Possibly via War department.	by 7/1948	12/1953
ANY 716	Thornycroft 'Handy' AE/FB4 (LWB)	25184	Wadham Bros.	B20F	6/1935	Ex F.J. John, Nantyffyllon, Maesteg. via: Lloyd, Pontrhydfendigaid, Cardiganshire.	8/1948	10/1949
JNY 273	Bedford OB	103521	Mulliner Mk III	B31F	4/1949	New	4/1949	by 7/1961
JNY 770	AEC 'Regal III'	9621E714	Harrington	C33F	6/1949	New	6/1949	7/1963
JNY 771	Bedford OB	108746	Mulliner Mk III	B31F	6/1949	New	6/1949	by 2/1958
JTG 34	Maudslay 'Marathon III'	70473	Burlingham	C33F	6/1949	New	6/1949	2/1963
JTG 622	Bedford OB	116375	Mulliner Mk III	B31F	9/1949	New	9/1949	11/1961
JTG 854	AEC 'Regal III'	9621E789	Duple 'A'	C33F	1/1950	New	1/1950	1/1966
JTG 901	AEC 'Regal III'	9621E715	Harrington	C33F	3/1950	New	3/1950	5/1966
JTX 152	AEC 'Regal III'	9621E651	Harrington	C33F	3/1950	New	3/1950	5/1966
JTX 153	AEC 'Regal III'	9621E652	Harrington	C33F	3/1950	New	3/1950	3/1963
JTX 358	Bedford OB	120739	Mulliner Mk III	B31F	3/1950	New	3/1950	4/1959
KNY 672	Bedford OB	142121	Mulliner Mk III	B31F	7/1950	New	7/1950	6/1955
KTG 764	AEC 'Regal III'	9621E1076	Longford	B40F	1/1951	New	1/1951	1/1968
KTX 741	AEC 'Regal III'	9621E1077	Longford	FC37F	5/1951	New	5/1951	5/1965
KTX 742	Bedford SB (Retrofitted Perkins P6 engine).	1046	Duple 'Vega'	DP33F	5/1951	New Coach body-shell, fitted bus seats from new.	5/1951	2/1966
LTX 170	AEC 'Regal IV'	9821E633	Roe	B44F	4/1952	New	4/1952	7/1967
LTX 470	AEC 'Regal IV'	9821E236	Duple 'Ambassador'	C41C	5/1952	New	5/1952	7/1972
MNY 335	AEC 'Regal IV'	9821E1380	Roe	B44F	12/1952	New	12/1952	by12/1964

Reg	Chassis	Serial	Body	Seating	Date	Notes	In	Out
OTG 600	Leyland 'Tiger Cub' PSUC1/1	535015	Weymann 'Hermes'	B44F	6/1954	New	6/1954	1972
OTG 601	AEC 'Reliance'	MU3RV197	Weymann 'Hermes'	B44F	7/1954	New	7/1954	by 6/1974
OTG 547	Bedford SBO	27285	Duple (Midland)	B40F	7/1954	New	7/1954	9/1968
OTX 697	Bedford SBO	29073	Duple (Midland)	B40F	7/1954	New	7/1954	9/1968
RTG 501	AEC 'Reliance'	MU3RV528	Duple 'Britannia'	C41F	5/1955	New	5/1955	1972
TTX 536	AEC 'Reliance'	MU3RV1068	Weymann 'Hermes'	B44F	7/1956	New	7/1956	by 1/1971
VTG 88	AEC 'Reliance'	MU3RV1633	Weymann 'Hermes'	B44F	6/1957	New	6/1957	by 8/1971
YNY 247	AEC 'Reliance'	MU3RV1891	Weymann 'Hermes'	B44F	5/1958	New	5/1958	5/1978
897 BTG	Albion 'Nimbus' NS3N	82051L	Willowbrook	B31F	4/1959	New	4/1959	7/1975
887 CTG	Leyland 'Tiger Cub' PSUC1/2	587131	Duple 'Britannia'	C41C	6/1959	New One of the few centre entrance Britannia's built.	6/1959	1/1973
212 FNY	AEC 'Reliance'	2MU3RV 1514	Weymann	B45F	4/1960	New	4/1960	by 5/1982
801 HTX	AEC 'Reliance'	2MU3RV 3072	Weymann	B45F	11/1960	New	11/1960	9/1983
98 KTG	AEC 'Reliance'	2MU3RV 3486	Plaxton 'Embassy'	C41F	5/1961	New	5/1961	1975
605 MNY	AEC 'Reliance'	2MU3RV 3706	Weymann	B45F	10/1961	New	10/1961	by 5/1982
277 PNY	AEC 'Reliance'	4MU3RA 4259	Plaxton 'Embassy'	C51F	5/1962	New Delivered in all-over Cream, from Arlington Motors' stock.	7/1962	1975
557 PTX	Bedford SB8	88845	Plaxton 'Embassy'	C41F	6/1962	New	6/1962	7/1975
278 TNY	AEC 'Reliance' 470 engine	4MU3RA 4122	Weymann	B53F	4/1963	New	4/1963	1/1988
433 UNY	Leyland 'Leopard' PSU3/3R	629350	Marshall 'Camagna' (BET style)	B59F	7/1963	New (3+2 seating).	7/1963	2/1979
873 WNY	Bedford SB5	93293	Plaxton 'Embassy III'	C41F	12/1963	New	12/1963	7/1975
ANY 135B	Bedford VAL14	1177	Plaxton 'Val'	C52F	5/1964	New	5/1964	c3/1982

Reg	Chassis	Serial	Body	Seats	New Date	Notes	In Service	Out
9572 F	Bristol SC4LK	121.050	Eastern Coachworks	B35F	12/1957	Ex Eastern National OC. Chelmsford (447).	7/1964	6/1970
608 JPU	Bristol SC4LK	121.037	Eastern Coachworks	B35F	5/1958	Ex Eastern National OC. Chelmsford (438).	7/1964	6/1970
DTG 676C	AEC 'Reliance'	4MU3RA 5627	Willowbrook (Duple Midland design)	DP49F	2/1965	New	2/1965	1/1988
JBO 56	Leyland 'Tiger Cub' PSUC1/1	542817	Weymann 'Hermes'	B44F	1/1954	Ex Western Welsh OC. (1056).	2/1966	by12/1972
HUH 41	Leyland 'Tiger Cub' PSUC1/1	534595	Weymann 'Hermes'	B44F	1/1954	Ex Western Welsh OC. (1041).	3/1966	by 3/1971
LNY 586D	Bedford VAM14	6842231	Duple 'Viscount'	C45F	8/1966	New	8/1966	4/1977
NTG 410E	Bedford VAL14	7828303	Duple 'Viceroy 36'	C52F	5/1967	New	5/1967	c3/1982
SNY 818F	Bedford VAL70	77456213	Duple 'Viceroy 36'	C52F	5/1968	New	5/1968	c3/1982
JTX 343	Bedford OB	122389	Duple 'Vista'	C29F	12/1949	Ex H.J. Uphill. Caerau, with the business.	6/1968 not operated	1970
KGU 667	Bedford OB	118428	Duple 'Almet'	B29F	1/1950	Ex H.J. Uphill. Caerau, with the business.	6/1968 lic 2/1969	1970
KTG 935	Bedford OB	146593	Duple 'Vista'	C29F	1/1951	Ex H. J. Uphill. Caerau, with the business.	c6/1968 not operated	1970
WNY 453H	AEC 'Reliance' AH505	6MU4R 6775	Plaxton 'Derwent'	B47F	8/1969	New	8/1969	by 1/1983
WTX 334H	Leyland 'Tiger Cub' PSUC1/12	951093	Willowbrook	DP45F to B45F 7/73	10/1969	New	10/1969	1/1988
TWN 557	AEC 'Reliance'	2MU3RV 2493	Willowbrook (1969)	B45F	10/1959	Acquired chassis only from N&C Express, Briton Ferry, 11/1968. See Note A page 141	11/1968 lic 10/1969	12/1984
BTG 577J	Ford R192	BC04JD 55715	Willowbrook	B45F	11/1970	New	11/1970	12/1984
BTG 737J	AEC 'Reliance' AH505	6MU4R 7475	Plaxton 'Panorama Elite'	C51F	12/1970	New	12/1970	1/1988
BTX 973J	AEC 'Reliance' AH505	6MU4R 7474	Plaxton 'Derwent'	B55F	12/1970	New	12/1970	by 10/1984
DTG 297J	AEC 'Reliance'	6MU4R 7792	Willowbrook	B45F	7/1971	New	7/1971	1/1988
KNY 968L	AEC 'Reliance'	6MU4R 8021	Willowbrook 'Expressway 002'	C51F	8/1972	New	8/1972	1/1988
LNY 589L	Bedford YRQ	2T474583	Duple 'Viceroy Express'	C45F	8/1972	New	8/1972	12/1984

Reg	Chassis	Body	Seating	New	History		
LTX 591L	AEC 'Reliance' 6MU4R 22663	Willowbrook 'Expressway 002'	C45F	11/1972	New Exhibited at 1972 Commercial Motor Show.	11/1972	1/1988
NKG 176M	AEC 'Reliance' AH505 6MU4R 24320	Willowbrook	B53F	8/1973	New	8/1973	1/1988
PTX 620M	AEC 'Reliance' AH760 6U32R 23778	Plaxton 'Panorama Elite Express III	C51F to C53F	8/1973	New	8/1973	1/1988
GKG 257N	AEC 'Reliance' AH760 6U32R 29337	Duple 'Dominant I'	C51F	11/1974	New	11/1974	1/1988
GNY 913N	Bedford YRT DW457173	Willowbrook 'Expressway 002'	C51F	1/1975	New Willowbrook demonstrator, at the 1974 Commercial Motor Show.	1/1975	1/1988
JHB 532N	Bedford YRQ EW452588	Duple 'Dominant I' Express	C45F	7/1975	New	7/1975	1/1988
JHB 533N	Bedford YRT EW453058	Duple 'Dominant I' Express	C53F	7/1975	New	7/1975	1/1988
MBO 516F	AEC 'Swift' AH505 MP2R194	Alexander 'W'	B47D+18 standees	6/1968	Ex Cardiff Corporation (516).	10/1975 lic 12/1975	3/1983
MBO 518F	AEC 'Swift' AH505 MP2R196	Alexander 'W'	B47D+18 standees	6/1968	Ex Cardiff Corporation (518).	10/1975 lic 12/1975	3/1983
MBO 521F	AEC 'Swift' AH505 MP2R199	Alexander 'W'	B47D+18 standees	6/1968	Ex Cardiff Corporation (521).	10/1975 lic 5/1976	by 5/1982
MBO 523F	AEC 'Swift' AH505 MP2R201	Alexander 'W'	B47D+18 standees	6/1968	Ex Cardiff Corporation (523).	10/1975	12/1984
MWO296P	AEC 'Reliance' AH760 6U32R 32781	Plaxton 'Supreme' Standard coachwork	C53F	6/1976	New	6/1976	4/1977
OUT 631R	AEC 'Reliance' 6U2R 33788	Plaxton 'Supreme II' Express	C53F	4/1977	New	4/1977 lic 5/1977	1/1988
WJF 378S	AEC 'Reliance' AH760 6U32R 36686	Duple 'Dominant II' Express	C53F	5/1978	New	5/1978	3/1984
YNY 459T	AEC 'Reliance' 6U32R 37179	Duple 'Dominant II' Express	C53F	1/1979	New	1/1979	3/1984
ANY 433B	2MU3RA 5497	Willowbrook	B45F	7/1964	New to Gelligaer UDC (13). Ex Rhymney Valley District Council (66).	8/1979 lic 9/1979	c10/1983
LTG 734D	2MU3RA 6537	Willowbrook	B45F	11/1966	New to Gelligaer UDC (34), as B42D. Ex Rhymney Valley District Council (73).	8/1979 lic 9/1979	by 1/1983
RTG 221M	Bedford YRT CW456664	Duple 'Dominant I' Express	C53F	12/1973	New to Gelligaer UDC (103). Ex Rhymney Valley District Council (87).	8/1979 lic 9/1979	1/1988
CEP 117V	Leyland "Leopard" PSU3F/5R 7903616	Plaxton 'Supreme IV' Express	C53F	12/1979	New	12/1979	1/1988
DHB 152F	Leyland "Leopard" PSU4/2R 703571	East Lancs	B42D	12/1967	Ex Merthyr Tydfil Borough Transport (152).	5/1980 lic 6/1980	8/1986

Registration	Chassis	Chassis number	Body	Seating	Date new	Notes	Date acquired	Date disposed
ECY 278V	Bedford YMT	KW451736	Plaxton 'Supreme IV' Express	C53F	6/1980	New	6/1980	1/1986
DHB 156F	Leyland 'Leopard' PSU4/2R	800433	East Lancs	B42D	1/1968	Ex Merthyr Tydfil Borough Transport (156).	9/1980 lic 12/1980	by 9/1985
EHB 265G	Leyland 'Leopard' PSU3A/2R	802952	East Lancs	B51F	10/1968	Ex Merthyr Tydfil Borough Transport (165).	11/1980	6/1986
GTH 536W	Leyland 'Leopard' PSU3F/5R	7904492	Plaxton 'Supreme IV' Express	C53F	3/1981	New	3/1981	1/1988
NNY 510E	AEC 'Reliance'	6MU4R 6529	Willowbrook (1969)	B45F	6/1967	Ex Taff-Ely Borough Council (97). **See Note B page 141.**	5/1981	12/1984
EHB 264G	Leyland 'Leopard' PSU3A/2R	802832	East Lancs	B51F	10/1968	Ex Merthyr Tydfil Borough Transport (164).	7/1981	1/1988
MEP 969X	Leyland 'Leopard' PSU3F/5R	8030935	Duple 'Dominant IV' Express	C53F	3/1982	New	3/1982	1/1988
MEP 970X	Dennis 'Lancet'	SD508/113	Wadham-Stringer 'Vanguard II'	B45F or B53F	4/1982	New	4/1982	1/1988
OYU 573R	AEC 'Reliance'	6U3ZR 35358	Duple 'Dominant II' Standard coachwork	C55F	7/1977	Ex National Travel (South East), London.	9/1982	2/1983
THG 852X	Leyland 'Tiger' TRCTL11/3R	8101584	Duple 'Goldliner III'	C50F	6/1982	Demonstrator on loan from Leyland Motors.	2/1983	5/1983
XDG 215S	Leyland 'Leopard' PSU5C/4R	7705461	Plaxton 'Supreme III' Standard coachwork	C55F	3/1978	Ex Cavalier, Hounslow, London. Previously South Wales Transport (215).	5/1983	1/1988
UPD 269X	Dennis 'Lancet'	SD503/102	Wadham-Stringer 'Vanguard II'	B45F	4/1982	Ex Demonstrator for Hestair-Dennis, Guildford.	5/1983	1/1988
A644 WCY	DAF MB200DKFL600	240336	Caetano 'Algarve'	C53F	1/1984	New Exhibited at the Coaching Symposium, NEC, Birmingham, 19/2/1984.	1/1984	1/1988
A504 WTH	DAF MB200DKFL600	240357	Caetano 'Algarve'	C53F to C48FT	3/1984	New	3/1984	1/1988
C950 GTH	DAF MB200DKFL600	241717	Lag 'Galaxy'	C53FT	1/1986	New	1/1986	1/1988
C22 KDT	Mercedes-Benz L608D	WDB30955-920700233	Reeve-Burgess	C21F	2/1986	New	2/1986	1/1988
YNY 71T	Ford A0609	BCLWUM-47318	Moseley 'Faro III'	C25F	1/1979	Ex Len Hopkins, Ogmore Vale, Mid-Glam.	4/1986	1/1988
948 RJO	Bedford YMT	GW451124	Plaxton 'Supreme III'	C53F	5/1977	Ex Tappin, Wallingford, Oxfordshire. Re-registered from *PRX 398R* in 4/1985.	5/1986	1/1988
556 DHO	Bedford YMT	FW455486	Plaxton 'Supreme III'	C53F	3/1977	Ex Tappin, Wallingford, Oxfordshire. Re-registered from *OJB 664R*, in 3/1986.	by 7/1986	1/1988
B697 VCX	DAF SB2300DHTD585	243414	Plaxton 'Paramount 3200'	C53F	8/1984	Ex Harris, Little Houghton, Northants.	by 1/1987	1/1988

MUA 45P	Bristol LHS6L (0.401)	LHS-242	Eastern Coachworks (7ft 6ins)	DP27F	7/1976	Ex Nottingham City Transport (731).	1/1987	1/1988
JUG 352N	Bristol LHS6L (0.401)	LHS-217	Eastern Coachworks (7ft 6ins)	DP27F	7/1975	Ex Nottingham City Transport (735).	4/1987	1/1988
D186 PWN	MCW 'Metrorider' MF150/7	MB8955	MCW	C25F	6/1987	New	6/1987	1/1988

Note A: AEC Reliance TWN 557, was new to N&C Coaches, James Street, Neath, in October 1959, with a Park Royal C41F body. It sustained extensive bodywork damage in a RTA involving a lorry, in 1968, and after removal of its body, the chassis was sold to Brewer's, who had it re-bodied for further use, in October 1969. *See photograph below, and page 71.*

Note B: Whilst in the ownership of Pontypridd UDC, AEC Reliance NNY 510E, was rebuilt with a new Willowbrook body, after an overturning accident in 1969.

Left: This was the twisted remains of the AEC 'Reliance' coach, **TWN 557**, owned by N&C Coaches, of Briton Ferry, after its accident with a lorry, on the A48 road at Bonvilston, in 1968.

The driver had a miraculous escape with minor injuries, and eventually returned to work as a conductor. However, he never drove a bus again!

The running chassis was sold to Brewer's Motor Services, in November 1968, who later dispatched it to Willowbrook for a new body. It returned in October 1969, for a further fifteen years' service, and in December 1984, it was sold to Joe Sykes, the Carlton dealer, who passed it on to Blue Bus Services, of Rugeley, Staffordshire, where it saw further service. A picture of it after re-bodying, can be found on page 71.

BREWERS MOTOR SERVICES – VEHICLE DISPOSALS

unknown	(Arrol-Johnson lorry). No further trace.
L 9530	Last licensed 10/1921. Totally destroyed in accident, 10/1921.
NY 2484	Withdrawn 1931. No further trace.
L 5492	Withdrawn 7/1935. No further trace.
NY 4610	Sold as a lorry, 2/1936.
BO 2378	No further trace.
L 8708	No further trace.
BO 1844	No further trace.
UH 313	Still operating 1935. No further trace.
BX 4384	Still operating 1935. No further trace.
UT 694	Sold to Price, Llanbadarn Fynydd, Radnorshire (Powys), unknown date.
AX 8743	No further trace.
DE 5861	Sold to unknown owner at Swansea, probably scrap dealer, 12/1934. Registration voided 12/1934.
WN 3424	No further trace.
RU 9716	Destroyed in a fire, 30/9/1937.
WN 4046	No further trace.
unknown	(Morris Commercial 'Viceroy'). Destroyed in garage fire, 5/1938.
unknown	(Morris Commercial 'Director'). Destroyed in garage fire, 5/1938.
WN 6788	Withdrawn 1/1960. Sold to scrap dealer at Pontyclun, Glam. 2/1962.
WN 7598	Withdrawn by 4/1953. Scrapped on site by Brewer's.
WN 8329	Last licensed 1946. No further trace.
WN 9952	Last licensed 12/1949. No further trace.
WN 1684	Sold to W. Leyland (Showman), London N4, unknown date. Withdrawn by Leyland, 9/1952.
WG 2315	Destroyed in garage fire, 5/1938.
BTX 599	Destroyed in garage fire, 5/1938.
TG 273	Sold to H.J. Uphill. Caerau, 12/1939. Last Licensed 1940.
CTX 865	Commandeered by War Dept., 7/1940. To E.R. Forse, Cardiff, c1942 (by 4/1943). Last licensed, 12/1953.
DNY 140	Commandeered by War Dept., 7/1940. To E.R. Forse, Cardiff, by 8/1943. To Hill, Dinas Powis. Last lic. 9/1957.
DNY 148	Last licensed 12/1950. Broken up by 12/1952.
WN 853	Sold to unknown showman at Salford, 8/1948.
DTG 77	Withdrawn 9-10/1952. Probably scrapped.
CS 1498	Sold to Wm. Evan Lloyd (Glanteifi Motors), Pontrhydfendigaid, Cardiganshire, by 1950.
ENY 712	Withdrawn 5/1959. No further trace.
ATG 491	Sold to W.J. Jones, Skewen, Glam. 10/1942.
WG 1177	Withdrawn 3/1951. Broken up by 12/1952.
UH 7201	Withdrawn by 1948. No further trace.
AWA 486	Sold to Wm. Evan Lloyd (Glanteifi Motors), Pontrhydfendigaid, Cardiganshire, 2/1948.
TH 9189	Last licensed 1948. Scrapped 1951.
TX 4264	Last Licensed 12/1952. Broken up by 12/1952.
FNY 420	(Guy Arab). Not operated. The Traffic Commissioners refused authority to operate double deck vehicles in the Caerau area, as the roads were 'unsuitable'. Brewer's retained the registration FNY 420, for use on a forthcoming Bedford OB, and sold the Guy to United Welsh Services, Swansea, 9/1943, where it was re-registered DWN 370.
FNY 405	Withdrawn 10/1957. Sold for use as a mobile shop at Pyle, Glamorganshire, by 1/1961. Still about 10/1965.
FNY 406	Withdrawn 1/1955. Noted at depot de-licensed 6/1959. Scrapped.
TG 8764	Licence expired 12/1944. No further trace.
FNY 420	(Bedford). Sold to D. Thomas. Llangynwyd, Maesteg, 11/1952. Last licensed, 12/1954.
FNY 731	Sold to D. Thomas. Llangynwyd, Maesteg, 11/1952.
FNY 732	Sold for use as a mobile shop, Bridgend, 11/1960.
FNY 889	Withdrawn 1/1953. Sold to H. J. Uphill, Caerau, 4/1953. Last licensed 12/1959.
FNY 894	Sold to Lewis & Jacob, Maesteg, 12/1952, re-seated B28F, 7/1956, and withdrawn by 9/1961.
FNY 895	Withdrawn 1/1966, but reported still licensed 5/66 & 11/67.
VJ 1252	Not operated. No further trace.
CTG 251	Withdrawn 3/1951. Still owned 4/1953. Scrapped by Brewer's in 1953.
FTG 479	Withdrawn 5-6/1960. Sold by 9/1961, used as a Farm lorry,
GNY 509	Withdrawn 5/1952, Sold to Fairhurst, Wallsend, Tyne & Wear, 6/1952.
GTG 438	Sold to Parish, Morda, Salop, 5/1952. To Sargeant Motors, Builth Wells, Breconshire, by 1/1958.

GTX 162	Withdrawn 7/1968. No further trace.
GTX 163	Withdrawn 8/1959. No further trace.
GTX 363	Withdrawn 5/1961. No further trace.
HTG129	Withdrawn 4-5/1961. No further trace.
HTG 528	Withdrawn 5/1952. Sold to Wade. Doncaster, South Yorks, 6/1952.
ANY 166	Withdrawn 12/1953. Scrapped.
ANY 716	Last licence expired 10/1949. Broken up by 9/1951.
JNY 273	Withdrawn 1961. Sold to Edwin Gamlin, Maesteg, and used as caravan. Later abandoned in a field & derelict.
JNY 770	Withdrawn 7/1963. No further trace.
JNY 771	Withdrawn by 2/1958. Sold to W.L. Jones, Cwmavon, Glam, by 2/1958. To Moble shop at Bridgend, 11/1960.
JTG 34	Withdrawn 2/1963. No further trace.
JTG 622	Withdrawn 11/1961. Sold 11/1961. Mobile shop with Mr. Lock, Cymmer, Glam, 1/1962. Still there 5/1971.
JTG 854	Withdrawn 1/1966. No further trace.
JTG 901	Withdrawn 5/1966. No further trace.
JTX 152	Withdrawn 5/1966. No further trace.
JTX 153	Withdrawn 3/1963. No further trace.
JTX 358	Withdrawn 4/1959. Sold to Porthcawl Recreations Ltd. (Non PSV operator), Porthcawl, for staff transport, 4/1959.
KNY 672	Withdrawn 6/1955. No further trace.
KTX 741	Withdrawn 5/1965. No further trace.
KTX 742	Sold to A.G. Reed (t/a Gwyn Reed), Bridgend, 2/1966. Withdrawn c3/1969. No further trace.
KTG 764	Withdrawn 1/1968. No further trace.
LTX 170	Withdrawn 7/1967. No further trace.
LTX 470	Withdrawn 7/1972. Gone by 12/1974. No further trace.
MNY 335	Withdrawn by 12/1964. No further trace.
OTG 600	Withdrawn 1972. Sold to Andrew Scott (Contractor) Port Talbot, 10-12/1972.
OTG 601	Withdrawn by 6/1974. Gone by 12/1974.
OTG 547	Withdrawn 9/1968. Scrapped by 1/1971.
OTX 697	Withdrawn 9/1968. Scrapped by 1/1971.
RTG 501	Withdrawn 1972. Gone by 12/1974. No further trace.
TTX 536	Withdrawn for spares by 1/1971.
VTG 88	Withdrawn for spares by 8/1971.
YNY 247	Withdrawn 5/1978. Scrapped 1982.
897 BTG	Withdrawn 7/1975. Sold to G.M. Jones, Morriston, Swansea, 1/1976. To J.M. Hutchins, Pontardawe, Glam. 3/1976.
887 CTG	Sold to Humphrey's Bros, Bridgend, 1/1973. To R.R. Prance, Cardiff, 4/1974.
212 FNY	Scrapped by 5/1982.
801 HTX	Withdrawn 9/1983, Sold to J. Hassan, Barry, 10/1983, for preservation. Still on DVLA website but no further trace.
98 KTG	Withdrawn 1975. In use as a site hut on M4 construction site, Stormy Down, near Bridgend, by 3/1979.
605 MNY	Scrapped by 5/1982.
277 PNY	Withdrawn 1975. Scrapped 5/1976.
557 PTX	Withdrawn 7/1975. Sold to Abercarn RFC, Abercarn, Caerphilly, by 2/1976.
278 TNY	Passed to 'Helproute Ltd' with the business, 9/1/1988. Re-registered AKG144A, 3/1988, unused & sold 3/1988.
433 UNY	Sold to Kenfig Motors (Mansel David & Son), Kenfig Hill, Mid-Glam, 2/1979. Withdrawn by 7/1982.
873 WNY	Withdrawn 7/1975. Sold to D.D. Jones, Pandy Mill, Meidrim, Carmarthenshire (Dyfed) by 3/1976.
ANY 135B	Sold to Jones Motors, Login, Carmarthenshire (Dyfed), for spares, c3/1982.
9572 F	Withdrawn 6/1970. Out of use 8/1971. Sold for use as mobile home, at Pontypridd, by 12/1973.
608 JPU	Withdrawn 6/1970. Sold to Bethlehem Church, Cefn Cribwr, Mid-Glam, by 11/1972.
DTG 676C	Passed to 'Helproute Ltd' with the business, 9/1/1988. To D.H. Stolzenberg. Maesteg, 2/1988. W/drawn by12/1989.
JBO 56	Sold to Andrew Scott (Contractor), Port Talbot, by 12/1972.
HUH 41	Withdrawn by 3/1971. Used for spares by 6/1972.
LNY 586D	Withdrawn 4/1977. Sold to Morris Travel, Pencoed, Mid-Glam, 5/1977.
NTG 410E	Sold to Jones Motors, Login, Carmarthenshire (Dyfed), for spares, c3/1982.
SNY 818F	Sold to Jones Motors, Login, Carmarthenshire (Dyfed), for spares, c3/1982.
JTX 343	Not operated. Sold to Scarrett, Llanharan, for scrap, 1970.
KGU 667	Was operated. Sold to Scarrett, Llanharan, for scrap, 1970.
KTG 935	Not operated. Sold to Scarrett, Llanharan, for scrap, 1970.
WNY 453H	Withdrawn by 1/1983. Body reduced to a frame by 1/1983.
WTX 334H	Passed to 'Helproute Ltd' with the business, 9/1/1988. Sold for preservation by 5/1988. Last licenced 10/1989.
TWN 557	Sold to Joe Sykes (dealer), Carlton, 12/1984. To Blue Bus Services, Rugeley, Staffs, 3/1985.

BTG 577J	Sold to Joe Sykes (dealer) Carlton, for scrap, 12/1984.
BTG 737J	Passed to 'Helproute Ltd' with the business, 9/1/1988. To D.H. Stolzenberg, Maesteg, 2/1988. W/drawn by 12/89.
BTX 973J	Withdrawn and sold by 10/1984. No further trace.
DTG 297J	Passed to 'Helproute Ltd' with the business, 9/1/1988. Used as a tow-bus by 7/1988.
KNY 968L	Passed to 'Helproute Ltd' with the business, 9/1/1988. Driver trainer with subsidiary company 'Skillplace', 4/1988.
LNY 589L	Sold to Joe Sykes (dealer) Carlton, 12/1984. To Blue Bus Services, Rugeley, Staffs (N° 6), 1/1985.
LTX 591L	Passed to 'Helproute Ltd' with the business, 9/1/1988. To C.T.C. Caerphilly (subsidiary of Cleverly Cwmbran), 4/88.
NKG 176M	Passed to 'Helproute Ltd' with the business, 9/1/1988. Sold by 6/1988. No further trace.
PTX 620M	Passed to 'Helproute Ltd' with the business, 9/1/1988. Sold to Wilkins, Cymmer, 4/1988.
GKG 257N	Passed to 'Helproute Ltd' with the business, 9/1/1988. To D.H. Stolzenberg, Maesteg, 3/1988. Returned to A.E. & F.R. Brewer, Caerau, (United Welsh Holdings), with Stolzenberg's business, 6/1990.
GNY 913N	Passed to 'Helproute Ltd' with the business, 9/1/1988. Sold to Brian Isaac Coaches, Morriston, 4/1988.
JHB 532N	Passed to 'Helproute Ltd' with the business, 9/1/1988. Sold to Watts Coaches, Bonvilston, South Glam, by 5/1988.
JHB 533N	Passed to 'Helproute Ltd' with the business, 9/1/1988. Sold to K & P John, Llanharry, Mid-Glam, 5/1988.
MBO 516F	Sold to K & P John, Llanharry, Mid-Glam, 3/1983. Withdrawn/used for spares by 5/1986. Sold for scrap 7/1988.
MBO 518F	Sold to K & P John, Llanharry, Mid-Glam, 3/1983. Withdrawn by 4/1988. Derelict 3/1989.
MBO 521F	Withdrawn by 5/1982. Scrapped.
MBO 523F	Sold to J. Sykes (dealer), Carlton, 12/1984. To unknown Cardiff NPSV operator by 10/1985.
MWO296P	Withdrawn 4/1977. Sold to Willetts, Yorkley, Gloucestershire, 5/1977.
OUT 631R	Passed to 'Helproute Ltd' with the business, 9/1/1988. To Warren, Neath, 4/1988, to R.M. Gower, Burry Port, 8/1990. Re-registered SIB 1304, 7/1992, withdrawn 5/1997, To Fussell & Gower, Swansea, 4/1998 (not operated).
WJF 378S	Sold to Moseley (dealer) 3/1984. To Eynon, Trimsaran (Dyfed), 6/1984. To Davies Bros (Pencader) Ltd., 6/1988. Sold for preservation 2/1997, project abandoned and vehicle scrapped.
YNY 459T	Sold to Moseley (dealer) 3/1984. To Bluebird (Warren), Neath, West Glam, 11/1984.
ANY 433B	Withdrawn c10/1983. No further trace.
LTG 734D	Sold to Martin & Billett. Pontycymmer, Mid-Glam, by 1/1983. To R.M. Appleton, Bridgend, 4/1985.
RTG 221M	Passed to 'Helproute Ltd' with the business, 9/1/1988. To Cwmavon RFC, 6/1988. To Morrison, Crynant, 10/1991.
CEP 117V	Passed to 'Helproute Ltd' with the business, 9/1/1988. To Merlyns Coaches, Skewen, 9/1988. Sold 3/1989.
DHB 152F	Sold to J. Sykes (dealer) Carlton, 12/1984. To Capitol Coaches (J.D. Cleverly), Swansea depot, for spares, 8/1986.
ECY 278V	Sold 1/1986. To Owen's, Yateley, Hants, 2/1986, and re-registered ONY 837 by Owen.
DHB 156F	Used as a towing vehicle by 9/1985. Withdrawn from towing duties by 5/1986, and scrapped by 8/1987.
EHB 265G	Sold to K & P John, Llanharry, Mid-Glam, 6/1986. Scrapped on site 2-6/1992.
GTH 536W	Passed to 'Helproute Ltd' with the business, 1/1988. To A.E. & F.R. Brewer Ltd, (United Welsh Holdings) 159, 5/1988. Re-registered 948 RJO, 3/88 to JTH 44W, 8/1992. Withdrawn 11/1993, No further trace.
NNY 510E	Withdrawn 12/1984 with fire damage. Scrapped 8/1986.
EHB 264G	Passed to 'Helproute Ltd' with the business, 1/1988. To Morriston Coaches, Morriston, Swansea, 5/1988.
MEP 969X	Passed to 'Helproute Ltd' with the business, 1/1988. Re-registered YBK 132, c7/1988. To NTH 156X, 4/1993, To Western National OC, Exeter, 11/1993.
MEP 970X	Passed to 'Helproute Ltd' with the business, 1/1988. To C.T.C. Caerphilly (subsidiary of Cleverly Cwmbran), 9/88.
OYU 573R	Passed to 'Helproute Ltd' with the business, 1/1988. Sold by 6/1988. No further trace.
THG 852X	Demonstration vehicle returned to Leyland Motors, 2/1983.
XDG 215S	Passed to 'Helproute Ltd' with the business, 1/1988. To Cwmavon RFC (NPSV), 8/1992.
UPD 269X	Passed to 'Helproute Ltd' with the business, 1/1988. To C.T.C. Caerphilly (subsidiary of J.D. Cleverly), 9/1988.
A644 WCY	Passed to 'Helproute Ltd' with the business, 1/1988. Re-registered 278 TNY in 3/1988. To A654 XWN, by 12/1993. To Yeomans. Canon Pyon, Hereford.
A504 WTH	Passed to 'Helproute Ltd' with the business, 1/1988. Re-registered 948 RJO in 3/1988. To A659 XWN, 3/1988. To Stuart. Hyde, Manchester, 1/1990, re-reg SXI 3627, 7/1990.
C950 GTH	Passed to 'Helproute Ltd' with the business, 1/1988. To Stuart. Hyde, Manchester, 10/1990.
C22 KDT	Passed to 'Helproute Ltd' with the business, 1/1988. To C.T.C. Caerphilly (subsidiary of J.D. Cleverly), 7/1988.
YNY 71T	Passed to 'Helproute Ltd' with the business, 1/1988. To Briggs Coaches, Swansea, 2/1988.
948 RJO	Passed to 'Helproute Ltd' with the business, 1/1988. Re-reg RWO 723R, 3/88. To Cooper & Ebdon. Romsey, 3/1988
556 DHO	Passed to 'Helproute Ltd' with the business, 1/1988. Re-reg. RWO 722R, 3/1988. To Edwards. Tiers Cross, 3/1988
B697 VCX	Passed to 'Helproute Ltd' with the business, 1/1988. Re-registered 556 DHO (f/n 556), in 3/1988. Withdrawn 12/1993. Sold to Wrekin District Council (NPSV), Shropshire, 3/1994.
MUA 45P	Passed to 'Helproute Ltd' with the business, 1/1988. To Stockdale, Selby, North Yorkshire, 2/1988, and after several owners, this vehicle is now in preservation with the Merseyside Preservation Trust.
JUG 352N	Passed to 'Helproute Ltd' with the business, 1/1988. To Stockdale, Selby, North Yorkshire, 2/1988.
D186 PWN	Passed to 'Helproute Ltd' with the business, 1/1988. To South Wales Transport (386), 10/1988.

BREWER'S MOTOR SERVICES. TICKETS USED

BREWER'S MOTOR SERVICES. PHOTOGRAPH INDEX

Reg N°	Page N°	Reg N°	Page N°	Reg N°	Page N°	Reg N°	Page N°
ANY 166	40/41	GTH 536W	88	LTX 170	48	TTX 536	55
ANY 716	255	GTX 162	37/38	LTX 470	49	TWN 557	71/141
ANY 135B	64	GTX 363	38/39	LTX 591L	75	UPD 269X	91
ANY 433B	84	HTG 129	39/45	MBO 516F	79	VTX 88	56
AWA 486	35	HTG 528	38	MBO 518F	79	WJF 378S	82
A504 WTH	92	HUH 41	66	MBO 523F	80	WN 3424	23
A644 WCY	92	JBO 56	66	MEP 969X	89	WN 6788	31
BTG 577J	71	JHB 532N	78	MEP 970X	90	WNY 453H	69/70
BTG 737J	72	JHB 533N	78	MNY 335	49	WTX 334H	70
BTX 973J	72	JNY 273	41	MUA 45P	96	XDG 215S	91
CEP 117V	85	JNY 770	42	MWO 296P	81	YNY 71T	96
C950 GTH	93	JTG 34	42/43	NKG 176M	75	YNY 247	56
DE 5861	24	JTG 622	31	NNY 510E	88	YNY 459T	82
DHB 152F	86	JTG 854	43	NTG 410E	67	98 KTG	59
DHB 156F	87	JTG 901	44/45	NY 2484	20	212 FNY	58
DTG 297J	73	JTX 152	44	NY 4610	21/22	277 PNY	60
DTG 676C	65	JTX 153	45	OTG 547	52	278 TNY	61
D186 PWN	97	JTX 358	45	OTG 600	51	433 UNY	62
ECY 278V	86	JUG 352N	96/97	OTG 601	51	557 PTX	61
EHB 264G	89	KNY 968L	74	OTX 697	52	605 MNY	60
EHB 265G	87	KTG 764	47	OUT 631R	81	608 JPU	65
ENY 712	31/34	KTX 741	47	OYU 573R	90	801 HTX	58
FNY 895	36	KTX 742	48	PTX 620M	76	873 WNY	62
FTG 479	36	L 5492	21	RTG 501	54/57	887 CTG	57
GKG 257N	77	LNY 586D	67	RTG 221M	85	897 BTG	57
GNY 913N	77	LNY 589L	74	SNY 818F	68	9572 F	64
GTG 438	38						

A.E. & F.R BREWER Ltd. PHOTOGRAPH INDEX
(UNITED WELSH HOLDINGS Ltd)

Reg N°	Page N°	Reg N°	Page N°	Reg N°	Page N°	Reg N°	Page N°
ANA 94Y	113	C210 HTH	105	H782 GTA	131	NWS 904R	110
ANA 644Y	132	C213 PNJ	106	JUH 230W	122	PJT 255R	108
AWN 812V	121	C479 BFB	111	J375 WWK	115	P620 VDW	128
A658 KUM	125	D520 FAE	123	J901 MAF	126	RWN 477S	106
BEP 981V	117	EWW 945Y	125	J916 WVC	115	SPK 116M	109
BEP 982V	117	E203 PWY	133	KUB 669V	102	UAR 598W	114
BVP 778V	127	F100 CEP	107	K9 BMS	116	UTF 723M	104
B221 WEU	118	F546 EJA	124	K11 BMS	116	VDH 244S	127
B440 WTC	111	F606 AWN	105	K404 BAX	118	XEU 859T	110
B905 DHB	124	F615 XWY	130	LRN 328J	104	YBK 132	101/113
B930 AAX	103	F721 FDV	129	L218 AAB	131	278 TNY	103
CSU 244	126	G261 LUG	120	L601 FKG	120	300 CUH	128
C200 PCD	112	G841 PNW	119	MBB 404X	100	556 DHO	101
C209 HTH	114	HHJ 379Y	112	NIL 2450	130	948 RJO	102

W.G. THOMAS
LLYNFI MOTOR SERVICES LTD

William George Thomas, the founder of Llynfi Motor Services, was born at 4 Picton Street, Carmarthen, on 20th July, 1878. He was the second of three sons born to Sarah, and David Thomas – a professional gardener. His elder brother, David John Thomas, born 1876, was one of the earliest passenger vehicle operators in Maesteg, and was the founder of Cream Line (Maesteg) Ltd., which is dealt with separately on page 252.

By early 1891, the family had moved to 2 Union Street, Carmarthen, but William, at the young age of 12 years 9 months had moved to live with relatives at Maesteg, to begin his working career as a coal miner.

Meanwhile, back in Carmarthen, the family's next door neighbour, was the head attendant at Carmarthen 'Lunatic Asylum', and assisted William in obtaining employment there.

William George Thomas accepted the position of an attendant at Carmarthen 'Lunatic Asylum', where he met Nurse Martha Jenkins, from Llandyfriog, Cardiganshire.

Martha and William were married at Newcastle Emlyn Parish Church on 14th May, 1902, and after their marriage, they moved to Maesteg (in the Parish of Cwmdu), where George took up the vocation of Colliery Engineman. The first of their six children, Glyn Haydn Thomas, was born in Maesteg, on 21st February, 1903, and in early 1911, the family settled down to live at 4 Exchange Street, Maesteg, where they also ran a 'boarding house'.

There are no archive records for William George Thomas between 1911 and 1919, but he claimed that he ran a vehicle on the Maesteg to Caerau route in 1921, and gave it up due to fierce competition. That statement is feasible, as he was granted a drivers licence (N° 27), with Maesteg Urban District Council, on 1st February 1921.

Presumably, he drove one of his brother's cars on the Caerau route, as his brother, David John Thomas mentioned above, was licenced to operate two cars in 1921. D.J. Thomas was one of the earliest licenced drivers on the Maesteg to Caerau route, receiving his first charabanc driver's licence (badge N° 1), from Maesteg UDC, on 27th April, 1915. He was granted his first 'omnibus' licence in December 1917, to legally run a motor car for hire and reward.

However, returning to 27th September, 1919, a national rail strike began, leaving the villagers of nearby Bryn, completely isolated. The 'Port Talbot Railway' was the villagers' only means of transport, so George appeared on the scene with a motor car, probably his brothers, and provided the villagers with an 'unlicensed' service between Bryn and Maesteg.

It must be pointed out that the village of Bryn at this point in time, had no direct road access to Cwmavon and Port Talbot. That particular road was still at planning stage, and W.G. Thomas become a lifeline to the villagers, who continued to support him when he later started running a regular service.

In the meantime, Cridland Brothers of Cardiff, asked Maesteg UDC, for a licence to ply between Maesteg and Bryn on 14th August 1923, but their application was deferred.

Meanwhile, construction of the new road between Bryn and Ynysygwas, (near Port Talbot) was going ahead, and with just one vehicle owned, William George Thomas applied in February 1924, to the Maesteg, and Port Talbot local authorities, for a licence to operate a service between the towns, when the new road opened. The new six mile 'Bryn Road' (B4282), costing £25,000, was jointly paid for by Maesteg, and Port Talbot Councils, and was officially opened on Saturday 3rd May, 1924, by the Minister of Transport, Mr Harry Gosling (1924-9).

After W.G. Thomas submitted his licence application to Port Talbot BC, they wrote to Maesteg UDC, stating *'that their council favourably entertained an application of The South Wales Transport Co. Ltd., for a licence to ply for hire between Port Talbot and Maesteg, and that the application received from W.G. Thomas was deferred, as they thought it a mistake to grant a licence to an individual who had only one or two conveyances'*.

Maesteg Licensing Committee replied stating *'they considered that licences should be granted to all applicants who undertook to maintain a regular service, according to their respective timetables'*, and in return, decided to defer an application made by South Wales Transport.

Both Councils eventually came to an amicable agreement, and licences were issued to both applicants, in March 1924, for a jointly operated service.

South Wales Transport Co., immediately wrote to Maesteg UDC, stating they propose to commence their new service between Aberavon and Maesteg on Monday 7th April, 1924.

However, the first vehicle licensed to W.G. Thomas was NY 4206, a Blue and Cream, 1918, Fiat 15TER, with a 25 hp engine, and Massey 14 seat bus bodywork, which he acquired from the War Department, in October 1923.

Eleven months later, in September 1924, he bought a new Daimler CKY, registered NY 6910, which was fitted with Massey 20 seat bodywork, and painted Cream and Navy Blue.

Above: This vehicle is said to be W.G. Thomas' new Daimler 'CKY', registered **NY 6910** in September 1924. Records show NY 6910 to be a 20 seat bus, so this charabanc was probably rebuilt as a bus. *(Courtesy Byron Gage).*

The next vehicle acquired by W.G. Thomas, who by now traded as Llynvi Motor Service, was a 1920 Daimler 'CK', 29 seater registered CW 2589. This was acquired from Helliwell, of Nelson, Lancashire, in July 1926, and was still licensed to him in 1934.

Above: This 1920 Daimler 'CK', 29 seat bus, **CW 2589**, was purchased by William Thomas in July 1926, when he started using the fleetname 'Llynvi Motor Service' (later spelt 'Llynfi Motor Service'). It had been rebuilt from a charabanc at an unknown date, probably the same time as it received those new wheels with pneumatic tyres on the front axle. From October 1928, the law regarding pneumatic tyres changed. Vehicles fitted with the 'softer tyres' all around, were permitted to have an increased speed limit from 12 mph to 20 mph, and two years later, that was increased to 30 mph. So this vehicle would have been restricted to 12 mph with that configuration. This view was taken outside E & A Laviers' Drapers Shop, in Commercial St., Maesteg, and features that cheerful little chap in front – who is also featured in one of the Brewer's views, on page 23. I wonder whether he 'jumped ship' to work for the opposition. *(Courtesy Byron Gage).*

Certain difficulties arose with the shared timetable on the Port Talbot route in March 1927, and the issue involving South Wales Transport, continued until 28th March, 1929, when new timetables were finally approved by the Maesteg Licensing Committee. Four months later, both operators fixed their joint timetable to the notice board in the new Maesteg Bus Station. On 3rd September, 1929, both parties agreed to extend their jointly operated service during the summertime, to reach Aberavon Beach, which was approved by both Licensing Committees.

Meanwhile, annual renewal of licences came around in February 1929, and W.G. Thomas relicensed his only three vehicles, NY 4206, NY 6910 and CW 2589.

At the same time, he renewed his driver's licence, together with the driver's licences of his eldest two sons, Glyn Haydn Thomas (26), and Dyfrig Llewellyn Thomas (20), and the first licence for his eldest daughter, Margaretta May Thomas (23), known as 'Gretta'.

It was very much a family concern in those far gone days, and 'Gretta' was able to claim the honour of being the first female omnibus driver in Maesteg! However, the family's driving licence renewals in January 1931, included William George Thomas junior (18), together with Hackney Carriage licences for vehicles, VA 4592, T 9054, and 'a newcomer', DE 5349.

Above: Bus number 6, **VA 4592**, arrived in May 1930. It was a 174 inch w/b, Leyland PLSC1 'Lion', fitted with Leyland B31F bodywork, and was new in February 1926, to an unknown owner in Lanarkshire. Not much other information is known about this vehicle, other than it passed to W. Browning & Sons, at nearby Cefn Cribwr, at a later stage!   *(Courtesy Byron Gage).*

Above: Bus number 7, **DE 5349**, was another Leyland PLSC1 'Lion', fitted with Leyland 31 seat bodywork, but this differed slightly, as it was rear entrance. It was new to the large Pembrokeshire operator, Green's Motors, of Haverfordwest, in May 1926, and arrived at Maesteg in March 1930. It was photographed here at this unknown location, with no headlights fitted, accompanied by VA 4592, which only had one headlamp! On the other hand, it could have been war-time!   Driving these buses without decent lighting on the dark roads between Maesteg and Port Talbot must have been horendous for those drivers. *(Courtesy Byron Gage).*

The next major event in the company's history however, was 'The Road Traffic Act 1930'. This Act of Parliament, which was passed in August 1930, gave the Ministry of Transport's Traffic Commissioners, full control of public service vehicles (PSVs), together with passenger services, and their licensing in Great Britain.

These Traffic Commissioners, with the power vested in them, brought about improved operating conditions, adherence to timetables, and stability of fares. All stage carriage and express carriage routes had to be licensed, and the granting of such licences, which had previously been under the jurisdiction of local authorities, were then only obtainable through the Traffic Commissioners. Licences to drive and conduct a PSV, also became the Traffic Commissioners responsibility.

Under this new licensing system, all PSV operators were issued with operator identification numbers, by which they were identified. Consequently, the number issued to Llynvi Motor Services, was TGR 434, with each road service licence applied for thereafter, given licence numbers beginning with the operator identification number.

After implementing the new Traffic Act fully, in April 1931, every bus and coach operator had to re-apply to the new authority for renewal of each licence held, and re-apply annually thereafter. Likewise, any changes to services, times, fares, or new routes, all had to be applied for, and the licences would only be granted when approved by the Traffic Commissioners.

Conforming to the new licensing rules, **Llynvi Motor Services**, of 4 Exchange Street, Maesteg, applied for renewal without change, of the only stage carriage service licence held by them during the past year. The following licence application was published in the Traffic Commissioners first 'Notices & Proceedings', dated 25th March, 1931:-

TGR 434/1   **Maesteg (Town Hall)** to **Aberavon Beach**,
via: Bryn, Penrhydwaelod, Ynysygwas, Saron, and Port Talbot.
Operated jointly with The South Wales Transport Co. Ltd. (TGR 421/35).
This licence was granted on 13th May, 1931.

On 17th June, 1931, the company asked for the following 'new' licence:-

TGR 434/2   To run a group of **Excursions & Tours** at inclusive fares only, starting from Ogmore, Llynfi, and Afan Valleys. *Tours within SWTA, to run throughout the year. Max number of vehicles to be used on this group of tours in 1 day, is 3.*
Granted 8th July, 1931.

When renewal of TGR 434/2 was asked for in January 1932, an objection was received from Western Welsh OC., resulting in a hearing held at Port Talbot Town Hall, on 11th May, 1932, where the licence was granted. Two years later, in April, 1934, a modification to this licence was asked for, with respect to operate an additional excursion to Blackpool, running on Wednesdays only, during June or July, using one vehicle (35 passengers). Fare, all inclusive, at £35.0.0 each. There was one objector, the Great Western Railway Co., and the modification was refused on 15th June, 1934. The licence was renewed as originally authorised.

For reasons unknown, Llynvi MS objected to the stage carriage licence renewal of David Jones & Sons, (Pantdu), for service between Aberavon and Tonmawr (TGR 365/1), in April 1932.

The service did not interfere with Llynvi MS route, so was allowed to continue as authorised.

In September 1933, the passenger services of the Port Talbot to Maesteg Railway ceased due to lack of public support. This was obviously beneficial to Llynvi Motor Services, as it gave them extra custom on their jointly operated service between Maesteg and Port Talbot. The railway remained open for goods and mineral traffic for some considerable time afterwards.

A year later in September 1934, the Port Talbot based Thomas Brothers family (pre - BET takeover), needed extra capital to absorb several competitors in their district. W.G. Thomas of Llynvi Motor Services, came to their rescue and purchased a 40% share in their business.

Shortly afterwards, in December 1934, W.G. Thomas' eldest son, **Glyn Haydn Thomas**, of 33 Salisbury Road, Maesteg, applied for his own Road Service Licence, as listed below:-

> TGR 2065/1 **Maesteg (Castle St. Bridge)** to **Onllwyn**. *Workmen's stage carriage service.*
> via: Nantyffyllon, Caerau Square, by-pass road to Maesteg General Hospital, Bryn, Port Talbot, Neath, Aberdulais, Seven Sisters, and Banwen.
> *(Previous licence granted to Reginald Edwin Greenslade, 18 Duke Street, Maesteg, on TGR 1283/1). 3 x shifts per day. Weekly fares not issued.*

The following short period licences were issued in order to continue operating the service:-

> TGR 2065/Sp/1   Issued to operate the above service. Period 1/1/1935 to 7/1/1935.
>
> TGR 2065/Sp/2   Issued to operate the above service. Period 8/1/1935 to 14/1/1935.
>
> TGR 2065/Sp/3   Issued to operate the above service. Period 15/1/1935 to 21/1/1935.
>
> TGR 2065/Sp/4   Issued to operate the above service. Period 22/1/1935 to 28/1/1935.
>
> TGR 2065/Sp/5   Issued to operate the above service. Period 29/1/1935 to 4/2/1935.

Licence TGR 2065/1 above, was finally granted on 20th February, 1935, and was withdrawn on 22nd December, 1937.

Only one other licence application was made by Glyn Thomas, and that was made on 21st December, 193<u>8</u>:-

> TGR 2065/2 **Port Talbot (Taibach Square)** to **Bryn Colliery**. Workmen's stage carriage via: Burgess Green, Chapel of Ease, and Ynysygwas.   *3 x shifts per day.*

After objections from Thomas Brothers (Port Talbot), the licence TGR 2065/2 was refused on 18th January, 1939.

No vehicles were licenced to Glyn Thomas, he used vehicles of the Llynvi fleet.

Returning to November 1935, Llynvi Motor Services entered negotiations with Western Welsh, regarding the possibility of a take-over. Negotiations however fell through.

At the same time, the company's founder, William George Thomas (snr) became ill, and after a two year illness, passed away at home (4 Exchange Street, Maesteg), on 17th August, 1937, aged 59. His effects were valued at £3,349-18-0.

On 15th September, 1937, George Thomas' widow, Martha Thomas, applied for her late husband's licences, which read:-

Llynvi Motor Services (Martha Thomas t/a), of 4 Exchange Street, Maesteg, applied for:-

TGR 3213/1   **Maesteg (Town Hall)** to **Aberavon Beach**. Stage carriage service, via: Bryn, Penrhydwaelod, Ynysygwas, Saron, and Port Talbot.
(Previous licence granted to the late W.G. Thomas, on TGR 434/1).

TGR 3213/2   **Excursions & Tours** starting from Maesteg.
(Previous licence granted to the late W.G. Thomas, on TGR 434/2).

The licences were granted on 27th October, 1937, with a new operator number TGR 3213, due to the change of entity from W.G. Thomas, to Martha Thomas.

Above: ACY 104 was a Leyland 'Tiger' TS7T (6 wheeler), with Massey B40R coachwork, and was dealer registered in Swansea. It was new to the company on 12th June, 1936, and delivered in fleet livery, Cream and Blue. *(Courtesy Byron Gage).*

Above: Another view of Llynvi Motors' (Llynfi Motors) rare Leyland 'Tiger' TS7T (6 wheeler), **ACY 104**, depicts it here at Cardiff Civic Centre. This vehicle was withdrawn in February 1951, and was refused a new 'Certificate of Fitness' in May 1953. It was still laid up at the company's Bryn premises, as late as June 1959, but there was no further trace. *(Courtesy Byron Gage).*

Above: In November 1937, the company purchased this 6 months old, Leyland 'Tiger' TS7, **BWX 722** (12), from Ripponden & District (f/n 1). It was originally fitted with B33F bodywork, built by Wise Coachbuilders, of Staines, but in May 1948, it was rebodied with this Santus C33F coachwork, and consequently renumbered with fleet number 41. *(Courtesy Byron Gage).*

Llynfi Motor Services
(PROPRIETOR: W. G. THOMAS)

PRIVATE PARTIES CATERED FOR
DISTANCE NO OBJECT.

GARAGE:
BRYN., PORT TALBOT.

4, EXCHANGE STREET,
MAESTEG,
GLAM.

25th November 1937.

Messrs, The West Riding County Council.,
14, St. John's North,
WAKEFIELD.

Dear Sirs,

<u>Leyland Tiger Coach BWX 722.</u>

    I beg to inform you that I have purchased the above numbered coach from Messrs, The Ripponden & District Motors Ltd., Commercial Garage, Ripponden, and I shall be glad if you will kindly register the change to me, and return the Registration Book as soon as possible.

    Thanking you in anticipation.

Yours faithfully,
FOR (MRS) M. THOMAS.

Above: This letter was sent by the company, to West Riding CC, in November 1937, asking for transfer of ownership of the Leyland 'Tiger' TS7, **BWX 722**, after its purchase (pictured on previous page). It will be noted that by this date, the company were using letterheads with the correct spelling of Llynfi Motor Services, but the spelling Llynvi, on the buses, was not finally phased out until around 1950. *(Courtesy of Cardiff Transport Preservation Group).*

Above: Pictured here at the company's Bryn depot, near Maesteg, is **FV 68**, a 1929 Leyland 'Tiger' TS1, which had been acquired from S & J Wood, Blackpool, by 1939. Its original body, built by Leyland Motors to C30R layout, was later replaced with a body built by Massey Bros, of Wigan, to C35R layout. *(Courtesy Byron Gage).*

Above: This 1930 AEC Regal, **TX 9497** was new to T. Davies (t/a Osborn Services), Neath, and passed to South Wales Transport (f/n 111), with the Osborn Services' business, in June 1937. In July 1938, it passed to D.J. Thomas (Cream Line Services) Maesteg, brother of the late W.G. Thomas (founder of Llynfi Motor Services). Confusingly, by June 1939, it passed to Llynfi Motor Services, with whom it is seen here at some point after WW2 ended. However, the hooded/masked headlights had been removed, but it was still carrying white edging to the front wings, and lifeguard rails – a legal requirement during the hostilities. By October 1945, this vehicle was with Gibbs, Pontllanfraith, Monmouthshire, and had passed to M & M Kidderminster, by June 1947.
(Courtesy Byron Gage).

World War 2 commenced on 3rd September, 1939, and within a few days the company were compelled to introduce an emergency timetable, in order to conserve fuel when fuel rationing began on 16th September. Services were reduced to a very basic frequency – merely maintaining services to accommodate workers. Licences to operate Excursions & Tours were suspended, in order to conserve fuel and rubber, as were the licences for Express Carriage services three years later. During the war years, licences to provide extra services, or any modification to existing services, had to be applied for as usual, but were only authorised by the Ministry of Defence (Ministry of War Transport).

In addition to this, War Department Officials toured all bus and coach operators in Britain, in July 1940, requisitioning buses and coaches for military use, usually taking the operators best buses and coaches, but in Llynfi Motor Services' case, nothing was commandeered.

As war progressed, business was quiet in comparison with their competitors. There are no records of 'workers services' being sanctioned to the company by the Ministry of War Transport, although two unrecorded road service licences were issued during the hostilities.

However, it is known that during WW2, South Wales Transport were instructed by the Ministry of War Transport, to abandon their share of the Port Talbot to Maesteg service. The service was drastically reduced, and operated solely by Llynfi Motor Services, in order to conserve fuel. After the hostilities were over, South Wales Transport restarted the service.

Reflecting upon the company's tranquillity during the war years, only one vehicle was acquired during that period, and that is pictured below.

Above: **BDW 474** was a 1938 Dennis 'Lancet II', acquired from W.A. Pugh, Newport (Mon), in July 1940. This view would have been taken after the WW2 hostilities were over, yet its Dennis 32 seat coachwork was still lettered with the old spelling of 'Llynvi'. It operated on hire to W.Gwyn Richards, Neath, from June, to October 1951, and was sold in 1954. *(Courtesy of The Bus Archive).*

Above: Another Dennis 'Lancet II' with Dennis B35F bodywork, was acquired in August 1944, and is seen here at Bethany Square, Port Talbot, with conductress Jenny Davies, and driver Gwyn Davies, about to depart for Maesteg. This vehicle was re-registered FTG 311, upon acquisition from the War Department, in August 1944, but had previously been registered EXH 985, or EXF 935, when new to Glenton Tours, of New Cross, London, SE14, in June 1938. *(Courtesy Byron Gage).*

In the meantime, the company corrected the spelling of their title to Llynfi Motor Services, whilst their rivals, Brewer's Motor Services, absorbed their last competitors on the Caerau - Maesteg route, with approval from the Ministry of War Transport. Brewer's firstly took over William John's share of the jointly operated service in 1940. This was followed by the share held by Frederick John, Nantyffyllon (William John's brother), in July 1943; Griffith Hughes, Caerau, in 1945; and lastly, in June 1945, the share of Cream Line (Maesteg) Ltd., operated by D.J. Thomas, brother of the late W.G. Thomas (founder of Llynfi Motor Services).

D.J. Thomas continued running his remaining stage carriage service between Maesteg Bus Station and Garth, until September 1947, and his workmen's service between Maesteg and Margam (Carbide Works), until July 1947, alongside his haulage business.

When D.J. Thomas applied for renewal of his licences in 1947, the only licence granted to him was for Excursions & Tours, starting from Maesteg. Renewal of his Maesteg to Margam Carbide Works, with an extension to start from Abergwynfi, was refused in July, 1947.

He then decided to wind up the PSV business, and concentrate on haulage only, offering the licence and two coaches to his sister-in-law, Martha Thomas (Llynfi Motor Services).

Martha applied for her brother-in-law's last remaining licence on 18th February, 1948:-

TGR 3213/6   **Excursions & Tours** starting from Maesteg (Town Hall).

The licence was granted on 28th April, 1948, allowing Martha to purchase the former Cream Line, Bedford OB coaches, GNY 856 and GTG 322, dating from 1947, along with the Excursions & Tours licence.

Above: This Bedford OB, **GTG 322**, was one of two OB's acquired in April 1948, with the remnants of the Cream Line (Maesteg) Ltd., business. This coach was bodied by W.L. Thurgood, of Ware, Hertfordshire, and passed to East Glam Motors, Nelson, in 1950. In the backdrop, the derelict remains of the company's first bus, **NY 4206**, are just visible. *(Courtesy Byron Gage).*

Above: The first new vehicle purchased by the company after wartime hostilities ended, was this Leyland 'Tiger' PS1/1, registered **GTX 437** (37), fitted with Massey B35F bodywok. It was delivered in September 1947, and was extensively rebuilt in 1957. The chassis was lengthened, and the bodywork from a point behind the drivers cab, was rebuilt by Neath Coachworks, to B39F layout, using some of the Massey framework. (The rebuilt vehicle can be seen on next page). *(John Jones collection).*

Above: This view of rebuilt Leyland 'Tiger' **GTX 437**, has been included for comparison of its rebuilt bodywork, against the original bodywork pictured on the previous page. It was withdrawn from service in December 1972, and sold to D. Gwyn John, Swansea, for preservation, and is currently in the care of the Swansea Bus Museum, at Viking Way, Winch Wen, Swansea.   *(John Jones).*

Above: Originally intended for N&C Express, of Neath, this AEC 'Regal III', **JTG 286**, which was bodied by N&C's subsidiary, Longford Coachworks, to C35F layout, was delivered to Llynfi in July 1949. It was withdrawn in June 1963, and eventually sold for scrap June 1966.   *(Copyright Roy Marshall / The Bus Archive).*

Above: Also received in July 1949, was this consecutively registered, Dennis 'Lancet III', **JTG 287**, with coachwork built locally by D.J. Davies, of Merthyr Tydfil, to C33F layout. In consideration, the company did not retained this vehicle very long, as it passed to W.G. Richards, of Neath, in April 1953. It has been stated that D.J. Davies' coachwork was not of good quality!
(Courtesy Byron Gage).

Above: It can be seen that Llynfi had a preferance for the Dennis chassis for a short while. This 1947 Duple 'A' bodied 'Lancet III', **GDG 795** (42), was acquired in December 1949, from Bennett, of Tongwynlais. However, it became the last Dennis' chassis purchased by the company, and left the fleet in November 1960, to be converted into a car transporter. *(Courtesy Byron Gage).*

Above: Another coach bodied locally by Longford Coachworks, Neath Abbey, was **JTX 746** (47). This Leyland 'Tiger' PS2/3, which was delivered in March 1950, was withdrawn in January 1967. It was then retained at Maesteg depot until August 1970, before its final disposal. *(Courtesy The Bus Archive / Roy Marshall).*

Above: This 1945 Bedford OWB, **FUP 159** (32), with Duple B30F bodywork, was acquired in January 1951, from Nicholson, New Washington, Co. Durham (33). It was new to Nicholson in October 1945, as B32F, but was downseated before its arrival in South Wales. The Bedford OB in the backdrop was ORF 564, owned by Pugh & Stanton, Ogmore Vale. *(Courtesy Byron Gage).*

Above: Having gained extra work from 'The Steel Company of Wales' in May 1951, the company set about buying extra buses and coaches. This AEC 'Regal, **GL 5060** (40), with Eastern Coachworks B35R bodywork, was one of a pair purchased from Bath Tramways (2222), in May 1951. However, its radiator badge incorrectly stated it was an AEC 'Renown'. *(Courtesy John Jones).*

Above: GL 5075 (46), was the second ECW bodied AEC 'Regal I', acquired from Bath Tramways (2224), in May 1951. It was used on stage carriage service, and contracts to Abbey Works, and the Llandarcy Oil Refinery. *(Courtesy Byron Gage).*

Returning to December 1946, the company applied for a licence to provide a 'new' workmen's stage carriage service:-

TGR 3213/5 **Maesteg** to **Port Talbot (Steelworks)** & **Taibach (Plastic Works)**.
via: Bryn, Ynysygwas, and Saron.

This application was objected to by South Wales Transport, but was granted on 5th March, 1947, with one condition: To carry employees of the Steelworks at Port Talbot, and the Plastic Works at Taibach only.

However, numerous modifications were made to this licence in due course, to serve the requirements of the 'new' Port Talbot Steelworks, known as Abbey Works, which was formally opened by its owners, The Steel Company of Wales Ltd., on 17th July, 1951.

Abbey Steelworks, planned in 1947, was built in phases, and was not fully operational until 1953, when it became the largest steel producing complex in Europe.

On 18th July, 1951, an additional workmen's journey to the new Abbey Works at Margam, (Port Talbot), was asked for, and [2] Revision of fares. [3] Removal of restriction to the service, with regard to the conveyance of workpeople employed at the Steelworks in Port Talbot, and Plastic Works in Taibach. Objections to this application were received from the South Wales Transport Co., and Port Talbot Borough Council, so the licence was renewed retaining its original conditions.

On 7th November, 1951, the company asked to run one extra journey per day, to accommodate day shift office workers. That modification was granted on 19th December, 1951.

Inevitably, rivals Brewer's Motor Service submitted an application on 5th December, 1951, (TGR 267/16), for a workmen's stage carriage service, from Caerau, to the Abbey Steelworks, via Nantyffyllon and Maesteg, with four return journeys per day, Monday to Friday, and one on Saturdays, covering all shift patterns.

That triggered off a very bitter fight between the rivals. A week later, Llynfi asked for another modification to their Maesteg to Port Talbot Steelworks service (TGR 3213/5). This time they asked to extend the service to start from Caerau. The application inevitably received an objection from Brewer's, which led to a public hearing held in Crown Court, at Swansea's Guildhall, on 28th January, 1952, where both operators objected to each other's applications. Brewer's application was refused in favour of Llynfi's modification for a route extension.

Additionally, Brewer's Motor Services unsuccessfully objected in March 1952, to Llynfi's application for a revised timetable on the Abbey Works service.

In the meantime, Llynfi Motor Services won a substantial contract from The Steel Company of Wales Ltd., to operate bus services within the confines of the vast Abbey Works site.

Gaining this additional work meant extra buses, resulting in a large influx of new and second-hand vehicles during 1951/2. Capital to pay for those buses, was received from a 'well timed' sale of Llynfi's 40% shareholding in Thomas Bros (Port Talbot) Ltd. The entire share capital of Thomas Bros (Port Talbot) Ltd., and its subsidiary, Afan Transport Co. Ltd., was purchased by BET (British Electric Traction Company Ltd.), in March 1951.

Above: Pictured here at the company's base in Maesteg, between duties on the Abbey Works contract, is this Leyland 'Tiger' PS2/15, **KTX 631** (59), with Massey B39F, 30ft bodywork. It was delivered in June 1951, and was the company's first 30ft long vehicle. When it was withdrawn 20 years later, it was snapped up by Smith's Enterprises, a Bridgend contractor, by August 1971, for further use as a staff bus. More recently, however, this vehicle is in preservation, currently undergoing major restoration, and resides in South Wales. *(Copyright Robert F. Mack).*

Above: Another fine view of the Leyland 'Tiger' PS2/15, **KTX 631** (59), taken at the Maesteg premises of Llynfi Motor Services, depicts its rear end design, and stylish lettering of its Massey bodywork. *(Courtesy Byron Gage).*

Above: The company's first underfloor engined vehicle, was this attractively designed Burlingham 'Seagull' C39C bodied, Leyland PSU1/15 "Royal Tiger". Delivered in June 1951, it was registered **KTX 869**, and received fleet number 58. After 22 years' of yeoman service, this vehicle was sold as a staff bus, to Porthcawl Recreations Ltd.   *(Copyright The Bus Archive / R. Marshall).*

Above: AEC 'Regal I', **FUP 782** (38), dating from May 1946, was one of a pair acquired from Trimdon Motor Services, in October 1951. It originally carried a B35F body built by Raine, but was rebodied as seen here, to B34F, by Neath Coachworks, in 1955. It was sold for scrap to W.H. Way, Cardiff, in August 1970, but saw further service with Jenkins, Pontardulais. *(John Jones collection).*

On 9th January, 1952, Llynfi Motor Services were one of six objectors against an application from George Davies & Co. Port Talbot, (George Selway Davies, Brynmor Charles Davies, Harry Davies, and Graham Davies), for an Express Carriage licence between Port Talbot and

Carmarthen. The partnership withdrew their application (TGR 4315/2), on 6th February, 1952.

February 1952, also witnessed the opening of Llynfi Motor Services new office at 29 Llynfi Road, Maesteg, which eventually became their travel office.

Above: A splendid rear view of the rebodied AEC 'Regal I', **FUP 782** (38), at the company's Bryn depot. *(John Jones Collection)*.

Above: The only photograph available of Llynfi's second former Trimdon MS., AEC 'Regal', **FUP 783** (39), is this one, whilst in service with Trimdon MS. This vehicle had bodywork built by Thurgood, to B35F layout, and was not rebodied. It was withdrawn in December 1957, with no further trace. *(Courtesy Byron Gage)*.

Above: CBX 733, was Bedford OWB, with Duple B32F bodywork, new to Davies Bros. (Pencader) Ltd., in November 1945. It was acquired by Llynfi Motor Services in December 1951, but was disposed of very quickly, passing to Wye Valley Motors Ltd, Hereford, on 2nd May, 1952, with whom it is seen here. *(Author's collection).*

Above: Another vehicle which passed through the Llynfi fleet very quickly, was this Whitson C33F bodied, Maudslay 'Marathon III', **HNY 80**. This arrived from D.H. Roberts (Pioneer), Newport, Pembrokeshire, in January 1952, but was part exchanged for a former Sentinal demonstrator two months later, in March 1952. It's seen here at Goodwick, whilst operating for D. H. Roberts. The Austin K4 lorry on the left of this view (JUV 446), was from the large fleet of parcel delivery vehicles operated by British Railways. *(Author's collection).*

Above: The first Sentinel acquired by the company in March 1952, was this former Sentinel STC6/44 demonstrator, **GUX 614**. Integrally built, with 44 seats, it was the very first STC6/44 demonstrator, and appeared at the 1950 Commercial Vehicle Show, albeit in Ribble livery. Withdrawn December 1958, it passed to Wooton, Wombwell, as a staff bus, April 1959. *(Author's collection).*

Above: Pictured here outside the company's Bryn depot, is **ARN 528** (62), a 1946 Burlingham B34F bodied Leyland 'Tiger' PS1, acquired from Viking, Preston (14), in December 1952. This was sold to Jones Motor Services (62), Aberbeeg (Mon), in September 1955, and scrapped in February 1960. *(Courtesy Byron Gage).*

Above: MTG 469 (49), was one of four prototype Leyland HR40 'Olympic' demonstrators, built by Leyland Motors Ltd., in 1949, and registered *KOC 234* in 1950. However, it received a 'new' 1953 Glamorganshire registration mark upon arrival at Maesteg in January 1953, and ran for almost 10 years before passing to Porthcawl Omnibus Co., in April 1962. This 'Olympic' was built at Metro-Cammell's Elmdon Works, Birmingham. They were Leyland Motors' first integrally built vehicles, and their first 'underfloor' engined vehicles, using the Leyland horizontal 0.600 power unit, coupled to a synchromesh gearbox. *(Author's collection).*

Above: Llynfi acquired this Leyland 'Tiger' PS1/1, **FVA 389** (50), with Plaxton C33F coachwork, in May 1953, from Park's of Hamilton, Scotland. It's seen here in Talbot Road, Port Talbot, making a right turn into Abbey Road. *(Copyright Roy Marshall).*

SERVICE No. **20** T.G.R. 421/35

The South Wales Transport Company Ltd.
Llynfi Motor Services
REVISED FARE TABLE—26th OCTOBER, 1953
ABERAVON—MAESTEG

Stage Nos.												
1	**ABERAVON BEACH**											
2	3d		Bethany Square					Weekly Tickets as per the authorised scale.				
3	3d	5d	*1½d	**PORT TALBOT, G.W.R.**				Season Tickets as per the anthorised scale.				
4	5d	9d	3d	2d	Saron							
5	6d	10d	4d	7d	3d	1½d	Curran Ddu					
6	7d	11d	5d	8d	4d	2d	1½d	Ynysgwas, Cwmavon Crossing				
7	9d	1/2	7d	11d	7d	11d	5d 9d	4d 7d	3d	Penywaelydd		
8	10d	1/2	8d	1/-	8d	1/-	6d 10d	5d 9d	4d 7d	2d	**BRYN, CROSS ROADS**	
9	10d	1/2	8d	1/-	8d	1/-	6d 10d	5d 9d	4d 7d	2d	1½d	Bryn, Royal Oak
10	1/-	1/6	10d	1/3	9d	1/2	8d 1/-	7d 11d	6d 10d	4d 7d	3d	3d	Maesteg, Mount Pleasant
11	1/1	1/8	11d	1/5	11d	1/5	9d 1/2	8d 1/-	7d 11d	5d 9d	4d 7d	4d 7d	2d	Maesteg Hospital
12	1/2 S	1/9 R	1/- S	1/6 R	1/- S	1/6 R	10d 1/3 S R	9d 1/2 S R	8d 1/- S R	6d 10d S R	5d 9d S R	5d 9d S R	3d S	2d S	**MAESTEG, TOWN HALL**

Additional Single Fares—

Burgess Green—Hospital Road ... 1½d Single Bethany Square—Abbey Road ... 2d Single
Bethany Sq.—Tanygroes St. (P.O.) ... 2d ,, Burgess Green—Port Talbot G.W.R. 2d ,,
Chapel of Ease—Saron ... 1½d ,, Aberavon Beach—Abbey Road ... 4d ,, 7d Return
Burgess Green—Aberavon Beach ... 2d ,, Burgess Green—Abbey Road ... 3d ,,
Burgess Green—Bethany Square ... 1½d ,,
Baldwin St., Bryn—Royal Oak ... 1½d ,,

Return, Weekly and Season Tickets are interavailable on the services of the South Wales Transport Co. Ltd. and Llynfi Motors.

* Available between Market and Port Talbot, G.W.R.

Above: A joint 'Fare Table' between South Wales Transport, and Llynfi Motor Services, dated 26th October, 1953. *(Steve Powell).*

Above: This Brush B32F bodied AEC 'Regal I', **SME 81** (43), was one of an identical pair acquired in November 1953. This one came from Victoria, Leigh-on-Sea, Essex, and was renumbered 48 in due course. *(Author's collection).*

Above: Pictured here on layover inside Abbey Works, Port Talbot, is Duple bodied Bedford OB, **CUX 527** (51), dating from 1945. This was acquired in November 1953, from Jenkins, Bargoed, and was new to Thomas, Bishops Castle, Shropshire.
(Author's collection).

Above: This Daimler CVD6SD, **FKV 472** (47 later 55), was one of two identical Burlingham C33F bodied Daimlers, purchased in November 1953, from Valliant Coaches, of Ealing, London W5. It was new in February 1948 to H & H Motors (Bunty Coaches), Coventry. It was withdrawn from service in November 1962, and sold for scrap in 1964.
(Author's collection).

Above: Pictured here at Maesteg Bus Station on lay-over, is this rather battered former Leyland Motors, prototype demonstrator, **KOC 241** (60). It was originally one of four prototype Leyland 'Olympic' HR40s built in 1949, three of which were acquired by Llynfi in 1953. This, and KOC 242 seen below, were subsequently aquired from J.T. Whittle, Highley, Salop, in November 1953, whilst *KOC 234*, (re-registered MTG 469), arrived 10 months earlier (see p170 for details). *(Copyright The Bus Archive / Roy Marshall).*

Above: Llynfi Motor Services always looked out for a bargain when buying replacement stock, and over a period of time, bought no less than eight former demonstration vehicles. **KOC 242** (61) [right], was the third former Leyland Motors prototype 'Olympic', absorbed into the fleet in November 1953. It is accompanied here at Maesteg Bus Station, by Llynfi's Saunders Roe bodied Leyland 'Tiger Cub', **OTC 738** (66), which was another former Leyland Motors demonstrator. Meanwhile, the lady on the right looks rather annoyed at having her picture taken! *(Copyright The Bus Archive / Roy Marshall).*

Above: **CTJ 84** (57), was a 1938 Leyland 'Tiger' TS8c, fitted with what Leyland Motors termed, 'Gearless' transmission, and Leyland B32R bodywork. The 'Gearless Bus' was an early form of automatic transmission, fitted with a torque converter (fluid flywheel), and pre-select gearbox. It was new to Accrington Corporation (37), in April 1938, and was acquired from them in December 1953. *(John Jones' collection).*

Above: This 1952 integrally built Sentinel STC6, **GTH 576** (64), with B44F layout, was acquired in July 1954, from W.J. Davies, Pencader (38), who traded as Davies Bros. It has been said that the Sentinel braking systems were troublesome, experiencing brake fade, yet this was the second of three Sentinels purchased by the company. However, this was sold three years later to Princess, of Clonmel, County Tipperary, in the Republic of Ireland, where it retained its registration **GTH 576**. *(Author's collection).*

Above: The third Sentinel purchased by the company was truely unique. **KUX 412** (65), was a Sentinel SLC6/30 demonstrator, built in 1954, as a joint venture with Newcastle Sentinel dealer, K & B, who specified a dual-door, service bus layout. It was built by a Sunderland company, Associated Coach Builders, and Llynfi purchased it from Moffit, of Acomb, Northumberland, as B40D. However, it was converted to B44F configuration, before entering service with Llynfi, in February 1955.   *(Author's collection).*

On 22nd July, 1953, the company asked to modify their existing Excursions & Tours licences TGR 3213/2 and 3213/6. They asked to pick up passengers at any point within the Maesteg UDC area, and for the maximum number of vehicles used on TGR 3213/2, to be increased from 2 to 9 vehicles, and to increase TGR 3213/6, from 3 to 6 vehicles. The modification regarding pick-up points was granted, but the change to the maximum number of vehicles used on tours was refused, after an objection from Brewer's.

At the same time, Brewer's applied to similarly modify their E&T licences, TGR 267/3 and 267/4, for a maximum number of vehicles used on any one day to be 20, and 7, respectively. In retaliation, Llynfi MS objected to Brewer's application, and it was refused. At the same hearing held on 14th September, 1953, the Traffic Commissioner granted Llynfi permission to use 10 vehicles on any one day, on both E&T licences, TGR 3213/2 and 3213/6.

Two years later, on 31st August 1955, the following Express Carriage licence was asked for:-

TGR 3213/7   **Maesteg (Town Hall)** to **Blackpool**.
  via: Port Talbot, A48 to Neath, A465 to Hirwaun, A4059 to Storey Arms, A470 to Brecon, and A438 into West Midlands TA.   Return same route.
  To be operated during the miners holiday period in this area, and during the period of Illuminations. Only to be operated for pre-booked parties on occasions when no excursions from the Maesteg Valley are operated by British Railways. Picking up points within the Maesteg UDC area, Cymmer (Avondale Hotel), and Abergwynfi (Great Western Hotel).

Proposed timetable:

Depart Maesteg (Town Hall) 9.00 am, arrive Shrewsbury 2.30 pm (lunch), depart 3.30 pm, arrive Blackpool 7.45 pm.

Return from Blackpool: Depart 1.30 pm, arrive Shrewsbury 5.30 pm for Tea, depart Shrewsbury 6.30 pm, arrive Maesteg (Town Hall) 12.00 midnight, OR at times suitable for Colliers, Factory Workers, and party organisers.

Proposed Fares: 3 days, 30/-; 4 days, 32/6; 5 days, 35/-; 8 days, 40/-. Children over 3 years, and under 14 years of age, two-thirds of adult fares.

Conditions: Not more than one vehicle shall be used on any one journey.

There were no objectors, and the licence was granted on 12th October, 1955.

On 23rd November, 1955, the company applied for permission to start all their journeys to the Abbey Steelworks, TGR 3213/5, from Caerau (Garages), Brewer's premises. Obviously, the application was once again objected to by their rivals, and the modification was refused on 1st February, 1956.

Above: It looked like a beautiful day for Aberavon Beach, with quite a number of passengers too. Aberavon Beach became a very popular seaside resort in the 1960s, and competed well against the amenities of Coney Beach, at nearby Porthcawl, until the beach became contaminated with industrial effects etc. The vehicle pictured here at Maesteg Bus Station, was another former Leyland Motors demonstrator, **OTC 738** (66), which was a Leyland 'Tiger Cub' PSUC1/1T, with lightweight B44F bodywork, built in 1952, by Saunders Roe, an Aerospace Engineering Company, famous for their overhaul and repair of flying boats during WW2, at Beumaris, Anglesey. **OTC 738**, gave the company excellent service until withdrawal at 24 years' old, passing to a Cardiff breaker by January 1977, and later to Trevor Wigley, another breaker at Carlton, Yorkshire, by May 1979.

(Copyright The Bus Archive / Roy Marshall).

Above: Another former demonstrator acquired in December 1955, was **210 AMP**, which is seen here at Abbey Works, Port Talbot, awaiting departure to Ynysygwas, a village situated between Port Talbot, and Maesteg. New in November 1953, **210 AMP** (67), was an experimental AEC 'Monocoach', integrally built by Park Royal Vehicles, to B44F layout, and appeared at the 1953 Scottish Motor Show, as a demonstrator for AEC Ltd., Southall. *(Copyright Robert Mack).*

Above: A splendid view of an attractive AEC 'Reliance' MU3RV, **LWN 119**, seen at the company's Maesteg depot on 21st February, 1971. The coachwork was built by Duple, to the style marketed as 'Elizabethan', with C41F layout. **LWN 119** was one of an identical pair of 'Reliances', new to Bryn Demery, of Beaufort Garage, Morriston, in May 1955, and was acquired by Llynfi in February 1956. After nineteen years' service, it passed to an unknown private owner in Cardiff, and passed to W.H. Way, the Cardiff breaker by January 1977. *(Copyright John Jones).*

Above: The first double deck vehicle purchased by Llynfi, was **FBW 886** (69), in May 1957. This was a 1952 Daimler CVD6, with Massey H32/26RD bodywork, which came from Heyfordian, of Upper Heyford, Oxfordshire. It is seen here outside the company's Bryn depot, with KBX 442, an Austin 'Loadstar' tipper truck, of 1954 vintage, fitted with 'gready boards', passing by. This decker was withdrawn in January 1967, and passed to W.H. Way, the Cardiff breaker, in August 1970. *(John Jones collection).*

Above: This vehicle registered **HVT 919** (44), is not what it appears to be. It was actually **BEH 963 masquerading as HVT 919**. Its Leyland 'Tiger' TS7 chassis was built in early 1935, receiving chassis number 6354, and fitted with Brush B32F bodywork. Delivered to Potteries Motor Transport in 1935, it received registration number BEH 963. In 1955, together with other withdrawn Potteries vehicles, it passed to a dealer, who rebodied it with a 1947, Brush B34F body, removed from another PMT vehicle. At the same time, the registration, and chassis plates, from another former PMT vehicle, a 1942 Leyland 'Tiger' TS11, were fitted before its sale to Hulley's of Baslow, Derbyshire, in August 1956. However, Hulley's became aware of its unauthorised background, and hurriedly exchanged it the following spring. It then found a home with Llynfi Motor Services, in June 1957, and is seen here at the Abbey Works, Port Talbot, on layover between shifts. It was withdrawn in August 1959. *(Author's collection).*

Above: In November 1957, the company acquired their second double decker, **GBW 337** (70), which was another Daimler CVD6 with identical Massey H32/26RD bodywork. It was acquired from the same source as its sister, FBW 886, Heyfordian, of Upper Heyford, Oxfordshire, and it operated in Heyfordian's fleet livery of Silver, for quite a while. It eventually received the usual smart fleet livery, of Blue and Cream, with Black wings, as displayed below. This photograph was taken at their Maesteg depot.

(John Jones collection).

Above: Another view of the former Heyfordian, Massey bodied Daimler CVD6, **GBW 337** (70), which was taken at Maesteg depot, sometime after receiving fleet livery. This vehicle was withdrawn in 1971, and sold to W.H. Way, the well known Cardiff scrap dealer, at Cardiff Docks, in April 1973.

(John Jones collection).

Above: The chromium plated (electroplated) radiator surround, fitted to Leyland 'Tiger' PS1s, were truly a classic feature. This particular 1948 Leyland PS1/1, **LVT 946** (71), with Willowbrook B34F bodywork, was acquired from Baxter of Hanley, Staffordshire (f/n 3), in April 1958, and passed to Parfitt's Motor Service, Rhymney Bridge, for further service in May 1963. *(Author's collection).*

Above: Some sources state that this Massey bodied Leyland 'Titan' PD3/4, **YTG 304** (72), was acquired brand new in July 1958. That was purely an assumption, due to its Glamorganshire registration number. To clarify the matter, with greatful thanks to Byron Gage, for his research, this vehicle was built in 1957, and supplied in 1957, to the United States Air Force, at Upper Heyford, Oxfordshire, and worked within the confines of the USAF camp, unregistered. It was sold to Llynfi Motors in July 1958, who registered it for the first time, receiving a brand new registraton mark, **YTG 304**. That is how the system worked in those far gone days! At first, it retained the previous owners livery of Silver, with Blue relief, but later received the appealing fleet livery, of Blue with Cream relief, as seen opposite. It's seen here negotiating Maesteg Town Hall roundabout, from Talbot Street, into Church Street, for its destination at Maesteg Bus Station. *(John Jones collection).*

Above: A superb view of Leyland PD3/4, **YTG 304** (72), alongside the 'Nissen Hut' style garage at Maesteg.   *(John Jones).*

Above: When **YTG 304** was withdrawn from service in 1987, it passed to Bevington Motors, a car sales outlet located at Margam, for use as a mobile advertisement for their buisiness. It was later sold and converted into a mobile Hotel. *(Copyright Byron Gage).*

In July 1959, the company were issued the following short period Express Carriage licence:-

TGR 3213/Sp/1   **Maesteg (Town Hall)** to **Margam (Royal Welsh Agricultural Show)**.
Period of operation, 22/7/1959 to 25/7/1959 inclusive.

Above: In January 1959, the company bought their first pair of Burlingham 'Seagull' bodied coaches. **NDA 23** (73), seen here, was numerically first of the pair, acquired from Don Everall Coaches, Wolverhampton. They had Leyland 'Tiger Cub' PSUC1/2T chassis, fitted with two speed rear axles, and the economical Leyland O.350 engines. *(R.H.G. Simpson).*

Above: NDA 24 (74), was the second Burlingham 'Seagull' C41C bodied Leyland 'Tiger Cub' acquired from Don Everall Coaches in January 1959. This one passed to Hardings Coaches, Birkenhead, in 1962. *(Author's collection).*

Above: This AEC 'Regent III', with Park Royal H30/26RD bodywork, **SMU 194** (75), was new in September 1950, to ACV Sales Ltd., Southall, as a demonstrator, but afterwards passed to D. Jones & Son (Pantdu), Port Talbot. Llynfi acquired it from Jones in 1959, and operated it until June 1971, when it passed to Andrew Scott (Contractor), Port Talbot. *(John Jones collection).*

Above: GCY 304 (86), was an AEC 'Regal III' fitted with Willowbrook B34F bodywork, which was acquired from The South Wales Transport Co. Ltd., (134), in September 1959. It was the first of nine Willowbrook bodied Regals received from South Wales Transport, in 1960/1, and is seen here at the Abbey Works, Port Talbot. In October 1964, it passed to C. Collier, Abertillery, Monmouthshire (Gwent), and was withdrawn by Collier, in April 1967. *(John Jones collection).*

Above: Following the arrival a year earlier, of two Burlingham 'Seagull' bodied Leyland 'Tiger Cubs', another pair, **OUJ 207/8**, arrived in February 1960, from J.T. Whittle, of Highley, Shropshire. These were almost identical to the earlier pair shown on page 182. The only noticeable difference was, that they were built to front entrance layout with 41 seats, and were new in April 1957. **OUJ 207** (78), seen here at an unknown location, was written off after an accident in December 1973.   *(John Jones collection).*

Above: The Burlingham 'Seagull' was a truly classic design. This particular Leyland 'Tiger Cub', **OUJ 208** (79), gave the company excellent service, and was withdrawn at the age of twenty years, in 1977. It was afterwards used as a seat store, and was finally broken up at the company's Bryn depot, in September 1979.   *(R.H.G. Simpson).*

Above: This former Devon General (DR 558), 1948 AEC 'Regent III', with Weymann H30/26R bodywork, **JUO 558**, became the second vehicle in the Llynfi fleet to carry fleet number (65). **JUO 558** arrived in July 1960, and this view was taken on 22nd July, 1963. The original Nº 65, was a Sentinel bus, registered KUX 412, which had been withdrawn six months earlier.
(Copyright Geoff Mead).

By 1959, the family owned unregistered business had been in existence for nearly 40 years, and with moderate expansion, they were operating a total of 37 vehicles, 17 Leyland, 8 AEC, 5 Bedford, 4 Daimler, 2 Sentinel, and 1 Dennis. It was at this point that the family decided to register the business as a Limited Company, in order to safeguard everyone involved.

With a capital of £25,000, incorporation took place on 10th July, 1959, receiving company number 00632464. The shareholders, all with one share each, were given as:

Mrs Martha Thomas (widow), 4 Exchange Street, Maesteg.

Glyn Haydn Thomas (son), (General Manager and Engineer), 'Woodlands', 33 Salisbury Road, Maesteg.

Dyfrig Llewellyn Thomas (son), 2 Smith Street, Maesteg.

William George Thomas (son), 45 Neath Road, Maesteg.

Margaretta May Evans (daughter), 4 Exchange Street, Maesteg.

Francis Enid Lloyd (daughter), secretary, 46 Neath Road, Maesteg.

Glyn Howell Davies (Solicitor), 13 Adare Street, Bridgend.

Ten months later, on 7th May, 1960, Mrs Martha Thomas, widow of the late W.G. Thomas, the founder of Llynfi Motor Services, passed away at the age of 81. Mrs Thomas had been at the helm since the death of her husband in 1937.

Her passing, and the change to a Limited company resulted in a change of entity to **LLYNFI MOTOR SERVICES Ltd.**, 29 Llynfi Road, Maesteg, in July 1960. A new operator licence, TGR 4862, was issued, together with new licence application numbers listed below:-

TGR 4862/1	Previously TGR 3213/1:	**Maesteg (Bus Station)** to **Aberavon (Beach)**.
TGR 4862/2	"	TGR 3213/2: **E&Ts** starting from **Maesteg (Town Hall)**.
TGR 4862/3	"	TGR 3213/5: **Caerau** to **Margam Abbey Wks**. (Vivian Bus Pk.)
TGR 4862/4	"	TGR 3213/6: **E&Ts** starting from **Maesteg (Town Hall)**.
		(Former Cream Line [Maesteg] Ltd licence).
TGR 4862/5	"	TGR 3213/7: **Maesteg** to **Blackpool**. (Express Carriage).

In the meantime, the following short term licences were issued, to continue running the above services during the interim period, ending 24th September, 1960:-

TGR 4862/Sp/1 **Maesteg (Town Hall)** to **Aberavon (Beach)**.
TGR 4862/Sp/2 **E&Ts** starting from **Maesteg (Town Hall)**.
TGR 4862/Sp/3 **Caerau** to **Margam (Abbey Works)**.
TGR 4862/Sp/4 **E&Ts** starting from **Maesteg (Town Hall)**.
TGR 4862/Sp/5 **Maesteg** to **Blackpool**. (Express Carriage).

TGR 4862/1, to 4862/5, were all granted without opposition on 9th November, 1960, and the old licences, TGR 3213/1, 2, 5, 6, 7, were all surrendered on 7th December, 1960.

Above: After purchasing their first AEC 'Regal III' from The South Wales Transport Co., in September 1959, more became available in February 1961, when the company bought a further eight of them, albeit, one was not operated and used for spares. Besides the one used for spares, numerically the first to arrive was **FWN 818** (81), which is seen here on the company's yard at Maesteg, with the Maesteg RFC, '7777' clubhouse, situated next door to the depot, visible in the backdrop. This particular 'Regal III', with Willowbrook B34F bodywork, was sold for further service to Henley's Bus Service, of Abertillery, Monmouthshire, in September 1965.   *(Copyright P.S.A. Redmond).*

Llynfi Motor Services
—LUXURY RADIO COACHES—

Proprietress: Mrs. M. THOMAS

Residence: 4 Exchange Street, Maesteg, Glam.

Garages: BRYN, Nr. Port Talbot
'Phone: Cwmavon 357

Private Parties catered for
(distance no object)

Offices:
29 LLYNFI ROAD,
MAESTEG — Glam.
(Tel.—Maesteg 3192)

Glamorgan County Council,
Licensing Authority,
68a, Cowbridge Road,
Cardiff.

4th. May. 1959.

Dear Sirs,

    Please find enclosed Registration Book in respect of Leyland Tiger BWX.722.

    This vehicle have been broken up and we are returning same.

               Yours faithfully,
       p.p. Llynfi Motor Services.

Above: This AEC 'Regal III', **FWN 819** (82), with Willowbrook B34F bodywork was previously numbered 125 in the South Wales Transport fleet, and arrived with Llynfi in February 1961. This was also sold to Henley's of Abertillery in September 1964.
(Author's collection).

Above: Two for the price of one! **FWN 822** (84) on the left, and **FWN 820** (83) on the right, were another two of the Willowbrook bodied AEC 'Regal IIIs' acquired from South Wales Transport in February 1961. This pair saw further use with Aaeron Jenkins, Fountain Garage, Pontardulais, after their withdrawal by Llynfi Motor Services, in 1970. Jenkins used these two buses for a short period only, on NCB contracted services to the local collieries at Betws, Graig Merthyr, and Brynlliw, until he ceased operations in late 1971.
(John Jones collection).

Above: Pictured here near 'The Promenade' at Aberavon, is former South Wales Transport 129, **FWN 823**, another 'Regal III' with Willowbrook B34F bodywork. This one became number 85 in the Llynfi fleet, in February 1961, and was withdrawn in March 1966, passing to Aaron Jenkins, Pontardulais, in October 1970, but it was not operated by Jenkins. *(John Jones collection).*

Above: This former South Wales Transport AEC 'Regal III' **GCY 306** (87), was also acquired in February 1961, but was the first former SWT 'Regal' to be withdrawn by the company, in May 1963. However, it was not disposed of until 1970, when it was sold for scrap to W.H. Way, the Cardiff breaker. *(Peter Yeomans).*

Above: Numerically the last AEC 'Regal III' acquired from South Wales Transport (138), in February 1961, was this Willowbrook bodied example, **GCY 472**, which received fleet number 88. However, it passed to Morris, Pencoed in November 1963, and in 1964, to Humphreys, Bridgend, passing to Edwards, Llangeinor, in August 1964. *(Alistair J. Douglas).*

Above: AEC 'Monocoach' **CHG 748** (82, later 80) was numerically the 54th of only 188 Monocoaches ever built. It was integrally built, and the majority were constructed by Park Royal – this being one example, with 44 seats. It was new to Ezra Laycock, Barnoldswick, Lancs, in October 1954, and was acquired by Llynfi in February 1961. *(Copyright The Bus Archive / Roy Marshall).*

Above: KNY 197 (another Nº 65), was a Daimler CVD6SD, new in 1950, to Neath & Cardiff Express, Neath. It was bodied by N&C subsidiary, Longford Coachworks, of Neath, to C33F layout, using a Duple shell. This vehicle was acquired from N&C in May 1961, but quickly passed to Jones (Reliance Coaches), of Llanishen, Cardiff, within a year. *(R.H.G. Simpson).*

Above: In April 1961, the company bought another pair of Burlingham 'Seagull' bodied Leyland 'Tiger Cubs' from J.T.Whittle, of Highley, Salop, PUJ 781/3. **PUJ 781** (89), is seen here at Maesteg in July 1973, and after giving seventeen years' of service to Llynfi Motor Services, the pair were reunited with Whittle in late 1978, for preservation. See next page. *(Copyright John Jones).*

Above: In late 1978, 'Tiger Cub' **PUJ 781**, returned to its original owner, J.T. Whittle, together with PUJ 783, pictured below, for preservation. **PUJ 781** is now privately owned, and still in preservation, whilst PUJ 783 did not make it. *(Authors collection).*

Above: PUJ 783 (90), was the the second Burlingham 'Seagull' bodied Leyland 'Tiger Cub' purchased from J.T. Whittle in April 1961. Seen here at Maesteg depot, on 20th May, 1973, this was converted into a mobile home after sale! *(Copyright John Jones).*

Above: This view of Llynfi's first Leyland 'Leopard', a L2 model, registered **620 NTG** (91), was taken at Aberavon Beach Coachpark, when it was still quite new in 1962. It was fitted with Willowbrook B45F bodywork, and is seen here accompanied by Leyland 'Tiger Cub' PUJ 781 (89), and Leyland 'Tiger' PS1/1, JTX 746 (47). **620 NTG** was withdrawn in March 1976, after an accident, and was scrapped in October 1976.
(Copyright The Bus Archive / Roy Marshall).

Above: The second new vehicle delivered in May 1962, was this AEC 'Reliance' 4MU3RA, registered **691 PNY**, carrying fleet number 92. Fitted with Plaxton 'Panorama' C51F coachwork, it was the first 'new' Plaxton coachwork purchased by the company, and the first of many. A feature of this coach was the name 'Llynfi Panorama', made from polished stainless steel, attached to both sides. However, it received a 1966/7 Plaxton front end in September 1969, after an accident, and was sold for further use in 1980, to a local Jazz Band 'The Avonaires', from Maesteg. **691 PNY** is captured here at King Edward VII Avenue, Cathays, Cardiff, near the Civic Centre.
(John Jones' collection).

On 24th October, 1962, the company submitted an application to the Traffic Commissioners, requesting a modification to their licence, TGR 4862/1. They asked to delete the words 'South Wales Transport Company Ltd.' from their conditions of service, and to substitute it with 'Llynfi Motor Services Ltd.' on existing timetables, to the intent that the service now operated by South Wales Transport Co Ltd., will in future be operated by Llynfi Motor Services Ltd. Objections were received from the South Wales Transport Co., and Thomas Bros (Port Talbot Ltd.), and the application was refused on 8th May, 1963.

Another point of interest, Llynfi MS, and South Wales Transport, made objections on 27th February, 1963, to an application made by an established local operator, Lewis & Jacob, for a workmen's 'Express Carriage' licence between Bryngurnos Street, Bryn, and Glyncorrwg Colliery. However, the licence was granted to Lewis & Jacob on 19th June, 1963.

A month later, Llynfi Motors asked permission to operate double deck vehicles on a relief basis, on their registered service, TGR 4862/1, between Maesteg, and Aberavon Beach (Jersey Beach Hotel). The intended route to Aberavon Beach was given as B4282 to Port Talbot, A48 to Baglan Roundabout, then via Sandfields Estate to Aberavon Beach, instead of the authorised route. That was due to a low railway bridge at Port Talbot town centre. Conditions to their application were given as: 'No passenger to be picked up after Abbey Road, Port Talbot, on inward journeys, and no passenger to be set down before Abbey Road on return journeys'. The licence was granted on 18th December, 1963.

Additionally, in 1963, the company established a 'Travel Agency' at their registered office, 29 Llynfi Road, Maesteg, marketing holiday tours, to provide additional revenue.

Above: This AEC 'Reliance' 2MU3RV, **545 AVA** (93), with Willowbrook B53F bodywork, was new to Irvine (Golden Eagle Coaches), Salsburgh, North Lanarkshire, in April 1961. Llynfi acquired this in March 1963, and it passed to the well known Cardiff dealer, Arlington Motors, in June 1967, and to Grenville Motors, of Cambourne, Cornwall, in July 1968. *(John Jones' collection).*

Above: Another second-hand purchase in December 1964, was this 1954 Leyland 'Tiger Cub', **NNY 56** (94), fitted with Weymann 'Hermes' B44F bodywork. This rather battered looking 'Tiger Cub' was one of eighteen, delivered to the BET group owned, Thomas Brothers fleet, at Port Talbot, in 1954. It gave eight years service at Llynfi, before moving on to R.M. Douglas (Contractors), Birmingham (f/n 97074) in March 1973. It worked from Douglas' Swansea depot. *(Copyright unknown. Author's collection).*

Above: Pictured here on the Eastern end of Aberavon Beach Promenade (opposite the Amusement Park), is **ORR 325** (98), another Saunders Roe B44F bodied Leyland 'Tiger Cub' PSUC1/1. I wonder whether the driver of this bus realised that the engine cover (side panel) was open! A danger to oncoming traffic on the narrow country roads between Aberavon and Maesteg, and an invitation for a PG9 from the Traffic Commissioners. This vehicle was acquired from East Midland Motor Services (B325), in June 1965, and ran with Llynfi Motors for just 20 months. It passed to Milburn Motors (dealer), of Walmer Bridge, near Preston, Lancashire, by July 1967, and later passed to a contractor in Lanarkshire. *(Copyright The Bus Archive / Roy Marshall).*

Above: A very wet day at Aberavon Promenade, as this Saunders Roe bodied Leyland 'Tiger Cub' PSUC1/1, **FCH 11** (96), awaits departure time for 'sunny' Maesteg. **FCH 11** was one of two 'Tiger Cubs' acquired from Trent Motor Traction, Derby, in November 1965. They both gave Llynfi Motors, ten years service, before passing to W.H. Way, the Cardiff breaker in December 1975, where they were both destroyed by fire. *(Copyright The Bus Archive / Roy Marshall).*

Above: Standing at exactly the same spot as FCH 11 (upper photograph), is its sister, **FCH 16** (97), another Saunders Roe bodied Leyland 'Tiger Cub' PSUC1/1, acquired from Trent Motor Traction (366), in November 1965. It's accompanied by another 'Tiger Cub' from the Western Welsh fleet, JBO 108 (1108). *(Copyright The Bus Archive/Roy Marshall).*

During this period in the 1960s, quite a lot of fleet renumbering took place, details of which can be found in the fleet lists which appear on pages 237 to 245.

By mid-1965, however, a new depot manager, Randolf T Rainford was employed by the company. Mr Rainford, had originally been employed by BET owned J. James & Sons, of Ammanford, as assistant manager until its demise in 1962, but had transferred to South Wales Transport as a traffic manager after absorption of the James undertaking. Mr Rainford was later succeeded by another former SWT manager, Donald Phillip Drew, who remained with Llynfi until its demise.

September 1966, saw a bunch of new stage carriage service licences being applied for by United Welsh Services Ltd., of Swansea. Amongst their applications was TGR 3357/231, a service competing with Llynfi Motor Services, on their Maesteg (Town Hall), to Aberavon Beach route, via Bryn, Ynysygwas, and Port Talbot. The timetable and fare table submitted by United Welsh, were those authorised to South Wales Transport on TGR 421/35, the service jointly operated with Llynfi Motor Services.

On the same date, The South Wales Transport Company applied for a licence to operate a new service from Swansea to Maesteg, but two months later in November, 1966, they withdrew their application.

By December 1967, a total of thirty-one vehicles were licensed by the company, plus five that were withdrawn and delicenced, a slight reduction since 1959.

Above: Another former Thomas Bros, Port Talbot, Leyland 'Tiger Cub' PSUC1/1, to enter the Llynfi fleet in 1966, was **NNY 60**, which is seen here at Maesteg. This Weymann 'Hermes' bodied example was purchased in March 1966, with accident damage, but was repaired before entering service in June 1966, and received fleet number 99. It was sold in March 1973, to R.M. Douglas (contractor), Birmingham, (f/n 97078), and used for staff transport. *(Robert Mack).*

Above: Pictured here in Bristol City Centre, dangerously travelling with the entrance door open, is Llynfi Motors' Bedford VAL14, **695 ETH** (100). This Plaxton 'Val', C52F bodied coach, fitted with a Leyland engine, was new to Samuel Eynon & Sons, of Trimsaran, Carmarthenshire, in May 1964, and was acquired by Llynfi Motor Services in July 1966. The name 'Llynfi Embassy' on its side panels, were fabricated from polished stainless steel. This was the only Bedford VAL operated by the company, and was disposed of in 1971, passing to Powell, of Little Tarrington, Hereford, in June that year. *(John Jones' collection).*

Above: RTG 286 (101, originally f/n 103), was a 1955 Willowbrook DP41F bodied Leyland 'Tiger Cub' PSUC1/2T. It was new to W.H. John, of Coity, Bridgend, in June 1955, who traded as Coity Motors, operating local stage carriage services between Bridgend and Coity. It was withdrawn by Coity Motors in June 1966, and was quickly snapped up by Llynfi, who licenced it in February 1967. This view was taken at the Maesteg depot, on 18th November, 1979. *(Copyright John Jones).*

Above: **4777 NE** (102) was a Leyland 'Leopard' L2T, with attractive Burlingham 'Seagull 70', C41F coachwork, acquired in March 1967, from Spencer's Tours, Manchester. It's seen here at Fulmer Avenue, Maesteg, and was one of two 'Seagull 70' coaches owned by Llynfi. Withdrawn after an accident in July 1974, it was rebuilt, not used, and scrapped in 1987. *(Copyright R.F. Mack).*

Above: Abbey Works Bus Station, Margam, Port Talbot, is the backdrop for this view of **YNR 549** (104), which was a 1961 Leyland 'Leopard' L1, with Willowbrook DP41F bodywork. This bus was acquired from Jones Omnibus Services (118), of Aberbeeg, Monmouthshire, in August 1967, via Arlington Motors (dealer), Cardiff. It was new in October 1961, to Irvine, of Salsburgh, North Lanarkshire, and arrived at Aberbeeg in November 1963. This view was taken on 5th June, 1976.

(Copyright John Jones).

Above: After withdrawal by Western Welsh OC (1113), in 1967, this Leyland 'Tiger Cub' PSUC1/1, **JBO 113** (106), found its way into the Llynfi fleet in November 1967. It was withdrawn in 1975, and sold for further use to Griffiths & Powell (Morriston Coaches). It is seen here at Maesteg, on 21st February, 1971, with extra beading added to the waist band of its Weymann 'Hermes' bodywork, making the waist band a perminant feature. The Leyland badge was donated by a withdrawn Leyland HR40 'Olympic'.

(Copyright John Jones).

As we have seen, rural bus services were in decline in the 1960s, and operators nationwide had campaigned for many years to the Tory Government, to have the heavy fuel tax abolished to assist failing services. Consequently, under Section 92 of the Finance Act 1965, 'Fuel Duty Rebate' was established, to assist operators of stage carriage bus services. The rebate amounting to 10d a gallon, was only 50% of the total fuel tax, but it was increased to 100% from January 1969, a tremendous help to rural bus operators such as Llynfi Motor Services. This vital financial assistance was given to the bus industry by a Labour Government that had taken control in 1964.

However, following the purchase of all those second-hand buses by the company in the 1960's, came some more good news, when the Minister of Transport announced details of the Road Traffic Act 1968.

The new Traffic Act, gave stage carriage bus operators financial grants of 25% towards the purchase of new service buses, provided that they complied with certain requirements of the Ministry of Transport, including for example, an extreme front entrance doorway under driver supervision, and suitable for one-person operation.

The intention of the grant scheme was to encourage operators to modernise their fleets, and make buses more competitive in terms of comfort with cars. The scheme applied initially, only to buses used primarily on stage carriage services.

By 1970, however, the grant was increased to 50%, and it was agreed that coaches could also qualify for grant, if used to a sufficient extent on such bus services, provided that their coach bodies were built with minor essential modifications, such as 'jack knife entrance doors' and other features which complied with the bus grant specification. Conditions attached to the 'New Bus Grant' stated that qualifying operators would have to refund the grant if they sold the vehicle, or ceased to use it for stage carriage service within five years of its delivery.

The scheme, which came into being on 1st September, 1968, and ended in March 1984, was a blessing to stage carriage operators all over the country, including Llynfi Motor Services, who modernised their fleet tremendously.

In addition to the bus grant, was the introduction of 'Rural Bus Grants' in order to subsidise un-remunerative bus services, besides an increase to the fuel duty rebate introduced in 1965, (mentioned earlier), from 50% to 100%. That figure meant an increase from 10d to 1/7d per gallon paid to operators of *rural services only*, from 1st January, 1969.

However, Llynfi Motor Services were very slow making use of the Government's 'New Bus Grant' scheme. The first vehicle purchased under this scheme, was not ordered until 1971, by such time the grant was 50%, and the scheme had changed to include coaches.

In the meantime, they had bought no less than eight second-hand vehicles, and due to a shortage of drivers at SWT, were operating SWT's share of the Port Talbot service from August 1970.

As a direct result of that, and with SWT's full approval, in June 1971, the company applied for the following modifications to their Maesteg to Aberavon Beach service:

[1] To incorporate into this licence, the facilities and conditions authorised to The South Wales Transport Co Ltd., on licence TGR 421/35. In the event of this application being granted, TGR 421/35 will be surrendered. [2] To remove the restriction of picking up and setting down passengers between Aberavon Beach and Abbey Road, on certain journeys at hourly intervals during the summer period of operation. (A similar modification was refused in October 1962).

The modifications were granted on 21st July, 1971, allowing Llynfi Motor Services to absorb SWT's share of the Maesteg (Town Hall) to Aberavon Beach service.

On 16th February, 1972, the following new Express Carriage licence was asked for:-

TGR 4862/6   **Maesteg (Cross Inn)** to **Kenfig Industrial Estate**. *3 shifts per working day via: Bridgend Rd, Maesteg (Bus Stn), Bryn, A4107, A48M, A48, & B4283. To run only when the Borg-Warner Ltd, plant is operating. Weekly fares: Maesteg Cross £1.30, Maesteg (BS) £1.15, Bryn £1.00, Ynysygwas £0.85.*

There was one objector to this application, local competitor, DLJ Private Hire (L.J. & D.H. Stolzenberg t/a), of 84 Turberville Street, Maesteg.

After receiving this objection, Llynfi Motor Services withdrew their application, and in return, objected to a similar application made by DLJ Private Hire, for an identical Express Carriage licence, Maesteg to Kenfig Industrial Estate, on TGR 5246/1.

Ironically, DLJ Private Hire, withdrew their application too, and sold their business to Llynfi, a month later, in March 1972. For further information see pages 205/107.

Above: Another former Western Welsh (1104), Leyland 'Tiger Cub' PSUC1/1, with Weymann 'Hermes' bodywork, **JBO 104** (88), entered the fleet in early 1969. This one came via Morris Travel, of Pencoed, and was similarly treated to a face lift, with modified waist band, Leyland badge, and indicators, by Llynfi, before entering service. It was sold in July 1976 for further service, to Griffiths & Powell, of Morriston Coaches. *(Copyright The Bus Archive / Roy Marshall).*

Above: This 1956 Leyland 'Tiger Cub' PSUC1/2, **PWO 49**, carried fleet number 105 for its entirety with the company, even though it was renumbered 106 in 1969. Fitted with Willowbrook DP41F bodywork, it came from Jones Omnibus Services, of Aberbeeg, Monmouthshire, in April 1969, together with former Western Welsh Leyland 'Tiger Cub', HUH 13, for spares. PWO 49 is seen here at Station Road, Port Talbot, loading up for the return journey to Maesteg. *(Copyright The Bus Archive / Roy Marshall).*

Above: This former Trent Motor Traction (373), of Derby, Leyland 'Tiger Cub' PSUC1/1, **FCH 23** (108), was another Weymann 'Hermes' B44F bodied vehicle to join the fleet in 1969. It was another vehicle acquired from Davies Bros (Pencader) Ltd., and was sold for further use to Griffiths & Powell (Morriston Coaches), Morriston, in August 1975. The history of Davies Bros [Pencader] Ltd., is published in my Davies Bros publication, available on www.vernonmorgan.com *(Copyright The Bus Archive/Roy Marshall).*

Above: Another secondhand Leyland 'Tiger Cub' taken into stock in August 1970, was this Willowbrook DP41F bodied PSUC1/2T example, **VTX 44**, purchased from W.H. John (Coity Motors), of Coity, Bridgend. This vehicle didn't receive a fleet number during its six year stay with Llynfi, and passed to Barry Comprehensive School in 1976. *(Copyright The Bus Archive / Roy Marshall).*

Above: In December 1970, the company purchased three 1966, Leyland 'Leopard' PSU3/3RT's, with Duple 'Commander' C51F coachwork, from Hall's of Hounslow, London, consecutively registered LYL 996-8D. Numerically the first, **LYL 996D** (107), is seen here at Maesteg on 18th April, 1973, and passed to Morris Bros, of Upper Bank, Swansea, in April 1976. *(Copyright John Jones).*

Above: **LYL 997D**, was numerically second of the three Leyland 'Leopard' PSU3/3RT, Duple 'Commander' coaches acquired in December 1970. This never received a fleet number, and passed to Morris Bros, of Swansea, in April 1976. Its previous owner, Hall's of Hounslow, did lots of airport work, including airside, hence the amber beacon on its roof. *(Copyright John Jones).*

Above: Numerically the third Leyland 'Leopard' PSU3/3RT acquired from Hall's of Hounslow, was **LYL 998D** (109), which is seen here at the Maesteg depot. This particular coach was the first of the trio to leave the fleet. It had passed to John Lewis Coaches, Morriston, Swansea, by July 1973. *(Author's Collection).*

Above: Captured here after a wash at the company's Maesteg depot, on 21st February, 1971, is **933 DVA** (105), a Burlingham 'Seagull 70' C41F bodied AEC 'Reliance'. This coach was purchased in May 1968, from Samuel Eynon & Sons, of Trimsaran, Carmarthenshire, and was one of a pair new to Irvine, Salsburgh, North Lanarkshire, in July 1962. After withdrawal in May 1975, it passed to Ferris, Taffs Well, near Cardiff, for further use. *(Copyright John Jones).*

In March 1972, Llynfi purchased the three vehicle business of local competitor, L.J. & D.H. Stolzenberg (t/a DLJ Transport), Maesteg. The vehicles were not used, and sold on. It appears that no conditions were applied to the sale agreement of Stolzenberg's business, as he later restarted under the same title, from the same address. Further information on p107.

Above & Below: In August 1971, the company purchased this pair of Willowbrook bodied AEC Regent V deckers, **VWN 956/7** (111/112, later renumbered 107/8), from The South Wales Transport Co. Both views were taken at Maesteg depot, on 8th July, 1976 (upper), and 3rd June, 1975 (lower), respectively, by the late John Wiltshire. *(Copyright held by John Jones).*

Above: A spledid view of the company's first 'Grant Aided' vehicle, **ETG 298K** (110), captured at Sophia Gardens, Cardiff on 9th June, 1973. This was a Leyland 'Leopard' PSU3B/2R, with Willowbrook B53F bodywork, delivered in July 1971, and licensed on 1st August, 1971. In later years, it received a repaint using far less cream paint. *(Copyright John Jones).*

Above: 119 LNY (113), was one of a trio of Harrington 'Cavalier' bodied coaches purchased from South Wales Transport (f/n 116), in April 1972. All three, 119/120 LNY, and 121 NTX, had AEC 'Reliance' 2MU3RA chassis, and were new to BET owned Thomas Brothers, of Port Talbot, in July 1961, and April 1962, respectively. *(Copyright Peter Yeomans).*

Above: This former Thomas Bros, Port Talbot, AEC 'Reliance', **120 LNY** (112), with Harrington 'Cavalier' C41F coachwork, was one of three 'Reliances' purchased from South Wales Transport, in April 1972. *(Copyright The Bus Archive / Roy Marshall).*

Above: This AEC 'Reliance' 2MU3RA, **121 NTX** (111), with Harrington 'Cavalier' C41F coachwork, was another cast off from the South Wales Transport fleet, in April 1972. These vehicles were surplus to requirement after the formation of National Bus Company, and the mergers of South Wales Transport, Thomas Bros, N&C Coaches, and United Welsh Services in 1971.
(Copyright The Bus Archive / Roy Marshall).

Above: JNY 881K (119), was a Leyland 'Leopard' PSU3B/4R, with Plaxton 'Panorama Elite Express II' coachwork, seating 51. This 'Grant Aided' coach entered service in July 1972, and is seen here visiting Shrewsbury, for the annual Flower Show on 14th August, 1982. It remained with Llynfi Motors until the company's demise in July 1988, passing to the United Welsh Holdings' subsidiary company, A.E. & F.R. Brewer, Caerau, with the Llynfi business. *(Copyright John Jones)*.

Above: JNY 882K (120), was another 'Grant Aided' coach, and identical to its stablemate JNY 881K above. This was also fitted with Plaxton 'Panorama Elite Express II' coachwork, but this one entered service a month earlier, in June 1972, and left the fleet in June 1979, when it was sold to Clarkes Coaches, London SE3. Clarkes re-registered this coach SRS 123, but in June 1991, it was re-registered again to DSN 551K. *(Copyright unknown)*.

Above: In 1972, the company placed an order for their first Bristol chassis, in the form of two 'Grant Aided' Bristol LH6Ls, with Plaxton 'Panorama Elite III' Express coachwork. However, that order was cancelled and changed for two 'Grant Aided' Bristol LHL6Ls with Plaxton 'Derwent' DP45F bodywork. The 'Panorama' bodied LH6Ls, were delivered to Silcox Motor Coach Co, Pembroke Dock, in February 1973, and registered GDE 374/5L. The Llynfi Motors' replacement order for two LHL6Ls, with Plaxton 'Derwent' bodies arrived in April 1973, as NTX 595/6L. **NTX 595L** (117), is seen here at Port Talbot Bus Station, en route to Aberavon Beach. Both LHL6L's passed to the newly formed A.E. & F.R. Brewer company, July 1988.   *(Copyright Roy Marshall).*

Above: NTX 596L (118), was the second Bristol LHL6L, with Plaxton 'Derwent' DP45F bodywork, delivered to the company in April 1973. It gave excellent service until the company's demise in July 1988, passing to its new owners, United Welsh Holdings subsidiary, A.E. & F.R. Brewer Ltd., Caerau.   *(Copyright The Bus Archive / Roy Marshall).*

Above: A splendid view of beautiful vehicle. This Leyland 'Leopard' PSU3B/4R, **PNY 633L** (121), with Plaxton 'Panorama Elite III' Express, C51F coachwork, was another 'Grant Aided' vehicle delivered in May 1973. I have always had an affection for the Leyland PSU3B/4R with Plaxton 'Panorama Elite III' Express, probably because I drove one daily for 4 years! *(John Jones).*

Above: **PTG 706L** (122), was another PSU3B/4R, 'Leopard', identical to its stablemate PNY 633L above. However, this 'Grant Aided' coach was delivered to Llynfi Motors a month later, in June 1973, and was photographed here at Taff Embankment, Cardiff, on 18th February, 1978, on the occasion of the WRU International, between Wales & Scotland. *(Copyright John Jones).*

Above: This former Provincial of Leicester (R15), 1960 AEC 'Reliance' 2MU3RA, with Duple 'Britannia' C41F coachwork, arrived at Maesteg in February 1974, from Barton Transport, Chilwell, Notts (1055). Registered **XBC 546**, it received reissued f/n 109, and was operational until 1980. It's seen here at King Edward VII Avenue, Cardiff, on 14th June, 1975.   *(Copyright John Jones).*

Above: Looking in good condition working a private hire to the Wales v Australia (Wallabies), WRU match at Cardiff, on 5th December, 1981, is **HPT 323H** (123). This former Trimdon Motor Services, of Co Durham, 1970 Leyland 'Leopard' PSU3A/4R, with Plaxton 'Derwent' B55F bodywork, was one of several Trimdon 'Leopards' to find homes in South Wales. It gave lengthy service, passing to A.E. & F.R. Brewer Ltd., Caerau, upon Llynfi's demise in July 1988.   *(Copyright John Jones).*

Above: This 1960 AEC 'Reliance' with Harrington 'Cavalier' C41F coachwork, **99 GAL**, arrived from Barton Transport, Chilwell, Notts (936), in August 1974, and for unknown reasons, was the third vehicle to receive fleet number 109. The company's fleet numbering system was absolutely atrocious. This was scrapped at Bryn depot in 1982. *(Copyright The Bus Archive/R. Marshall).*

On 22nd May, 1974, the company applied for two more new stage carriage licences as follows:-

TGR 4862/7   Blaengwynfi to Kenfig Industrial Estate.
              via: Abergwynfi, A4107, A4063 to Caerau, and Maesteg, B4282 to Bryn, and
              Ynysygwas, A4107 Chapel of Ease, A48M Groes, A48, B4283.

TGR 4862/8   Glyncorrwg to Kenfig Industrial Estate.
              via: A4063, A4107 to Croeserw, A4063 to Cymmer, A4107 to Pontrhydyfen,
              Ynysygwas, and Chapel of Ease, A48M Groes, A48, B4283.

Both licences were granted without objections on 17th July, 1974.

Llynfi Motor Services Ltd
TRAVEL AGENTS
28a TALBOT STREET, MAESTEG, GLAMORGAN
Telephones : Maesteg 3192 & 3355

Our ref. DPD/EB   5th June, 1974

The Traffic Manager,
Western Welsh Omnibus Co. Ltd.,
253 Cowbridge Road, West,
Ely,
Cardiff.

Above: This former Ribble Motor Services (1044), 1961, Leyland 'Leopard' L2T, **PCK 626** (124), with Harrington 'Cavalier' C39F coachwork, arrivied in September 1974, from Davies Bros (Pencader) Ltd. (94). It had only worked for 6 months at Pencader, having previously operated for R.G.M. Mathews, Pontypool (Gwent), from April to June 1973. Mathews was absorbed by J.D. Cleverly (Capitol Coaches), Pontypool in June 1973, who ran it until February 1974. However, after the brief period at Pencader, it spent the rest of its days with Llynfi, and was scrapped at Maesteg depot in 1985. *(Copyright The Bus Archive / Roy Marshall).*

Above: Pictured here outside the company's original Bryn Garage, is **800 ABX** (126), a 1961 Leyland 'Leopard' L2, with coachwork built by Duple Motor Bodies, to a design named 'Donington', and C43F layout. This coach arrived in May 1975, from Davies Bros (Pencader) Ltd, (65), and was withdrawn and broken up on the same day of its accident, in February 1978. *(Byron Gage).*

<u>Above:</u> In June 1975, the company purchased a pair of Plaxton 'Panorama II' bodied 1968 Leyland 'Leopard' PSU3A/2RT coaches, TRK 5/6F, from Silverline, of Hounslow, London. **TRK 5F** (127), is seen here at Wood Street, Cardiff, dropping off passengers in the middle of a busy road. This coach had previously worked airport/airside work at Heathrow, hence the amber beacon on its roof dome. Both coaches passed to Eynon's of Trimsaran, in 1981. *(Copyright The Bus Archive / Roy Marshall).*

<u>Above:</u> **TRK 6F** (128), was numerically the second Plaxton 'Panorama II' bodied Leyland 'Leopard' acquired in June 1975, from Silverline, Hounslow. Fitted with a pneumocyclic gearbox, 2 speed rear axle, and exhaust brake, TRK 6F is accompanied here at the Maesteg depot by former Wallace Arnold 'Leopard' 9905 UG. *(Copyright The Bus Archive / Roy Marshall).*

Above: August 1975 saw the arrival of two Leyland L1 'Leopards', from Portsmouth Corporation. Registered YBK 132/8, their Weymann bodies were converted from B42D to B44F and B45F respectively, before entering service. **YBK 132** (129), dating from December 1961, is seen here at Maesteg Bus Station on 22nd March, 1977, looking rather sad, but it continued operational until the demise of Llynfi Motors in 1988, passing to A.E. & F.R. Brewer Ltd., with the business in July 1988. *(Copyright John Jones).*

Above: YBK 138 (130), pictured here at Maesteg depot, was the second L1 'Leopard' received from Portsmouth CT in August 1975. This also gave lengthy service, it was withdrawn by June 1986, and scrapped in December 1987. *(Copyright Byron Gage).*

In July 1975, a comparatively new competitor, I.B. Jones & Son, of Square Garage, Caerau, applied for three local express carriage licences:-

TGR 5478/1 **Llangynwyd** to **Port Talbot (Revlon Factory)**, via Caerau, and Maesteg.
Mon to Fri., Sat & Sun if required. Only employees of Revlon to be carried.

TGR 5478/2 **Glyncorrwg** to **Maesteg (Revlon Factory, Ewenny Road Ind. Estate)**.
via: Cymmer, Croeserw Site, Caerau, & Nantyffyllon. *Same conditions.*

TGR 5478/3 **Glyncorrwg** to **Maesteg (Revlon Factory, Ewenny Road Ind. Estate)**.
Same conditions.

Jones was granted three short period licences to operate those services, but in the meantime, objections were received from Llynfi Motor Services; Brewers Motor Services; and South Wales Transport Co. Ltd. The application was supported by West Glam CC.

Much to the disappointment of the objectors, the licences were all granted on 8th October 1975.

However, I.B. Jones & Son, had ceased operating by May 1982. The business and one remaining vehicle passed to R.G. Millington, Cefn Cribwr, Kenfig Hill (G & M Coaches).

Returning to December 1976, Llynfi Motor Services applied for permission to change their long standing bus terminus at Bethany Square, Port Talbot, to the new Port Talbot Bus Station. Permission for the change was granted on 9th February, 1977.

Above: Former Wallace Arnold Coaches, Leeds, Plaxton 'Embassy' bodied Leyland L2 'Leopard', **9905 UG**, received f/n 131 in the Llynfi fleet, and was acquired from R.R. Prance, Cardiff, in February 1976. It was scrapped by February 1978. *(Byron Gage).*

Above: Dealer registered **LFB 681P**, never carried a fleet number, but was allocated f/n 131. This was a 'Grant Aided' Leyland 'Leopard' PSU3C/4R, with Plaxton 'Panorama Elite Express III' coachwork, which passed to A.E. & F.R. Brewer Ltd., upon take over of Llynfi in July 1988, but was immediately sold on to Brian Isaac, Morriston. *(Copyright The Bus Archive / Roy Marshall).*

Above: In July 1976, four Glasgow PTE Leyland 'Atlanteans' were acquired ready for the new academic year in September. All four, registered AGA 112/126/128/129B, were 1964 PDR1/1, Mk 1 Atlanteans, with Alexander 'A type' H44/34F bodywork, and gave the company many years' service. **AGA 112B** (133), is seen here at Maesteg depot on 19th March, 1978. *(John Jones).*

Above: Former Glasgow PTE (LA187), Leyland 'Atlantean' **AGA 126B** (134), is seen here on the B4282 road, climbing out of the village of Bryn, en route for Port Talbot on 21st July 1982. The 'Royal Oak' public house is visible in the backdrop.
(Copyright John Jones).

Above: Another view of the former Glasgow PTE, Leyland PDR1/1 'Atlantean' (Mk 1), **AGA 126B** (134). This also had Alexander 'A type' H44/34F bodywork, and gave the company excellent service for nine years before its disposal. It's seen here at the Maesteg depot in 1980, with Leyland 'Titan' LHG 537 (146) parked behind it. *(Copyright Robert Edworthy).*

Above: Former Glasgow PTE (LA189), Leyland 'Atlantean' **AGA 128B** received f/n 135, and is seen here at Maesteg depot, between duties, with CYS 570B (142), another Glasgow PTE, Alexander bodied 'Atlantean' on the left. To the right, is former Coity Motors' Leyland 'Tiger Cub', RTG 286 (101). *(Copyright Robert Edworthy).*

Above: Numerically the last Glasgow PTE, 'Atlantean' acquired by the company in July 1976, was **AGA 129B** (136), which is seen here about to leave the depot, to take up its school contract duty. This vehicle was withdrawn in November 1982, and scrapped in 1988. *(Author's collection. Copyright unknown).*

Above: This former Southdown Motor Services, 1963 Leyland 'Leopard' PSU3/1RT, **267 AUF** (144), with Marshall B49F bodywork (and Willowbrook badge added by Llynfi), arrived in September 1976, via East Kent Road Car Co. Originally allocated f/n 137, it was not licenced until August 1979, and is seen here at Croeserw, on 18th November, 1979. *(Copyright John Jones).*

Above: The second former Southdown (671), Leyland 'Leopard' PSU3/1RT acquired by Llynfi in September 1976, was **271 AUF** (138), which is seen here at the Maesteg depot on 19th May, 1977. It was identical to its sister above, and came from the same source, East Kent RCC. Licensed in January 1977, it was withdrawn after an accident in February 1979. *(Copyright John Jones).*

Above: This Leyland 'Leopard' PSU3D/4R, **OHY 789R** (141) was delivered in July 1977, and was another 'Grant Aided' vehicle. Fitted with Plaxton 'Supreme II Express' C51F coachwork, it is seen here at the Taff Embankment, Cardiff, on the occasion of the WRU International, Wales v France (22-12), on 6th February, 1982. *(Copyright John Jones).*

Above: This Ford R1114, with Duple 'Dominant I' Express bodywork, **HNM 926N** was hired by Llynfi Motor Services, from an unknown dealer, from June 1977, to January 1978. It had been new to R.I. Davies, Tredegar, in March 1975, passing to 'Stonnis' Tredegar, February 1977, after the collapse of R.I. Davies' business in September 1976. *(Author's collection).*

Above: In November 1977, another former Glasgow PTE, Leyland 'Atlantean' PDR1/1, **CYS 570B** (142), arrived. This also had Alexander 'A type' H44/34F bodywork, and is seen here at the depot on 31st October, 1978, ready to depart on a schools journey.
(Copyright of the late John Wiltshire).

Above: FCX 287C (143), was another Leyland 'Leopard' PSU3/1R, with Weymann B53F bodywork, and arrived in October 1977, from Yorkshire Traction (395). It entered service in January 1978, and had left the fleet by 1985, with no further trace.
(Copyright unknown / Author's collection).

A clerical error in June 1978, led to the company's failure to renew four road service licences. The Traffic Commissioners enquired on 18th July, 1978, as to why licences TGR 4862/2, 3, 4, & 5, had not been renewed.

TGR 4862/5, **Maesteg** to **Blackpool** (Express Carriage) was not re-applied for, but the other three were reapplied for under new application numbers, due to their expiry:-

TGR 4862/9 **Excursions & Tours** starting from Maesteg *(all tours listed individually). Previously licensed on TGR 4862/2, which expired 30/6/1978, and had not been renewed.*

TGR 4862/10 **Excursions & Tours** starting from Maesteg (all tours listed individually). *Previously licensed on TGR 4862/4, which expired 30/6/1978, and had not been renewed.*

Temporary short period licences TGR 4862/Sp/6, and 4862/Sp/7 were issued for the above two applications, with an operational period of 19/7/1978, to 12/9/1978.

Full term licences TGR 4862/9, and 10, were granted in October 1978, but the stage carriage licence issued under TGR 4862/3, was not re-applied for until December 1978, as below:-

TGR 4862/11 **Caerau** to **Port Talbot (British Steel Corporation, Abbey Works)**.
via: Maesteg, Bryn, Ynysygwas, Saron, BSC (Vivian Bus Shelter), & BSC (PHG Dept.). *To operate Monday to Friday. 3 x shifts per day.*

TGR 4862/11 was granted as applied for, on 18th April, 1979.

Above: A coachload of very excited looking passengers are admiring the scenery here at Hayle, Cornwall, on 5th September, 1978. This coach was dealer registered, **TOU 634T**, a brand new Leyland 'Leopard' PSU3E/4R, with 'Grant Aided' Plaxton 'Supreme III Express', C51F coachwork, which had been delivered to the company a month earlier. *(Copyright John Jones).*

Above: This former Burnley, Colne & Nelson (237), Leyland 'Titan' PD3/6, **LHG 537** (146), with East Lancs H41/32F bodywork arrived at Maesteg in October 1978, from Lancaster CT (537). It gave the company four years service before withdrawal in November 1982, passing to Bevington Motors, a motor car dealer, at Margam, in July 1983, for further use as a mobile all-over advertisement. This view was taken on 25th May 1982. *(Copyright John Jones).*

Above: In November 1978, the company bought two Leyland 'Tiger Cubs', with Alexander 'Y type' bodies fitted with 'Panoramic' windows, from the Trent Motor Traction Co., Derby. Numerically first of the pair was **HRC 100C** (148), pictured here at Croeserw. This was withdrawn May 1984, and scrapped by 1988. *(Copyright unknown / Author's collection).*

Above: **HRC 103C** (149), seen here at Maesteg Bus Station on 19th January, 1980, was the second of a pair of Alexander C41F bodied, Leyland PSUC1/1T 'Tiger Cubs', received from Trent MT in November 1978. This 1965 vehicle gave excellent service, passing to the Brewer's undertaking with the business, in July 1988. It was immediately disposed of to Brian Isaac Coaches, Morriston, for further use, and finally passed to Golden Coaches, Llantwit Major, in March 1991.   *(Copyright John Jones).*

In the meantime, a new Conservative Government embarked upon a programme of deregulation and privatisation of bus services, and brought into being The Road Traffic Act, 1980. The Act which came into effect on 1st October, 1980, was basically the beginning of deregulation, allowing Express Carriage services over 30 miles in distance, to be freed from licensing regulations, and Excursions and Tours would no longer require licensing at all. Additionally, the restrictions of advertising Excursions & Tours were lifted.

The Act also abolished the licensing of bus conductors from 19th May, 1980, and reduced the minimum age for PSV (later PCV) drivers from 21 years, to 18, with a restriction that under 21's may only drive a PSV within a 30 mile radius of their base. The Act also brought about the new 'coloured' operator licence discs indicating, National (blue); International (green); and Restricted, or Special Restricted (orange). At the same time, operator licence numbers were changed from TGR xxx prefix, to PG xxx prefix (in SWTA), with other traffic areas following suit with their own appropriate Traffic Area letters. The Transport Minister, Mr Norman Fowler, also announced that the 'New Bus Grant' scheme would cease by 31st March, 1984.

The company took advantage of the Minister's advanced warning regarding withdrawal of the 'New Bus Grant Scheme', by ordering two 'Grant Aided' Leyland 'Leopard' coaches, which unknowingly, were to become their final brand new vehicles in 1981 – pictured opposite.

Above: Pictured here at Cwmdu, Swansea, on 22nd January, 1982, is dealer registered **ETC 309W** (152), a 'Grant Aided' Leyland 'Leopard' PSU3F/5R, with Plaxton 'Supreme IV Express' C53F coachwork. It was one of a pair (ETC 309/310W), delivered in April 1981, passing with the business, to A.E. & F.R. Brewer Ltd., on 11th July 1988. *(Copyright John Jones).*

Above: The last two brand new vehicles purchased by Llynfi Motor Services, were captured here together on an excursion to Bath in 1984. **ETC 309/310W**, were originally an identical pair of Leyland PSU3F/5R 'Leopards', fitted with ZF manual gearboxes, and Plaxton 'Supreme IV Express' C53F coachwork, built to full grant specification. Both coaches passed to United Welsh Holdings subsidiary, A.E. & F.R. Brewer Ltd., on 11th July 1988. *(Copyright unknown / Author's collection).*

Above: Seen here on Neath Road, Maesteg, on 10th September, 1983, is former Southdown Motor Services (202), **KUF 202F**, a 1968 Willowbrook bodied, Leyland 'Leopard' PSU3/1RT. It was acquired by Llynfi Motor Services in February 1981, and received fleet number 151.
(Copyright John Jones).

Above: In August 1981, Llynfi Motors acquired three Newport Corporation Leyland PDR1/1 'Atlanteans', with Alexander 'A type' H43/31F bodies. **KDW 79F** (155), seen here on Taff Embankment, Cardiff, on 5th December, 1981, was numerically the first, and was the first of the trio to be withdrawn, after it was decaputated in a low bridge accident at Nantyffyllon, on 18th June, 1984.
(Copyright John Jones).

Above: This was the scene at Nantyffyllon after the accident involving **KDW 79F** (155), on 18th June, 1984. *(Copyright unknown).*

Above: **KDW 81F** was never allocated a fleet number by Llynfi Motor Services. It was another Alexander bodied Leyland PDR1/1 (Mk 1) 'Atlantean' acquired from Newport Corporation (81), in August 1981, ready for the new academic school year beginning in September. This view was taken at the companys Maesteg depot, on 16th February, 1983, by the late John Wiltshire.

Above: Former Newport Corporation (84), **KDW 84F**, is pictured here on the B4282 road between Bryn and Port Talbot, making a dead journey to Port Talbot, to collect school children for their homeward journey to Maesteg, on 21st July, 1982. **KDW 84F** (156), was one of the three Alexander bodied Leyland 'Atlanteans' acquired in August 1981. *(Copyright John Jones).*

Above: Pictured here at the company's Bryn depot, on 11th June, 1988, is another former Newport Corporation (100), Leyland 'Atlantean', **PDW 100H**. This one was acquired direct from Newport in July 1982, and had chassis type PDR1A/1, fitted with identical Alexander 'A type' H43/31F bodywork. It was one of the vehicles absorbed by A.E. & F.R. Brewer Ltd., with the Llynfi business, on 11th July, 1988. Note the entrance doors were still in Newport's livery, six years later. *(Copyright John Jones).*

Licences PG 4862/7 and 4862/8, were not renewed on 16th March, 1983, whilst PG 4862/11, (Caerau to Abbey Works), was surrendered on 28th March, 1984.

In April 1984, the following eight short period licences were issued to the company:-

PG 4862/Sp/9 **Bryn (Royal Oak)** to **Dyffryn Upper Comp. School, Port Talbot**.
Period of operation: 30/4/1984 to 13/7/1984.

PG 4862/Sp/10 **Travellers Rest, Briton Ferry** to **Glanafan Upper Comprehensive School, Port Talbot**. *Period of operation: 30/4/1984 to 13/7/1984.*

PG 4862/Sp/11 **Maes-Ty-Canol, Baglan** to **Glanafan Upper Comprehensive School, Port Talbot**. *Period of operation: 30/4/1984 to 13/7/1984.*

PG 4862/Sp/12 **Baglan Library** to **Glanafan Upper Comp. School, Port Talbot**.
Period of operation: 30/4/1984 to 13/7/1984.

PG 4862/Sp/13 **Sunnycroft** to **Glanafan Lower Comprehensive School, Port Talbot**.
Period of operation: 30/4/1984 to 13/7/1984.

PG 4862/Sp/14 **Old Road, Baglan** to **Glanafan Lower Comp. School, Port Talbot**.
Period of operation: 30/4/1984 to 13/7/1984.

PG 4862/Sp/15 **Travellers Rest** to **St Joseph's R.C. Junior School, Port Talbot**.
Period of operation: 30/4/1984 to 13/7/1984.

PG 4862/Sp/16 **Travellers Rest** to **St Joseph's R.C. Comp. School, Port Talbot**.
Period of operation: 30/4/1984 to 13/7/1984.

Due to major changes in Road Service Licensing, all 'School Services' had to be registered, and on 1st August, 1984, the following school service licences were asked for:-

PG 4862/12 **Bryn (Royal Oak)** to **Dyffryn Lower & Upper Comprehensive Schools**.
via: Ynysygwas, Penycae, B4107 Talcennau Road, and Bertha Road.
To operate on schooldays only, and will be available to the general public. Passengers on the forward journey, to be set down only at the schools, and on the return journey, passengers are to be picked up only at the schools. On the forward journey, passengers will not be picked up after Penycae, and on the return journey, passengers will not be set down before Penycae.

PG 4862/13 **Travellers Rest (Briton Ferry)** to **Glanafan Upper Comprehensive School**.
via: Old Road, Baglan, Crawford Road, and Ashgrove.
Same condition as 4862/12 (except pick up and set down before Ashgrove).

PG 4862/14 **Maes-Ty-Canol (Baglan)** to **Glanafan Upper Comprehensive School**.
via: Blaenbaglan School, Baglan Church, St Illtyd's Drive, and Station Road.
Same condition as 4862/12 (except pick up/set down before 'Jet Garage' A48).

PG 4862/15 **Baglan Library** to **Glanafan Upper Comprehensive School**.
via: Sunnycroft, Baglan Church, Lodge Drive, and Station Road.
Same condition as 4862/12 (except pick up/set down before 'Jet Garage' A48).

PG 4862/16 **Sunnycroft** to **Glanafan Lower Comprehensive School**.
via: Maes-Ty-Canol, and Baglan Church.
Same condition as 4862/12 (except pick up/set down before Baglan Church).

PG 4862/17 **Old Road (Baglan)** to **Glanafan Lower Comprehensive School**.
via: Greenwood Road, and Baglan Church.
Same condition as 4862/12 (except pick up/set down before 'Jet Garage' A48).

PG 4862/18 **Travellers Rest (Briton Ferry)** to **St Joseph's RC Comprehensive School**.
via: Baglan Library, Baglan Church, and Plasnewydd.
Same condition as 4862/12 (except pick up/set down before Plasnewydd).

PG 4862/19 **Travellers Rest (Briton Ferry)** to **St Joseph's Junior School**.
via: Crawford Road, Maes-Ty-Canol, Plasnewydd, St Theresa's RC School, St Joseph's RC Infants School, and St Joseph's RC Junior School.
Same condition as 4862/12 (except pick up/set down before Plasnewydd.

The above licences PG 4862/12 to 19, were all granted as applied for, on 7th November, 1984, and the following short period licences were issued with an 'undecided period of operation', in order to continue operating the services.

PG 4862/Sp/17 **Bryn (Royal Oak)** to **Dyffryn Upper Comprehensive School**.

PG 4862/Sp/18 **Travellers Rest** to **Glanafan Upper Comprehensive School**.

PG 4862/Sp/19 **Maes-Ty-Canol (Baglan)** to **Glanafan Upper Comp. School**.

PG 4862/Sp/20 **Baglan Library** to **Glanafan Upper Comprehensive School**.

PG 4862/Sp/21 **Sunnycroft** to **Glanafan Lower Comprehensive School**.

PG 4862/Sp/22 **Old Road (Baglan)** to **Glanafan Lower Comprehensive School.**

PG 4862/Sp/23 **Traveller's Rest** to **St Joseph's RC Junior School**.

PG 4862/Sp/24 **Traveller's Rest** to **St Joseph's RC Comprehensive School**.

A year later, on 11th September, 1985, another new stage carriage licence was applied for:-

PG 4862/20 **Afan Argoed Country Park** to **Glyncorrwg**.
To operate on schooldays only.
On morning journeys, passengers will only be set down at Dyffryn Afan Primary School. On afternoon journeys, passengers will only be picked up at Dyffryn Afan Primary School, Cymmer Clock, and Glyncorrwg Primary School.

The licence PG 4862/20 was granted on 4th December, 1985, but in the interim period, the following short term licence was issued, in order to operate the new service immediately:-

PG 4862/Sp/25 **Afan Argoed Country Park** to **Glyncorrwg**.
Period of operation: 2/9/1985 to 1/3/1986.

Above: The last two vehicles acquired by Llynfi, arrived in December 1984, and are seen on this page. **MDW 389G** above, was another former Newport Corporation Leyland 'Atlantean', which was acquired from Nicholson, Borve (Isle of Lewis), Scotland. MDW 389G entered service in April 1986, never received a fleet number, and is seen here on 24/2/1987. *(Copyright John Jones).*

Above: YSD 343L was a 1973 Leyland 'Leopard' PSU3/3R, with Alexander 'Y type' C49F coachwork, acquired from Highland Scottish (L35), in December 1984. Pictured here on 24th February, 1987, this vehicle, and the 'Atlantean' above were the last two vehicles acquired by Llynfi, and passed to A.E. & F.R. Brewer Ltd., with the business, in July 1988. *(Copyright John Jones).*

The next major issue in the company's history was 'Deregulation', brought about by The Road Traffic Act (1985). The Act, scheduled to be implemented on 26th October, 1986, was basically to transfer the operation of bus services from public bodies, to private companies, as legislated by the Act. It abolished 'Road Service Licensing' and allowed the introduction of competition on local bus services, for the first time since 1931. To operate a service, all an accredited operator was required to do was to provide 56 days' notice to the Traffic Commissioner, of their intention to commence, cease, or alter operation on a route.

The transition into deregulation, led by Transport Secretary, Nicholas Ridley, actually began on 6th January, 1986, with various provisions of the Act coming into force on that day:-

[1] The term 'Stage Carriage Service' changed to 'Local Service'.

[2] Licensing 'Stage Carriage Services' abolished - changed to 'Local Service Registrations'.

[3] The term 'Express Carriage' was abolished.

[4] Requirement to notify 'Express Services' abolished.

From 1st March, 1986, the layout of 'Local Service Registrations' (previously 'Stage Carriage' licensing), changed to a different format, and the following registrations are in accordance with paragraph 10, of schedule 6, of the Transport Act (1985). It lists all the 'Local Services' Llynfi Motor Services registered with the Traffic Commissioners, on 1st March, 1986:-

PG/0750/4862 **Maesteg (Bus Stn)** to **Port Talbot (Bus Stn)**. **Route Nº 1**
(Extends to Aberavon Beach on summer service), via: Bryn, Ynysygwas, and British Steel Corporation (Vivian Park), on certain departures.
Local service. Mon to Sat. Hourly frequency. D/D operation.

PG/0751/4862 **Baglan (Junct. Hilltop Close, & Tyn-y-Twr)** to **Port Talbot (Glanafan Upper Comp. School)**, via: Baglan Estate, and A48. *Schooldays only.*
Local service. 1 x return journey. D/D operation. **Route Nº 10**

PG/0752/4862 **Baglan (Junction Pinewood Terrace, & A48)** to **Port Talbot (Glanafan Upper Comp. School)**, via: Baglan Estate, and A48. *Schooldays only.*
Local Service. 1 x return journey. D/D operation. **Route Nº 11**

PG/0753/4862 **Baglan (Junction Cedar Gardens, and Sunny Mount)** to **Port Talbot (Glanafan Lower Comp. School)**, Velindre, via: Baglan Estate, and A48.
Local service. 1 x return journey daily. Schooldays only. D/D operation.
Route Nº 12

PG/0754/4862 **Baglan (Junction of Albion Road, & Old Baglan Road)** to **Port Talbot (St Joseph's RC Upper Comprehensive School)**, via: Baglan Estate, Sandfields Estate (including St. Theresa's RC School). *Schooldays only.*
Local service. 1 x return journey daily. D/D operation. **Route Nº 13**

PG/0755/4862 **Baglan (Shops), Church Crescent** to **Port Talbot (St Joseph's RC Upper Comp. School**, via: Westlands Estate, and Windsor Estate. *Schooldays only. Local service. 1 x return journey daily. D/D operation.* **Route Nº 14**

PG/0756/4862 **Cynonville** to **Glyncorrwg (Bridge Street).** Route Nº 15
via: Dyffryn Rhondda, Cymmer (Clock), Heol-y-Glyn, and Abercregan.
Local service. Schooldays only. 3 outward & 2 inward journeys. D/deck.

PG/0757/4862 **Caerau (Blaencaerau)** to **Swansea (Oystermouth Road).**
via: Caerau, Nantyffyllon, Maesteg, Bryn, and Ynysygwas.
Wed & Sat only, one return journey. Twice daily after commencement of 'Miners Fortnight', to end of August, and during Nov/Dec.   Double deck.

Twenty-two months later, on Saturday, 9th January, 1988, the company's long standing opposition, Brewer's Motor Services, ceased trading. Their complete business passed to 'United Welsh Holdings Ltd', the holding company of the newly privatised South Wales Transport Co., who formed a new subsidiary, 'Helproute Ltd', to take over the Brewer's undertaking from 10th January, 1988. However, the title Helproute, was soon discontinued in favour of A.E. & F.R. Brewer Ltd., Heol Gwyrosydd, Penlan, Swansea, SA5 7BN.

On 9th March, 1988, Llynfi Motor Services' applied for renewal of their 'O' licence, asking for 14 single deck, and 4 double deck vehicles, a 50% reduction since 1967. The 'Operating Centre' was given as 29 Llynfi Road, Maesteg, which was the company's office address, and the Transport Manager was recorded as Donald Phillip Drew.

The 'O' licence was granted as applied for, on 6th May, 1988, surprisingly, for one year only, expiring 30th April, 1989.

It later emerged that negotiations had taken place between Llynfi Motor Services Ltd., and United Welsh Holdings Ltd., with regard to a take-over of the business.

After 64 years of bitterness and rivalry, the Thomas family decided to call it a day, they'd had enough. What was their motive just six months behind their rivals, Brewers Motor Services.

It was known that the business had not recorded a profit for several years, and with ever increasing costs and mismanagement, coupled with the downward trend in passenger loadings, there was also the constant threat of competition from competitors since deregulation in 1986.

Besides all that, the management, brothers Glyn and George Thomas, (who did not confer between each other), decided to retire. Their brother Dyfrig Thomas, had passed away two years earlier, in May 1986, aged 77, besides, they were aged 85, and 76, respectively.

United Welsh Holdings purchased the Llynfi Motor Services undertaking, and amalgamated it with their AE & FR Brewer subsidiary, taking control from 10th July, 1988. Llynfi's garages at Maesteg and Bryn were not taken over, but Maesteg depot was used temporarily. Llynfi's Travel agents shop at 28A Talbot St, Maesteg, was absorbed with the business, and operated under the name of another United Welsh Holdings subsidiary, Travelwise (Wales) Ltd.

All Llynfi Motor Services staff transferred to the new company except management, and all Llynfi's licences were cancelled by 10th July, 1988.

Glyn Haydn Thomas died 7 years later in June 1995, aged 92. His brother George, was an eccentric, and weighed 6½ stone when he died in March 1992, yet it took 6 men to carry his coffin. It was laden with his complete collection of bus marque badges, saved off scrap buses.

Above: A very young bus conductor from the 1920s period, in full uniform complete with Cash Bag, Bell Punch, Ticket Rack, and Whistle. Unfortunately, she was not in posession of the mandatory 'licensed conductors badge'. I wonder which company employed her. She *may* have been one of W.G.Thomas' three daughters!

Having no connection with Llynfi Motor Services, a new business partnership was formed fourteen months later, between Vivian Benjamin Thomas, D. Cranshaw, and D.P. Lindenburn, who traded as 'Bryn Travel'.

The partnership rented the 'Old Llynfi Garage' Maesteg Road, Bryn, Port Talbot, and on 6th September, 1989, they applied to the Traffic Commissioners for an operator's licence to operate three single deck vehicles, from the operating centre stated above.

A five year licence, PG 6530/SI was granted, expiring 30th September, 1994, and two Duple 425 coaches were purchased. Both vehicles were sold after five months trading, in March 1990, and their licence was surrendered on 18th April, 1990.

LLYNFI MOTOR SERVICES – VEHICLE DETAILS

f/n	Reg Nº	Chassis make & type	Chassis number	Body make & type	Seating	Date new	Remarks / Additional Information Previous owner	Date acquired	Date withdrawn
	NY 4206	Fiat 15TER 25hp uw 2t 5cwt	66490	Massey	B14	1918	Ex War Dept. (Livery Cream & Blue).	10/1923	7/1926
	NY 6910	Daimler 'CKY' uw 3t 18cwt 2qr	4360	Massey	B20	11/1924	New (Livery Navy Blue & Cream).	14/11/1924	3/1930
	CW 2589	Daimler 'CK'	3303	?	B29	1/1920	Ex Helliwell, Nelson, Lancs.	7/1926	27/1/1931
	T 9054	Daimler 22hp	?	Charabanc Re-bodied by Massey B- -D	Ch18	7/1920	Ex Autocars, Ilfracombe, Devon.	by12/1929	?
6	VA 4592	Leyland 'Lion' PLSC1 5.1 litre (174 inch w/b)	45012	Leyland	B31F	2/1926	Ex -?-	by 5/1930	?
7	DE 5349	Leyland 'Lion' PLSC1 5.1 litre engine	45114	Leyland	B31R	5/1926	Ex Green's Motors, Haverfordwest. Pembrokeshire.	by 3/1930	3/1930
	VW 5135	Leyland 'Lion' PLSC3 5.1 litre (192 inch w/b)	47030	Dodson	B32R	6/1928	Ex Sheffield United Tours (w/d 1932). via: Pro Bono Publico, London.	c1932-3	6/1938
	VT 6537	Leyland 'Lion' LT2	51618	Leyland	B32	1931	Ex OK Bus Services, Derby.	?	?
	HE 3839	Thornycroft 'A6'	16219	?	B20	4/1928	Ex Yorkshire Traction (388).	1934	12/1936
	ACY 104	Leyland 'Tiger' TS7T (6 wheeler)	9822	Massey	B40R	3/1936	New (Livery Cream & Blue).	12/3/1936	2/1951
12 to 41	BWX 722	Leyland 'Tiger' TS7	12920	Wise Coachbuilders, Staines. Re-bodied by Santus 5/1948.	B33F	5/1937	Ex Ripponden & District (1). (Livery Cream & Blue).	11/1937	5/1959
	FV 68	Leyland 'Tiger' TS1	60149	Leyland Re-bodied by Massey C35R.	C30R to C35R	4/1929	Ex S & J. Wood, Blackpool.	by 1939	c1947
	TX 9497	AEC 'Regal I'	662206	Re-bodied by Romilly, Cardiff 1936. Original body Metcalf.	B31R	5/1930	Ex D.J. Thomas (Cream Line), Maesteg.	by 6/1939	by 10/1945
	CWW 494	AEC 'Regal I' Retrofitted with oil engine.	6622466	Wise Coachbuilders, Staines.	FC32F	6/1938	Ex Ripponden & District (114)	by 4/1939	7/1940
	BDW 474	Dennis 'Lancet II'	175519	Dennis	C32F	4/1938	Ex W.A. Pugh. Newport, Mon.	7/1940	9/1954
	CLG 429	Dennis 'Lancet I'	170389 or 170897	?	B32F	1935	Ex Watson, Runcorn, Cheshire.	11/1943	10/1953
	FNY 694	Bedford OWB	19821	Duple (utility)	B32F to B30F	5/1944	New	5/1944	3/1951

	Reg	Chassis	Serial	Body	Seating	New	History	Acquired	Disposed
18	FTG 311	Dennis 'Lancet II'	176394	Dennis	B35F	6/1938	Ex Glenton Tours, EXH 985 or EXF 935, London, SE14, via: War Department. Re-registered FTG 311 in 8/1944.	8/1944	1/1952
37	GTX 437	Leyland 'Tiger' PS1/1	471761	Original Massey B35F body rebuilt & lengthened by Neath Coachworks to B39F in 1957.	B35F to B39F	9/1947	New	9/1947	12/1972
	GNY 856	Bedford OB	45204	Duple Vista	C29F	3/1947	Ex D.J. Thomas (Cream Line), Maesteg.	4/1948	10/1951
	GTG 322	Bedford OB	46241	Thurgood	C29F	5/1947	Ex D.J. Thomas (Cream Line), Maesteg.	4/1948	4/1950
	GZ 2236	Bedford OWB	22288	Duple	B28F to B30F	9/1944	Ex Northern Ireland Rail Transport Board (X325).	2/1949	5/1951
45	JTG 286	AEC 'Regal III'	9621E737	Longford	C35F	7/1949	New. Originally intended for N&C, (Neath & Cardiff Express Coaches).	7/1949	6/1963
	JTG 287	Dennis 'Lancet III'	63203	D.J. Davies (Merthyr).	C33F	7/1949	New	7/1949	3/1953
42	GDG 795	Dennis 'Lancet III'	300J3	Duple 'A'	C35F	10/1947	Ex Bennett, Tongwynlais, Glam.	12/1949	11/1960
47	JTX 746	Leyland 'Tiger' PS2/3	494588	Longford	C35F	3/1950	New	3/1950	1/1967
33	HYP 681	Bedford OB	57205	Mulliner	B32F	8/1947	Ex BOAC. London.	5/1950	1/1956
34	HYP 686	Bedford OB	58758	Mulliner	B30F	9/1947	Ex BOAC. London.	5/1950	9/1956
35	HYO 704	Bedford OB	?	Mulliner	B32F to B30F	1947	Ex BOAC. London.	9/1950	1951
31	EU 7948	Bedford OWB	12718	Duple	B32F to B30F	11/1945	Ex Embassy Motors. Brynmawr, Brecs.	12/1950	3/1961
24	CXD 366	AEC 'Regal I'	6621832	Harrington	C33F	4/1936	Ex Grundon. Eltham. London SE9.	c1951	11/1953
32	FUP 159	Bedford OWB	31151	Duple	B30F	10/1945	Ex Nicholson. New Washington (33), Co Durham.	1/1951	4/1961
36	FDM 914	Bedford OB	117100	Mulliner	B28F	10/1949	Ex W. Bellis & Son, Buckley, Flintshire.	3/1951	5/1961
40	GL 5060	AEC 'Regal I'	06622315	Eastern Coachworks	B35R	7/1937	Ex Bath Tramways (2222).	5/1951	9/1960
46	GL 5075	AEC 'Regal I'	06622311	Eastern Coachworks	B35R	8/1937	Ex Bath Tramways (2224).	5/1951	6/1953

#	Reg	Chassis	Chassis no.	Body	Layout	New	In service	Notes	Withdrawn
59	KTX 631	Leyland 'Tiger' PS2/15 (225" wheelbase)	501267	Massey (30ft long body)	B39F	6/1951	6/1951	New. The company's first 30ft vehicle after introduction of the Act in 7/1950.	by 8/1971
58	KTX 869	Leyland 'Royal Tiger' PSU1/16 (air brakes)	510173	Burlingham 'Seagull'	C39C	6/1951	6/1951	New	2/1973
38	FUP 782	AEC 'Regal I'	06624729	Raine B35F (orig). rebuilt by Neath Coachbuilders, 4/1955, to B34F	B35F	5/1946	10/1951	Ex Trimdon Motor Services. Trimdon Grange, Co Durham.	by 4/1970
39	FUP 783	AEC 'Regal I'	06624728	Thurgood	B35F	5/1946	10/1951	Ex Trimdon Motor Services. Trimdon Grange, Co Durham.	12/1957
	CBX 733	Bedford OWB	32147	Duple	B32F	11/1945	12/1951	Ex Davies Bros (Pencader) Ltd. (23).	5/1952
	HNY 80	Maudslay 'Marathon III'	70058	Whitson	C33F	11/1947	1/1952	Ex D.H. Roberts. Newport, Pembs.	3/1952
63	GUX 614	Sentinel 'STC6'	STC6/44/95	Sentinel	B44F to B36F	1950	3/1952	Ex Sentinel demonstrator. Appeared at 1950 Commercial Motor Show.	12/1958
62	ARN 528	Leyland 'Tiger' PS1	461060	Burlingham	B34F	8/1946	12/1952	Ex Viking. Preston, Lancs. (14).	3/1955
49	MTG 469 (KOC 234)	Leyland-MCW 'Olympic' HR40 (Integrally built).	L4/494308	Metro-Cammell	B40F	1949	1/1953	This was one of four prototype Leyland 'Olympics' built in 1949, as KOC 234. Re-registered MTG 469 upon purchase.	4/1962
50	FVA 389	Leyland 'Tiger' PS1/1	496284	Plaxton	C33F	2/1950	5/1953	Ex Park. Hamilton, South Lanarkshire.	3/1965
56	BUX 745	Bedford OWB	11437	Mulliner	UB28F B26F	12/1942	10/1953	Ex Mid-Wales. Newtown, Montgomery.	3/1961
51	CUX 527	Bedford OB	11029	Duple	B30F B28F	11/1945	11/1953	Ex Jenkins. Bargoed, Mon.	3/1961
43 48	SME 81	AEC 'Regal I'	06625078	Brush	B32F	7/1947	11/1953	Ex Victoria. Leigh-on-Sea, Essex.	11/1960
48 63	SME 83	AEC 'Regal I'	06625564	Brush	B32F	7/1947	11/1953	Ex Venture. Hendon, London NW4.	11/1962
53	RN 8773	Leyland 'Tiger' TS8	301583	Burlingham	B32F	8/1939	11/1953	Ex Ribble MS (2208). via C.G. Hill, Tredegar, Mon.	9/1959
54	GDU 276	Daimler CVD6SD	13585	Burlingham	C33F	5/1947	11/1953	Ex Valliant. Ealing, London W5.	9/1959
47 55	FKV 472	Daimler CVD6SD	13293	Burlingham	C33F	4/1947	11/1953	Ex Valliant. Ealing, London W5.	11/1962
60	KOC 241	Leyland-MCW 'Olympic' HR40	L2/494043	Metro-Cammell	B40F	8/1950	11/1953	KOC 241/2, were originally prototype 'Olympic' demonstrators (with MTG 469 referred to above). Both were acquired via: J.T. Whittle. Highley, Salop	6/1970
61	KOC 242	Leyland-MCW 'Olympic' HR40	L2/494307	Metro-Cammell	B40F	7/1950	11/1953		8/1970

57	CTJ 84	Leyland 'Tiger' TS8c	Leyland	300232	B32R	4/1938	Ex Accrington Corporation (37).	12/1953	11/1960
64	GTH 576	Sentinel 'STC6'	Sentinel	6/44/98	B44F	1/1952	Ex Davies Bros (Pencader) Ltd (38).	7/1954	1957
65	KUX 412	Sentinel 'SLC6'	Associated Coachbuilders	6/30/7	B44F	-/1954	Converted from B40D, upon arrival from Moffit, Acomb, Northumberland, 2/1955.	2/1955	1/1960
66	OTC 738	Leyland 'Tiger Cub' PSUC1/1T	Saunders Roe	515176	B44F	6/1952	Ex Leyland Motors demonstrator. (1952 Commercial Motor Show Exhibit).	3/1955	by 1/1977
67	210 AMP	AEC 'Monocoach'	Park Royal	U163531	B44F	11/1953	Ex AEC Ltd, Southall, demonstrator. (1953 Scottish Motor Show Exhibit).	12/1955	4/1973
68	LWN 119	AEC 'Reliance'	Duple 'Elizabethan'	MU3RV129	C41F	5/1955	Ex Bryn Demery. Morriston, Swansea.	2/1956	12/1974
69	FBW 886	Daimler CVD6DD	Massey	17181	H32/26RD	1/1952	Ex Heyfordian. Upper Heyford, Oxford.	5/1957	1/1967
44	HVT 919 (BEH 963)	Leyland 'Tiger' TS7	Brush (1947). (S/H body fitted in 1955).	6354	B34F	1935	Ex Potteries, BEH 963, masquerading as HVT 919. (See full details page 178). Acquired via Hulley, Baslow, Derbyshire	6/1957	8/1959
70	GBW 337	Daimler CVD6DD	Massey	18485	H32/26RD	2/1953	Ex Heyfordian. Upper Heyford, Oxford.	11/1957	by 11/1971
	HD 6300	Leyland 'Tiger' TS7	Roe		B32F	1937	Acquired for spares	by 4/1958	not operated
71	LVT 946	Leyland 'Tiger' PS1/1	Willowbrook	481544	B35F B34F	10/1948	Ex Baxter, Hanley, Staffs (3).	4/1958	5/1963
72	YTG 304	Leyland 'Titan' PD3/4	Massey	571786	H41/31F	1957	Ex USAF. Upper Heyford, Oxfordshire. (**This was acquired unregistered**).	7/1958	c10/1987
73	NDA 23	Leyland 'Tiger Cub' PSUC1/2T	Burlingham 'Seagull'	543120	C41C	6/1954	Ex Don Everall. Wolverhampton.	1/1959	by 10/1974
74	NDA 24	Leyland 'Tiger Cub' PSUC1/2T	Burlingham 'Seagull'	543121	C41C	6/1954	Ex Don Everall. Wolverhampton.	1/1959	5/1962
75	SMU 194	AEC 'Regent III'	Park Royal	9612E 5337	H30/26RD	9/1950	Ex AEC Ltd. Southall, demonstrator. Via: D. Jones, Pantdu, Port Talbot.	7/1959	6/1971
86	GCY 304	AEC 'Regal III'	Willowbrook	6821A264	B34F	1950	Ex South Wales Transport (134).	9/1959	7/1964
	HNY 415	Leyland 'Tiger' PS1/1	Burlingham	472596	C33F	1/1948	Ex Thomas Bros. Port Talbot.	3/1960	6/1962
78	OUU 207	Leyland 'Tiger Cub' PSUC1/2	Burlingham 'Seagull'	567161	C41F	4/1957	Ex J.T. Whittle, Highley, Salop.	2/1960	12/1973
79	OUU 208	Leyland 'Tiger Cub' PSUC1/2	Burlingham 'Seagull'	567162	C41F	4/1957	Ex J.T. Whittle, Highley, Salop.	3/1960	1977

#	Reg	Model	Chassis #	Body	Body date	Seating	Notes	In	Out
65	JUO 558	AEC 'Regent III'	09611233	Weymann	4/1948	H30/26R	Ex Devon General Omnibus & Touring Co (DR558).	7/1960	11/1965
	FWN 804	AEC 'Regal III'	6821A244	Willowbrook	1949	B34F	Ex South Wales Transport (120), via Western Welsh OC (3110), for spares	by 2/1961	not operated
81	FWN 818	AEC 'Regal III'	6821A258	Willowbrook	1949	B34F	Ex South Wales Transport (124).	2/1961	6/1965
82	FWN 819	AEC 'Regal III'	6821A259	Willowbrook	1949	B34F	Ex South Wales Transport (125).	2/1961	9/1964
83	FWN 820	AEC 'Regal III'	6821A260	Willowbrook	1949	B34F	Ex South Wales Transport (126).	2/1961	by 1/1971
84	FWN 822	AEC 'Regal III'	6821A026	Willowbrook	1949	B34F	Ex South Wales Transport (128).	2/1961	by 8/1970
85	FWN 823	AEC 'Regal III'	6821A027	Willowbrook	1949	B34F	Ex South Wales Transport (129).	2/1961	3/1966
87	GCY 306	AEC 'Regal III'	6821A266	Willowbrook	1950	B34F	Ex South Wales Transport (136).	2/1961	5/1963
88	GCY 472	AEC 'Regal III'	6821A477	Willowbrook	1950	B34F	Ex South Wales Transport (138).	2/1961	11/1963
82 80	CHG 748	AEC 'Monocoach'	MC3RV054	Park Royal	10/1954	B44F	Ex Ezra Laycock, Barnoldswick, Lancs (51).	2/1961	7/1967
65	KNY 197	Daimler CVD6SD	17204	Longford	5/1950	C33F	Ex N&C Express Coaches, Neath.	5/1961	5/1962
89	PUJ 781	Leyland 'Tiger Cub' PSUC1/2	577966	Burlingham 'Seagull'	4/1958	C41F	Ex J.T. Whittle, Highley, Salop.	4/1961	by 12/1978
90	PUJ 783	Leyland 'Tiger Cub' PSUC1/2	578370	Burlingham 'Seagull'	4/1958	C41F	Ex J.T. Whittle, Highley, Salop.	4/1961	12/1978
	JUO 557	AEC 'Regent III'	09611232	Weymann	3/1948	H30/26R	Ex Western Welsh OC (1557). Acquired for spares.	by 6/1961	not operated
91	620 NTG	Leyland 'Leopard' L2	612464	Willowbrook	5/1962	B45F	New	5/1962	3/1976
92	691 PNY	AEC 'Reliance'	4MU3RA 4050	Plaxton 'Panorama'	5/1962	C51F	New	5/1962	by 7/1980
93	545 AVA	AEC 'Reliance'	2MU3RV 3452	Willowbrook	4/1961	B43F	Ex Irvine, Salsburgh, North Lanarkshire. (Golden Eagle Coaches).	3/1963	7/1966
94	NNY 56	Leyland 'Tiger Cub' PSUC1/1	534060	Weymann 'Hermes'	1954	B44F	Ex Thomas Bros (BET), Port Talbot.	12/1964	3/1973
98	ORR 325	Leyland 'Tiger Cub' PSUC1/1	534400	Saunders Roe	3/1954	B44F	Ex East Midland Motor Services (B325).	6/1965	2/1967

No.	Reg	Chassis	Body	Chassis No.	Seating	History	In	Out
96	FCH 11	Leyland 'Tiger Cub' PSUC1/1	Saunders Roe	534720	B44F	6/1954	Ex Trent Motor Traction, Derby (361).	11/1965	12/1975
97	FCH 16	Leyland 'Tiger Cub' PSUC1/1	Saunders Roe	534785	B44F	7/1954	Ex Trent Motor Traction, Derby (366).	11/1965 lic 1/1966	12/1975
99	NNY 60	Leyland 'Tiger Cub' PSUC1/1	Weymann 'Hermes'	534208	B44F	1954	Ex Thomas Bros (BET), Port Talbot. Acquired accident damaged & repaired	by 3/1966 lic 6/1966	3/1973
100	695 ETH	Bedford VAL14	Plaxton 'Val'	1254	C52F	5/1964	Ex S. Eynon & Sons, Trimsaran, Carms.	7/1966	6/1971
103 101	RTG 286	Leyland 'Tiger Cub' PSUC1/2T	Willowbrook	553312	DP41F	6/1955	Ex W.H. John (Coity Motors), Coity, Bridgend, Glam.	2/1967	11/1980
102	4777 NE	Leyland 'Leopard' L2T	Burlingham 'Seagull 70'	612000	C41F	5/1962	Ex Spencer's Tours, Manchester.	3/1967	7/1974
104	YNR 549	Leyland 'Leopard' L1	Willowbrook	611385	DP41F	10/1961	Ex Jones Omnibus Services, Aberbeeg, Monmouthshire (118).	8/1967	by 4/1980
106	JBO 113	Leyland 'Tiger Cub' PSUC1/1	Weymann 'Hermes'	543491	B44F	10/1954	Ex Western Welsh OC (1113). **Note**: It carried f/n 105 inside, and on fuel tank.	11/1967	7/1975
105	933 DVA	AEC 'Reliance'	Burlingham 'Seagull 70'	2MU3RA 3983	C41F	7/1962	Ex Irvine, Salsburgh, North Lanarkshire, via S. Eynon & Sons, Trimsaran, Carms.	5/1968	5/1975
	HUH 13	Leyland 'Tiger Cub' PSUC1/1	Weymann 'Hermes'	534314	B44F	2/1954	Ex WWOC (1013), via Jones OS, Aberbeeg (126). Acquired for spares.	4/1969	not operated
105 106	PWO 49	Leyland 'Tiger Cub' PSUC1/2	Willowbrook	565251	DP41F DP43F	7/1956	Ex Jones Omnibus Services, Aberbeeg (76).	4/1969 lic 5/1969	10/1976
88	JBO 104	Leyland 'Tiger Cub' PSUC1/1	Weymann 'Hermes'	543385	B44F	10/1954	Ex Western Welsh OC (1104), via: Morris, Pencoed, Bridgend.	by 2/1969	7/1976
108	FCH 23	Leyland 'Tiger Cub' PSUC1/1	Weymann 'Hermes'	534838	B44F	6/1954	Ex Trent Motor Traction, Derby (373), via Davies Bros (Pencader) Ltd (74).	by 10/1969	8/1975
	VTX 44	Leyland 'Tiger Cub' PSUC1/2T	Willowbrook	574998	DP41F	6/1957	Ex W.H. John (Coity Motors), Coity, Bridgend.	by 8/1970 lic 9/1970	5/1976
107	LYL 996D	Leyland 'Leopard' PSU3/3RT	Duple 'Commander' (Northern)	L61192	C51F	6/1966	Ex Hall, Hounslow, London.	12/1970	4/1976
	LYL 997D	Leyland 'Leopard' PSU3/3RT	Duple 'Commander' (Northern)	L61191	C51F	8/1966	Ex Hall, Hounslow, London.	12/1970	4/1976
109	LYL 998D	Leyland 'Leopard' PSU3/3RT	Duple 'Commander' (Northern)	L62076	C51F	8/1966	Ex Hall, Hounslow, London.	12/1970	by 7/1973
110	ETG 298K	Leyland 'Leopard' PSU3B/2R	Willowbrook	7102418	B53F	7/1971	New	8/1971	7/1987
111 107	VWN 956	AEC 'Regent V'	Willowbrook	2D3RA778	H39/32F	1960	Ex South Wales Transport (740).	8/1971	3/1982

Fleet No	Reg	Chassis	Chassis No	Body	Seating	Date	Notes	Acquired	Disposed
112/108	VWN 957	AEC 'Regent V'	2D3RA779	Willowbrook	H39/32F	1960	Ex South Wales Transport (741).	8/1971	3/1982
113	119 LNY	AEC 'Reliance'	2MU3RA 3213	Harrington 'Cavalier'	C41F	7/1961	Ex Thomas Bros (Port Talbot) Ltd. via: South Wales Transport (116).	4/1972	6/1981
112	120 LNY	AEC 'Reliance'	2MU3RA 3214	Harrington 'Cavalier'	C41F	7/1961	Ex Thomas Bros (Port Talbot) Ltd. via: South Wales Transport (117).	4/1972	1980
111	121 NTX	AEC 'Reliance'	2MU3RA	Harrington 'Cavalier'	C41F	4/1962	Ex Thomas Bros (Port Talbot) Ltd. via: South Wales Transport (122).	4/1972	12/1983
	JLJ 68E	Ford R192	BC04EE 21301	Plaxton 'Panorama I'	C41F	3/1967	New to Excelsior, Bournemouth. Acquired with business of Stolzenberg, Maesteg. (DLJ Transport).	3/1972	not operated
	530 CER	Bedford SB5	91678	Duple 'Bella Vega'	C41F	2/1963	Acquired with business of Stolzenberg, Maesteg.	3/1972	not operated
	DTG 580J	Bedford CF	822862	Dormobile	12	5/1971	Acquired with business of Stolzenberg, Maesteg.	3/1972	not operated
119	JNY 881K	Leyland 'Leopard' PSU3B/4R	7201366	Plaxton 'Panorama Elite II' Express	C51F	7/1972	New	7/1972	7/1988
120	JNY 882K	Leyland 'Leopard' PSU3B/4R	7201363	Plaxton 'Panorama Elite II' Express	C51F	6/1972	New	6/1972	8/1978
	order cancelled	2 x Bristol LH6L	LH658 LH659	Plaxton 'Panorama Elite III' Express	C45F	1973	Delivered to Silcox, Pembroke Dock, 2/1973, as GDE 374/375L respectively.	order cancelled	
117	NTX 595L	Bristol LHL6L	LH675	Plaxton 'Derwent'.	DP45F	4/1973	New	4/1973	7/1988
118	NTX 596L	Bristol LHL6L	LH676	Plaxton 'Derwent'	DP45F	4/1973	New	4/1973	7/1988
121	PNY 633L	Leyland 'Leopard' PSU3B/4R	7300423	Plaxton 'Panorama Elite III' Express	C51F	5/1973	New	5/1973	6/1981
122	PTG 706L	Leyland 'Leopard' PSU3B/4R	7300823	Plaxton 'Panorama Elite III' Express	C51F	6/1973	New	6/1973	7/1988
109	XBC 546	AEC 'Reliance'	2MU3RA 3049	Duple 'Britannia'	C41F	3/1960	Ex Provincial, Leicester (R15). via: Barton Transport. Chilwell, Notts (1055).	2/1974	by 4/1980
123	HPT 323H	Leyland 'Leopard' PSU3A/4R	903732	Plaxton 'Derwent'	B55F	2/1970	Ex Trimdon Motor Services. Trimdon Grange, Co Durham.	4/1974 lic 5/1974	7/1988
109	99 GAL	AEC 'Reliance'	2MU3RA 2984	Harrington 'Cavalier'	C41F	6/1960	Ex Barton Transport. Chilwell, Notts. (936).	8/1974 lic 9/1974	c7/1982
124	PCK 626	Leyland 'Leopard' L2T	610585	Harrington 'Cavalier'	C39F	8/1961	Ex Ribble Motor Services (1044). via: Davies Bros (Pencader) Ltd (94).	9/1974	by 6/1985
126	800 ABX	Leyland 'Leopard' L2	612607	Duple 'Donington'	C43F	11/1961	Ex Davies Bros (Pencader) Ltd (65).	5/1975 lic 6/1975	2/1978

#	Reg	Chassis	Serial	Body	Seats	Date	History	In	Out
127	TRK 5F	Leyland 'Leopard' PSU3A/2RT	802605	Plaxton 'Panorama II'	C51F	7/1968	Ex Silverline. Hounslow, London (80).	6/1975	7/1981
128	TRK 6F	Leyland 'Leopard' PSU3A/2RT	802710	Plaxton 'Panorama II'	C51F	7/1968	Ex Silverline. Hounslow, London (79).	6/1975 lic 7/1975	7/1981
129	YBK 132	Leyland 'Leopard' L1	611692	Weymann	B44F	12/1961	Ex Portsmouth Corporation (132). (Converted from B42D, before service).	8/1975	by 6/1988
130	YBK 138	Leyland 'Leopard' L1	611788	Weymann	B45F	12/1961	Ex Portsmouth Corporation (138). (Converted from B42D, before service).	8/1975	by 6/1986
131	9905 UG	Leyland 'Leopard' L2	603364	Plaxton 'Embassy'	C41C	2/1961	Ex Wallace Arnold; Wood, Blackpool; Edwards, Joys Green; Bebb. Llantwit Fardre; and Prance, Cardiff.	2/1976 lic 3/1976	1977
131	LFB 681P	Leyland 'Leopard' PSU3C/4R	7505791	Plaxton 'Panorama Elite III' Express	C51F	3/1976	New	3/1976 lic 4/1976	7/1988
133	AGA 112B	Leyland 'Atlantean' PDR1/1	L02041	Alexander 'A'	H44/34F	5/1964	Ex Glasgow PTE (LA173).	7/1976	4/1984
134	AGA 126B	Leyland 'Atlantean' PDR1/1	L03113	Alexander 'A'	H44/34F	5/1964	Ex Glasgow PTE (LA187).	7/1976	c1985
135	AGA 128B	Leyland 'Atlantean' PDR1/1	L03286	Alexander 'A'	H44/34F	5/1964	Ex Glasgow PTE (LA189).	7/1976 lic 9/1976	c1985
136	AGA 129B	Leyland 'Atlantean' PDR1/1	L03312	Alexander 'A'	H44/34F	5/1964	Ex Glasgow PTE (LA190).	7/1976 lic 10/1976	11/1982
137 144	267 AUF	Leyland 'Leopard' PSU3/1RT	623768	Marshall	B49F	3/1963	Ex Southdown Motor Services (667). via: East Kent Road Car Co.	9/1976 lic 8/1979	by 6/1986
138	271 AUF	Leyland 'Leopard' PSU3/1RT	623811	Marshall	B49F	3/1963	Ex Southdown Motor Services (671). via East Kent Road Car Co.	9/1976 lic 1/1977	2/1979
	PCK 625	Leyland 'Leopard' L2T	610544	Harrington 'Cavalier'	C41F	8/1961	Ex Ribble Motor Services (1043). via: Price. Barry, South Glam.	1/1977	not operated
141	OHY 789R	Leyland 'Leopard' PSU3D/4R	7607822	Plaxton 'Supreme II' Express	C51F	7/1977	New	7/1977	7/1988
	HNM 926N	Ford R1114	BC04PP 66800	Duple 'Dominant I' Express	C53F	3/1975	Operated on hire from a dealer.	6/1977	1/1978
142	CYS 570B	Leyland 'Atlantean' PDR1/1	L23033	Alexander 'A'	H44/33F	1964 1/1965	Ex Glasgow PTE (LA224).	11/1977	by 5/1982
143	FCX 287C	Leyland 'Leopard' PSU3/1R	L40546	Weymann	B53F	9/1965	Ex Yorkshire Traction (395).	10/1977 lic 1/1978	by 1985
	JHB 500L	Ford R1014	BC04LM 47272	Willowbrook 'Expressway'	C45F	8/1972	Ex Morlais. Merthyr.	5/1978	not operated
	TOU 634T	Leyland 'Leopard' PSU3E/4R	7800477	Plaxton 'Supreme III' Express	C51F	8/1978	New	8/1978	7/1988

Fleet No	Reg	Chassis	Body	Seating	Chassis No	New	History	In	Out
146	LHG 537	Leyland 'Titan' PD3/6	East Lancs	H41/32F	610136	4/1961	Ex Burnley, Colne & Nelson (237). via: Lancaster CT. (537).	10/1978	11/1982
	101 EUA	Leyland 'Leopard' PSU3/3R	Plaxton 'Panorama'	C49C	629572	4/1963	Ex Thomas. Rhoose, Cardiff, (for spares).	11/1978	not operated
148	HRC 100C	Leyland 'Tiger Cub' PSUC1/11T	Alexander 'Y'	C41F	L52218	12/1965	Ex Trent Motor Traction (100).	11/1978	5/1984
149	HRC 103C	Leyland 'Tiger Cub' PSUC1/11T	Alexander 'Y'	C41F	L52298	12/1965	Ex Trent Motor Traction (103).	11/1978	7/1988
151	KUF 202F	Leyland 'Leopard' PSU3/1RT	Willowbrook (BET style)	B45F	703136	2/1968	Ex Southdown MS. (202).	2/1981	by 6/1986
152	ETC 309W	Leyland 'Leopard' PSU3F/5R	Plaxton 'Supreme IV' Express	C53F	8030844	4/1981	New	4/1981	7/1988
	ETC 310W	Leyland 'Leopard' PSU3F/5R	Plaxton 'Supreme IV' Express	C53F	8030845	4/1981	New	4/1981	7/1988
155	KDW 79F	Leyland 'Atlantean' PDR1/1	Alexander 'A'	H43/31F	703124	2/1968	Ex Newport Corporation (79).	8/1981	6/1984
	KDW 81F	Leyland 'Atlantean' PDR1/1	Alexander 'A'	H43/31F	703794	2/1968	Ex Newport Corporation (81).	8/1981	7/1988
156	KDW 84F	Leyland 'Atlantean' PDR1/1	Alexander 'A'	H43/31F	703876	2/1968	Ex Newport Corporation (84).	8/1981	7/1988
	PDW 100H	Leyland 'Atlantean' PDR1A/1	Alexander 'A'	H43/31F	903242	1/1970	Ex Newport Corporation (100).	7/1982	7/1988
	MDW 389G	Leyland 'Atlantean' PDR1A/1	Alexander 'A'	H43/31F	803483	2/1969	Ex Newport Corporation (89). via: Nicholson. Borve, Isle of Lewis, Scotland.	by 12/1984 lic 4/1986	7/1988
	YSD 343L	Leyland 'Leopard' PSU3/3R	Alexander 'AY'	C49F	7202500	2/1973	Ex Western SMT (2383). via: Highland Scottish (L35).	c12/1984	7/1988

Service Vehicles:

No	Reg	Vehicle	Type	History	In	Out
103	GDW 775	Austin A40	Pick up		1967	c6/1975
125	SBO 699	Land Rover	Service vehicle	Ex Wales Gas Board	by 6/1975	1978
	PDE423G	Land Rover	Service Vehicle		1978	1979
	BVT 543H	Leyland 'Badger'	Recovery vehicle			
		Leyland Firemaster (fire engine)	Leyland 'Leopard' Chassis	Manchester Fire Brigade (acquired for spares).		1979

LLYNFI MOTOR SERVICES – VEHICLE DISPOSALS

	NY 4206	Withdrawn 7/1926. No further trace.
	NY 6910	Withdrawn 3/1930. Scrapped 1934.
	CW 2589	Licence withdrawn, 27/1/1931.
	T 9054	No further trace.
6	VA 4592	Sold to W. Browning, Cefn Cribwr, Glam, unknown date.
7	DE 5349	Sold to Bird, Neath (dealer), unknown date. To D.T. Breeze, Merthyr Tydfil, last licensed, 6/1941.
	VW 5135	Last licensed, 6/1938.
	VT 6537	Sold to Tighe Bros, Mendlesham, Suffolk, unknown date.
	HE 3839	Last licensed, 12/1936. No further trace.
	ACY 104	Withdrawn 2/1951. Refused C o F, 5/1953. Still at Bryn garage 6/1959. No further trace.
12	BWX 722	Withdrawn 5/1959. No further trace.
	FV 68	Withdrawn c1947, still at Bryn garage 1958. No further trace.
	TX 9457	Sold to Gibbs. Pontllanfraith, Mon, by 10/1945. To M&M Kidderminster, Worcs, by 6/1947.
	CWW 494	To War Department, Hereford, 7/1940. Abandoned on Dunkirk beaches, 1940.
	BDW 474	Hired to G. Richards. Neath, 2/1951 to 6/1951. Withdrawn 9/1954. Sold to Campbell, Nottingham, 12/1954.
	CLG 429	Withdrawn 10/1953. Still at Bryn garage 1955. Scrapped c1962.
	FNY 694	Withdrawn 3/1951. Sold to Mainwaring. Gilfach Goch, Glamorganshire, 10/1951.
18	FTG 311	Last licensed 1/1952. Derelict at Stormy Down, Glam, 1960.
37	GTX 437	Sold to D. Gwyn John for preservation 12/1972. Now in the care of Swansea Bus Museum (2024).
	GNY 856	Withdrawn 10/1951. Sold to Byley Garage, Byley, Cheshire, 1/1952.
	GTG 322	Withdrawn 4/1950. Sold to East Glam Motors, Nelson, Glam, 5/1950.
	GZ 2236	Sold to Mainwaring, Gilfach Goch, Glamorganshire, 5/1951.
45	JTG 286	Withdrawn 6/1963. To W.H. Way (Scrap dealer), Cardiff, 6/1966, for scrap.
	JTG 287	Withdrawn 3/1953. Sold to Gwyn Richards, Neath, Glam. 4/1953.
42	GDG 795	Withdrawn 11/1960. Sold / Converted into transporter for motor racing equipment, noted Neath, 4/1963.
47	JTX 746	Withdrawn 1/1967. Still at Maesteg, 8/1970. No further trace.
33	HYP 681	C o F expired 1/1956. No further trace.
34	HYP 686	Withdrawn 9/1956. No further trace.
	HYO 704	Withdrawn 1951. No further trace.
31	EU 7948	Withdrawn 3/1961. Sold to R.M. Douglas (Contractor), Birmingham, by 8/1961.
24	CXD 366	Sold to Bantam Coaches, Coventry, 11/1953.
32	FUP 159	Withdrawn 4/1961. Sold to R.M. Douglas (Contractor), Birmingham, 5/1961. Based at Swansea.
36	FDM 914	Sold to R.M. Douglas (Contractor), Birmingham, 5/1961. Based at Swansea.
40	GL 5060	Sold to Everall (dealer) Wolverhampton 9/1960. To Showman at Bristol, 5/1961.
46	GL 5075	Sold to Arnould. Fleur-de-Lys, Monmouthshire, 6/1953. To Peake, Pontypool, 2/1955.
59	KTX 631	Sold to Smith's Enterprises (Contractor), Bridgend, by 8/1971. In preservation, at South Wales, 2024.
58	KTX 869	Withdrawn 2/1973. Sold to 'Porthcawl Recreations Ltd.' (non PSV operator), for staff transport, 5/1973.
38	FUP 782	Sold to W.H. Way (scrap dealer), Cardiff, 8/1970. To A. Jenkins, Pontardulais, 9/1970, licensed 10/1970.
	FUP 783	Withdrawn 12/1957. No further trace.
	CBX 733	Sold to Wye Valley Motors, Hereford, between 5/1952 and 8/1953.
	HNY 80	Sold to Sentinel Motors (dealer), Shrewsbury, 3/1952. To Smith, Groby, Leicestershire, by 7/1953.
63	GUX 614	Sold to Everall (dealer), Wolverhampton, 12/1958. To Wootton. Wombwell, S.Yorkshire (staff bus), 4/1959.
62	ARN 528	Withdrawn 3/1955. Sold to Jones OS, Aberbeeg, Mon. (62), 9/1955. To scrap, 2/1960.
49	MTG 469	Sold to: Porthcawl Omnibus Co. Porthcawl, Glam. 4/1962.
50	FVA 389	Sold to Stanton, Ogmore Vale, Glamorganshire, 3/1965.
56	BUX 745	Withdrawn 3/1961. Sold to Don Everall (dealer), Wolverhampton, by 8/1961.
51	CUX 527	Withdrawn 3/1961. Sold to R.M. Douglas (Contractor). Birmingham & Swansea, by 8/1961.
43	SME 81	Withdrawn 11/1960. Sold to Don Everall (dealer), Wolverhampton, 1960.
48	SME 83	Withdrawn 11/1962. Sold to W.H. Way (scrap dealer), Cardiff, for scrap, 4/1963.
53	RN 8773	Withdrawn 9/1959. Sold to Branscombe, Blackheath, London, 3/1960. To Everall (dealer), Wolverhampton.
54	GDU 176	Withdrawn 9/1959. Sold to Drake, Cardiff, 5/1962.
55	FKV 472	Withdrawn 11/1962. Sold to Sold to W.H. Way, Cardiff for scrap, 4/1964 – 11/1964.
60	KOC 141	Sold to W.H. Way (scrap dealer), Cardiff, 6/1970, for scrap.
61	KOC 142	Sold to W.H. Way (scrap dealer), Cardiff, 8/1970, for scrap.
57	CTJ 84	Withdrawn 11/1960, To Don Everall (dealer), Wolverhampton, by 8/1961.
64	GTH 576	To Everall (dealer), Wolverhampton. To Princess. Clonmel, Co Tipperery, 7/1957, where it ran as GTH 576.

65	KUX 412	Sold to Don Everall (dealer), Wolverhampton, 1/1960. To Simpson. Cardenden, Fife, 8/1960.
66	OTC 738	Sold to W.H. Way (scrap dealer), Cardiff, by 1/1977. To Wigley. Carlton, for scrap, by 5/1979.
67	210 AMP	Withdrawn 4/1973. Sold to W.H. Way (scrap dealer), Cardiff, 4/1975, for scrap.
68	LWN 119	Withdrawn by 12/1974. To private owner Cardiff, 5/1975. To W.H. Way (scrap dealer), Cardiff, by 1/1977.
69	FBW 886	Withdrawn 1/1967. Sold to W.H. Way (scrap dealer), Cardiff, 8/1970, for scrap.
44	HVT 919	Withdrawn 8/1959. Sold to W.H. Way (scrap dealer), Cardiff, 4/1960. Other research states it passed to Don Everall (dealer), 4/1960, and was still at Everall's yard in 9/1961.
70	GBW 337	Withdrawn by 11/1971. Sold to W.H. Way (scrap dealer), Cardiff, 4/1973, for scrap.
	HD 6300	Acquired for spares, and broken up.
71	LVT 946	Sold to Parfitt's. Rhymney Bridge, Monmouthshire, 5/1963.
72	YTG 304	Sold to Bevington Motors (car dealer), Margam, Mid-Glam, 10/1987, as an all over advertisement hoarding. It was later sold for use as a mobile hotel.
73	NDA 23	Withdrawn by 10/1974. Sold to a private owner at Cardiff, by 3/1975.
74	NDA 24	Sold to Harding, Birkenhead, 5/1962.
75	SMU 194	Sold to Andrew Scott (Contractor), Port Talbot, 6/1971.
86	GCY 304	Withdrawn 7/1964. Sold to C. Collier, Abertillery, Monmouthshire, 10/1964. Withdrawn 4/1967.
	HNY 415	Sold to W.F. Sing. (Cardiff Motorways), Cardiff. 6/1962.
78	OUJ 207	Withdrawn 12/1973. Written off after accident.
79	OUJ 208	Withdrawn 1977. Used as seat store, 2/1978. Being scrapped at Bryn depot, by 9/1979.
65	JUO 558	Withdrawn 11/1965. Believed scrapped, 5/1970.
	FWN 804	Acquired for spares. Scrapped 8/1961.
81	FWN 818	Sold to Henley's. Abertillery, Mon, 6/1965.
82	FWN 819	Sold to Henley's. Abertillery, Mon, 9/1964.
83	FWN 820	Sold to A. Jenkins. Pontardulais, West Glam, by 1/1971. Licensed 10/1971, and used for spares 1971.
84	FWN 822	Withdrawn by 8/1970. Sold to A. Jenkins. Pontardulais, West Glam, by 1/1971. Licensed 4/1971.
85	FWN 823	Withdrawn 3/1966. Sold to A. Jenkins. Pontardulais, West Glam, 10/1970. Not operated.
87	GCY 306	Withdrawn 5/1963. Sold to W.H. Way (scrap dealer), Cardiff, between 10/1969 and 8/1970, for scrap.
88	GCY 472	Sold to Morris Travel. Pencoed, Bridgend, 11/1963. To Humphreys. Bridgend, 3/1964. To D.S. Edwards. Llangeinor, Glam, 8/1964. Withdrawn 9/1969. No further trace.
82	CHG 748	Sold to Arlington Motors (dealer), Cardiff, 7/1967. To Weaver, Ton Pentre, Mid Glam, 8/1967.
65	KNY 197	Sold to Jones (Reliance Coaches), Llanishen, Cardiff, 5/1962.
89	PUJ 781	Sold to its original owner, J.T. Whittle. Highley, Salop, for preservation in 1978. Now splendidly restored.
90	PUJ 783	Sold to its original owner, J.T. Whittle. Highley, Salop, 1978, and later sold for a mobile home conversion.
	JUO 557	Acquired for spares. Scrapped by 8/1961.
91	620 NTG	Withdrawn 3/1976, after accident. Scrapped 10/1976.
92	691 PNY	Sold to 'Avonaires Jazz Band' (non PSV operator), Maesteg, by 7/1980.
93	545 AVA	Withdrawn 7/1966. To Arlington Motors (dealer), Cardiff, 6/1967. To Grenville. Camborne, Cornwall, 7/1968.
94	NNY 56	Sold to R.M. Douglas (Contractor), Birmingham & Swansea (f/n 97074), 3/1973.
98	ORR 325	Withdrawn 2/1967. To Millburn Motors (dealer), Preston, by 7/1967. To contractor, Lanarkshire, by 12/1970.
96	FCH 11	Sold to W.H. Way (scrap dealer), Cardiff, 12/1975. Destroyed by fire at Way's yard.
97	FCH 16	Sold to W.H. Way (scrap dealer), Cardiff, 12/1975. Destroyed by fire at Way's yard.
99	NNY 60	Sold to R.M. Douglas (Contractor), Birmingham & Swansea (f/n 97078), 3/1973.
100	695 ETH	Sold to Powell. Little Tarrington, Hereford, 6/1971.
101	RTG 286	Sold to Hartwood Exports (dealer), Birdwell, Barnsley, South Yorkshire, 11/1980.
102	4777 NE	Withdrawn 7/1974, after accident. Rebuilt, but not used, and scrapped 7/1987
104	YNR 549	Withdrawn by 4/1980. Sold after 6/1981, with no further trace.
106	JBO 113	Sold 7/1975. To Griffiths & Powell (Morriston Coaches), Morriston, Swansea, 8/1975.
105	933 DVA	Withdrawn 5/1975. To R. Ferris. Taffs Well, South Glam, 6/1975. To C.K. Coaches, Cardiff, 10/1975. To 'The Spastics Society' (Non PSV), Sully, Cardiff, by 2/1977. To Jazz Band (Non PSV), Caerleon, by 4/1985.
	HUH 13	Acquired for spares. Remains to W.H. Way (scrap dealer), Cardiff, 1/1972.
105	PWO 49	Withdrawn 10/1976, with no further trace.
88	JBO 104	Sold to Griffiths & Powell (Morriston Coaches), Morriston, Swansea, 7/1976.
108	FCH 23	Sold to Griffiths & Powell (Morriston Coaches), Morriston, Swansea, 8/1975.
	VTX 44	Sold to Barry Comprehensive School (Non PSV) by 5/1976.
107	LYL 996D	Sold to Morris Bros. Swansea, 4/1976.
	LYL 997D	Sold to Morris Bros. Swansea, 4/1976.
109	LYL 998D	Sold to John Lewis Coaches, Morriston, Swansea, by 7/1973.
110	ETG 298K	Stolen by vandals and excessively damaged. Scrapped 7/1987.

111 107	VWN 956	Sold to Booth (dealer), Rotherham, 3/1982. To D. Hoare. Chepstow, 3/1982, To West of England Transport Collection, Winkleigh, Devon, 7/1982, for spares.
112 108	VWN 957	Sold to D. Hoare. Chepstow, 3/1982. To Durham. Meopham, Kent, 1982. To WETC, Winkleigh, Devon, 7/1982, with no further trace.
113	119 LNY	Withdrawn 6/1981. No further trace.
112	120 LNY	Withdrawn 1980. Sold to F. Williams, Swansea, for preservation, 3/1981, but eventually scrapped.
111	121 NTX	Sold to G. Ripley, Carlton, South Yorkshire, for scrap, by 12/1983.
	JLJ 68E	Not operated. Sold to Don Everall (dealer), Wolverhampton, by 6/1972.
	530 CER	Not operated. To Southern Coach Centre. Robertsbridge, E. Sussex, 3/1972. To Denning. Newport, 5/1972.
	DTG 580J	Not operated. Sold to Jones. Blackmill, Bridgend, 3/1972.
119	JNY 881K	Passed to A.E. & F.R. Brewer Ltd., Caerau, 7/1988, with the business. **N.B.** The new Brewer's company later moved to Maesteg, and afterwards, Port Talbot. To Brian Isaac Coaches, Morriston, Swansea, 7/1988.
120	JNY 882K	Sold to Arlington Motors (dealer), 8/1978. To Clarke's Coaches, London SE3, 6/1979.
117	NTX 595L	Passed to A.E. & F.R. Brewer Ltd., Caerau, 7/1988, with the business. Tax expired 8/1988.
118	NTX 596L	Passed to A.E. & F.R. Brewer Ltd., Caerau, 7/1988, with the business. Tax expired 21/8/1989.
121	PNY 633L	Sold to Parfitt's, Rhymney Bridge, Gwent, 6/1981.
122	PTG 706L	Passed to A.E. & F.R. Brewer Ltd., Caerau, 7/1988, with the business. To Brian Isaac Coaches, Morriston, Swansea, 7/1988. Burnt out in garage fire, remains to scrap dealer, 9/1988.
109	XBC 546	Withdrawn by 4/1980. Scrapped by 6/1988.
123	HPT 323H	Passed to A.E. & F.R. Brewer Ltd., Caerau, 7/1988, with the business. Tax expired 30/4/1989.
109	99 GAL	Scrapped at Bryn depot, 7/1982.
124	PCK 626	Scrapped at Maesteg depot, by 6/1985.
126	800 ABX	Withdrawn 2/1978, and broken up on the same day.
127	TRK 5F	Sold to S. Eynon & Sons, Trimsaran, Dyfed, 7/1981.
128	TRK 6F	Sold to S. Eynon & Sons, Trimsaran, Dyfed, 7/1981.
129	YBK 132	Withdrawn by 6/1988. Passed to A.E. & F.R. Brewer Ltd., Caerau, 7/1988, re-reg: AKG 219A, not operated.
130	YBK 138	Withdrawn by 6/1986. Scrapped, 12/1987.
131	9905 UG	Withdrawn 1977. Used for spares by 2/1978.
131	LFB 681P	Passed to A.E. & F.R. Brewer Ltd., Caerau, 7/1988, with the business. To Brian Isaac Coaches, Morriston, Swansea, 7/1988. To Greenhous (dealer), Hereford by 6/90. To Crump. Malvern, 6/1990, w/drawn 1/1997.
133	AGA 112B	Sold to Geoff Ripley (dealer), Carlton, South Yorkshire, 4/1984, for scrap.
134	AGA 126B	Still in use 10/1984. Sold by 1985. No further trace.
135	AGA 128B	Still in use 10/1984. Sold by 1985. No further trace.
136	AGA 129B	Withdrawn 11/1982. Scrapped by 6/1988.
137	267 AUF	Withdrawn by 6/1986. Scrapped by 12/1987.
138	271 AUF	Withdrawn 2/1979, after accident.
140	PCK 625	Not operated. Used as a store shed, 6/1977, last noted 6/1981. Later scrapped.
141	OHY 789R	Passed to A.E. & F.R. Brewer Ltd., Caerau, 7/1988, with the business. No further trace.
	HNM 926N	Returned to dealer off hire, 1/1978. To Pioneer Coaches, Laugharne, Dyfed, 8/1978.
142	CYS 570B	Sold by 5/1982. No further trace.
143	FCX 287C	Sold by 1985. No further trace.
	JHB 500L	Not operated. Sold to Arlington (dealer) Bristol, 5/1978. To Wilkins Coaches, Cymmer, Mid-Glam, by 7/1980.
	TOU 634T	Passed to A.E. & F.R. Brewer Ltd., Caerau, 7/1988, with the business. To Westerham Coaches, Kent.
146	LHG 537	Withdrawn 11/1982. Sold to Bevington Motors (car dealer), Margam, Mid-Glam, 7/1983, used as a static all over advertisement hoarding.
	101 EUA	Acquired for spares. Scrapped by 12/1978.
148	HRC 100C	Withdrawn 5/1984. Scrapped by 7/1988.
149	HRC 103C	Passed to A.E. & F.R. Brewer Ltd., Caerau, 7/1988, with the business. To Brian Isaac Coaches, Morriston, Swansea, 7/1988. To Golden Cs. Llantwit Major, S-Glam, 3/1991, believed unused, tax expired 8/1991.
151	KUF 202F	Withdrawn by 6/1986. Tax expired 1/1987. No further trace.
152	ETC 309W	Passed to A.E. & F.R. Brewer Ltd., Caerau, 7/1988, with the business. No further trace.
	ETC 310W	Passed to A.E. & F.R. Brewer Ltd., Caerau, 7/1988, with the business. To Aspden. Blackburn, Lancs.
155	KDW 79F	Decapitated in low bridge accident at Nantyffyllon, 18/6/1984. Sold for scrap by 8/1986.
156	KDW 84F	Passed to A.E. & F.R. Brewer Ltd., Caerau, 7/1988, with the business. Unused & sold for scrap.
	KDW 81F	Passed to A.E. & F.R. Brewer Ltd., Caerau, 7/1988, with the business. Unused & sold for scrap.
	PDW 100H	Passed to A.E. & F.R. Brewer Ltd., Caerau, 7/1988, with the business. Unused & sold for scrap.
	MDW389H	Passed to A.E. & F.R. Brewer Ltd., Caerau, 7/1988, with the business. Unused & sold for scrap.
	YSD 343L	Passed to A.E. & F.R. Brewer Ltd., Caerau, 7/1988, with the business. Unused. Tax expired 2/1989.

Above: This Leyland 'Badger', BVT 543H, was Llynfi Motors' recovery vehicle in the late 1970s. *(Copyright Byron Gage).*

Above: Llynfi Motor Services' Maesteg depot, February 1971. The site is nowadays a Tesco Superstore. *(Copyright John Jones).*

LLYNFI MOTOR SERVICES. TICKETS USED

LLYNFI MOTOR SERVICES. PHOTOGRAPH INDEX

Reg Nº	Page Nº	Reg Nº	Page Nº	Reg Nº	Page Nº	Reg Nº	Page Nº
ACY 104	153/154	FWN 822	188	KTX 631	165	SME 81	171
AGA 112B	218	FWN 823	189	KTX 869	166	SMU 194	183
AGA 126B	219	GBW 337	177/179	KUF 202F	228	TOU 634T	224
AGA 128B	220	GCY 304	183/189	KUX 412	175	TRK 5F	215
AGA 129B	220	GCY 306	189	LFB 681P	218	TRK 6F	215
ARN 528	169	GCY 472	190	LHG 537	225	TX 9497	156
BDW 474	157	GDG 795	161	LVT 946	180	VA 4592	150
BWX 722	154	GL 5060	163	LWN 119	177	VTX 44	203
CBX 733	168	GL 5075	163	LYL 996D	204	VWN 956	206
CHG 748	190	GTG 322	159	LYL 997D	204	VWN 957	206
CTJ 84	174	GTH 576	174	LYL 998D	205	XBC 546	212
CUX 527	172	GTX 437	159/160	MDW 389G	233	YBK 132	216
CW 2589	149	GUX 614	169	MTG 469	170	YBK 138	216
CYS 570B	223	HNM 926N	222	NDA 23	182	YNR 549	199
DE 5349	150	HNY 80	168	NDA 24	182	YSD 343L	233
ETC 309W	227	HPT 323H	212	NNY 56	195	YTG 304	180/181
ETC 310W	227	HRC 100C	225	NNY 60	197	99 GAL	213
ETG 298K	207	HRC 103C	226	NTX 595L	210	119 LNY	207
FBW 886	177/178	HVT 919	178	NTX 596L	210	120 LNY	208
FCH 11	196	JBO 104	202	NY 6910	148	121 NTX	208
FCH 16	196	JBO 113	200	OHY 789R	222	210 AMP	177
FCH 23	203	JNY 881K	209	ORR 325	195	267 AUF	221
FCX 287C	223	JNY 882K	209	OTC 738	173/176	271 AUF	221
FKV 472	172	JTG 286	160	OUJ 207	184	545 AVA	194
FTG 311	158	JTG 287	161	OUJ 208	184	620 NTG	193
FUP 159	162	JTX 746	162	PCK 626	214	691 PNY	193
FUP 782	166/167	JUO 556	185	PDW 100H	230	695 ETH	198
FUP 783	167	KDW 79F	228/229	PNY 633L	211	800 ABX	214
FV 68	156	KDW 81F	229	PTG 706L	211	933 DVA	201
FVA 389	170	KDW 84F	230	PUJ 781	191/192	4777 NE	199
FWN 818	186	KNY 197	191	PUJ 783	192	9905 UG	217
FWN 819	188	KOC 241	173	PWO 49	202		
FWN 820	188	KOC 242	173	RTG 286	198		

Right:
FUP 782, at Llynfi Motor Services' Bryn Depot, Nr Maesteg. *(Copyright John Jones).*

D.J. THOMAS
CREAM LINE (MAESTEG) Ltd

David John Thomas, was one of the earliest passenger vehicle operators licensed in Maesteg.

He was born in Carmarthen, in April 1876, and was the elder brother of William George Thomas, the founder of Llynfi Motor Services, Maesteg.

Beginning his working career as a grocer's assistant in Carmarthen, he left the town to become a collier in Maesteg, and this is where he met Sarah, who became his wife in 1901.

By 1911, the family were living at 17 Llwydarth Road, Maesteg, with their three children, William Edgar (8), Annie (7), and Illtyd (4). At the same time, he obtained the Post Office's mail carrier's contract for Maesteg, and was recorded as a 'Posting Master'.

At the princely sum of five shillings, he was issued his first charabanc drivers licence by the Maesteg Authority, in April 1915, and by this time had moved into larger premises at 28 Talbot Street, Maesteg, where he later set up a motor garage, known as Talbot Garages.

On 29th December, 1917, he was granted an 'omnibus' licence to operate a motor car, along with a few other car owners, between Maesteg and Caerau. (Page 9, explains the unique Hackney Carriage licensing system adopted by the Maesteg Licensing Authority).

Upon examination of local authority records, he was one of the first licensed 'omnibus' proprietors working the Maesteg to Caerau route, but after the World War 1 hostilities were over, he was joined by as many as twenty other licensed *motor car* operators on that route.

In February 1920, D.J. Thomas bought a Daimler lorry which was also 'Hackney' licenced. This was actually the beginning of his haulage business, but it must be said, he regularly utilised his lorries to carry passengers too, by fitting loose bench type seats, on the lorry platform. Unbelievably, the lackadaisical local authority accepted that dangerous practice.

By February 1921, he was issued with driving licence Nº 1, and drivers badge Nº 1, by the Maesteg Authority, and was granted 'omnibus licences' for two Ford model 'T' motor cars registered L 5820 and L 6561. At this point in time however, his brother William George Thomas, assisted with driving, and D.J. Thomas' son, William Edgar Thomas, received his first driving licence to join the conflict a year later, in February 1922.

Rivalry, overcrowding of cars, and violation of Hackney Carriage bye-laws, became commonplace, which inevitably led to numerous prosecutions amidst the rivals. D.J. Thomas was prosecuted and fined £2.0.0, on 19th October, 1921, for interchanging registration pates between two model 'T' Fords, L 6561 and NY 480. The reason for his foolishness was that NY 480 had arrived brand new, and had not received its inspection for an 'Omnibus licence'.

However, as the number of Hackney Licensed motor car owners dwindled in October 1925, Maesteg UDC, issued a licence to newcomer, Frederick James John, of 36 Barnardo Street, Nantyffyllon, to run a bus service on the competitive Maesteg to Caerau route. Frederick John soon became disliked, as he continuously defied everyone including the Licensing Committee, and was constantly in trouble. Frederick John's business is documented on pages 261-5.

Right: This view of Church Street, Maesteg, taken from the Town Hall, show how the 'Taxis', licensed as 'Omnibuses', had to queue up in order, and leave in turn, with their passengers to Caerau. The licensing conditions stated that all cars had to continue running the complete service route to Caerau Square, even though their passengers had alighted before reaching that point. Upon arrival at Caerau Square, it was the same procedure, queue up for passengers in sequence, and not to leave until passengers had been taken up. See notes on page 9.

D.J. Thomas' second son, Illtyd, was also a driver in the business, and by September 1928, he was officially warned about his unacceptable conduct towards the Council's Hackney Carriage Inspector.

Concurrently, several operators of the Maesteg-Caerau service were looking to expand their service network, and three of them asked the Maesteg Licensing Committee for permission to run into Bridgend. Frederick John successfully achieved his goal, but Brewer's application of 12th June, 1928, and D.J. Thomas' application of 7th May, 1929, were continuously deferred. Eventually, Maesteg UDC were in favour of issuing the licences, to allow a 15m frequency, jointly with Western Welsh, the successor of South Wales Commercial Motors. The licences however, were rejected by 'Joint Licensing Committee' members, Penybont RDC, and Bridgend UDC, triggering off a lengthy, bitter, battle, between the three Councils. Maesteg Council allegedly accused both Bridgend authorities of being bias, with an apparent desire to grant a monopoly to Western Welsh. The issue was finally left in the hands of the Ministry of Transport's Traffic Commissioners, when they took control of all licensing matters in April 1931.

However, D.J. Thomas' application was refused by the Traffic Commissioners in 1931, and his lengthy appeal was concluded with a refusal, in January 1938. Further details on next page.

Returning to September 1928, the Maesteg UDC, in vengeance, refused to licence the Great Western Railway (Road Motor Services), for a bus service from Bridgend to Caerau, via Maesteg, and in May 1929, D.J. Thomas complained to the Licensing Committee, of his difficulties in obtaining satisfactory settlements of interchangeable return tickets, with certain joint operators of the Caerau service. The Council immediately decided to abolish the issue of return tickets in favour of singe fares only, issued at a reduced rate.

In May 1930, the Licensing Committee, renamed themselves 'The Omnibus & Hackney Carriage Committee', and four months later, revived the feasibility of running a municipal bus service. They also decided that a timetable for local omnibus services should be drawn up as soon as possible, and given a trail period of three months, if the local services were still unsatisfactory, they should seriously consider the advisability of operating a municipal service. Consequently, they decided to obtain prices for 20 seater, and larger buses, and on 17th November, 1930, the secretary of the Maesteg Labour Party, was encouraging the Council to establish a municipal bus service. However, the issue was discussed no further. Perhaps the expense was too much of a burden upon the rate payers!

Irregular timekeeping nevertheless continued, and in October 1930, the Hackney Carriage Inspector made enquiries into the provision of time recording clocks, to ensure that timetables were strictly observed. Nothing further became of that issue either.

On the other hand, on 17th February, 1931, D.J. Thomas asked the Council for a licence to operate a new service between Maesteg Bus Station and Garth. Surprisingly, the licence was granted to him on 17th March, just 14 days before the responsibility of all aspects of PSV licensing, passed to the Ministry of Transport's Traffic Commissioners.

Introduction of 'The Road Traffic Act 1930', was the next major event in the company's history. Details of which can be found on page 28.

Under the new Traffic Act in April 1931, D. J. Thomas applied for renewal of *four* licences. His existing two road service licences, together with two 'new' applications. The applications carried a new entity: **CREAM LINE SERVICES,** Talbot Garages, 28 Talbot Street, Maesteg, and he was issued with operator identification number, TGR 432. The office address was registered at his home address, 47 Neath Road, Maesteg.

The licences applied for, were services which he *claimed* to have operated during the preceding year:-

TGR 432/1   **Maesteg** to **Caerau**, via: Nantyffyllon.

TGR 432/2   **Maesteg** to **Garth**, via: Castle Street, and Bridgend Road.

TGR 432/3   **Maesteg** to **Bridgend**, via: Llangynwyd, Tondu, and Aberkenfig.

TGR 432/4   **Excursions & Tours** starting from Maesteg & District.

TGR 432/1, 432/2, and 432/4, were granted on 8th July, 1931, but TGR 432/3 was refused.

On 2nd December, 1931, **Maesteg - Bridgend** was reapplied for as a 'new' service:-

TGR 432/5   **Maesteg** to **Bridgend**, via: Llangynwyd, Coytrahen, Tondu, & Aberkenfig.

The ongoing issue was again refused on 31st December, 1931. However, on 9th March, 1932, the company submitted the same application under appeal, stating that it was a new application, and the frequency of the service would be such as to provide a joint service with the present operators, every 15 minutes. Western Welsh OC, were the only objector, and after several postponements, and hearings, the application was finally refused on 19th January, 1938.

Above: This photograph of D.J. Thomas' long wheel base Thornycroft A1 (FB4), **TX 1380**, fitted with Hall Lewis B20D bodywork, was taken at Caerau Railway Station, circa 1926, when it was new. The coachwork was painted Cream, with Black wings, and it had an unladen weight of 3 tons. *(Byron Gage collection)*.

Above: This Thornycroft 'Handy', fitted with 'Pay As You Enter' style 20 seat coachwork, was built by Wadham Bros., of Waterlooville, Hampshire, and has been identified as being **ANY 716**, delivered in 1935. It also featured a sunshine roof, and a sliding front entrance door, passing to William E. Lloyd, Pontrhydfendigaid, Cardiganshire, in June 1946, before returning again to Maesteg, in August 1948, to Brewers Motor Services. *(Cardiff Transport Preservation Group collection)*.

Further Road Service Licences granted were:-

TGR 432/6   **Excursions & Tours** starting from Abergwynfi.
Granted 28th September, 1932.

TGR 432/7   **Maesteg (Bus Stn)** to **Maesteg (Old Park)**, via: Commercial St, Garn Road, and Alma Road. *Mon to Sat. 6 x return journeys daily.* Objectors: WWOC, and David Thomas, Llangynwyd. *Granted 1st February, 1935.*

On 31st March, 1937, D.J. Thomas asked for permission to introduce weekly tickets on service TGR 432/1, with an unlimited number of journeys at 2/6d, and 12 x single journeys, 1/6d. The tickets would unfairly, only be interchangeable on the joint service of Griffith Hughes, numbered TGR 343/1, and not interchangeable on the services of the other four joint operators.

At the same time, the introduction of an unlimited number of journeys for 2/0d, was asked for on his service TGR 432/2, Maesteg to Garth.

Modification to TGR 432/1 was objected to by Brewer's MS, and refused, whilst TGR 432/2 was objected to by Western Welsh OC, and refused.

On 26th June 1939, D.J. Thomas' business was incorporated, with company N° 00354350, and registered as **CREAM LINE (MAESTEG) Ltd.**, 47 Neath Road, Maesteg.

Three weeks later, on 19th July, 1939, Cream Line (Maesteg) Ltd., applied to the Traffic Commissioners for transfer of all licences held by the previous licensee, David John Thomas (t/a Cream Line Services). That was a legal requirement due to a change of entity. At the same time, a new operator identification number, TGR 3427, was issued to the company, and all five Road Service Licences listed below, were formally transferred to the new company, on 13th September, 1939, just a few days after World War 2 had been declared.

TGR 3427/1   **Maesteg (Bus Stn)** to **Caerau (Blaenllynfi Hotel)**. Previously TGR 432/1

TGR 3427/2   **Maesteg (Bus Stn)** to **Garth**.   Previously TGR 432/2

TGR 3427/3   **Excursions & Tours** starting from Maesteg.   Previously TGR 432/4

TGR 3427/4   **Excursions & Tours** starting from Abergwynfi.   Previously TGR 432/6

TGR 3427/5   **Maesteg (Bus Stn)** to **Maesteg (Old Park)**.   Previously TGR 432/7

It must be noted that to provide extra services during the war, licences had to be applied for as usual, but were only authorised by the Ministry of Defence (Ministry of War Transport), as were all other aspects of licensing during the hostilities. Licences to operate Excursions & Tours were suspended during the war years, in order to conserve fuel and rubber, as were the licences for Express Carriage services, three years later.

The MOWT also decided to drastically cut stage carriage services, and withdraw unnecessary services to conserve fuel. Additionally, if a route had more than one operator, they would encourage the larger operator to absorb the smaller one.

Service TGR 3427/1, was absorbed by their competitor Brewer's Motor Services, in June 1945, and incorporated into Brewer's timetable. TGR 3427/2, Maesteg to Garth, also passed to Brewer's in June 1945, and continued to run on a defence permit in Brewer's name, until officially transferred to Brewer (TGR 267/11), on 17th September, 1947.

TGR 3427/5, **Maesteg** to **Old Park,** was suspended during WW2, together with their Excursions & Tours licence.

Nevertheless, the company did receive one workmen's stage carriage service during the hostilities, which was:-

TGR 3427/6   **Maesteg** to **Margam** (**Carbide Works**), via: Bryn and Port Talbot.

In September 1946, the Traffic Commissioners regained control of licensing, and in most cases, services returned to normal pre-war working patterns.

However, Cream Line (Maesteg) Ltd., only reapplied for two licences, which were:-

TGR 3427/3   **Excursions & Tours** starting from Maesteg.   *Granted 28/4/1948.*

TGR 3427/6   **Maesteg** to **Margam** (**Carbide Works**), via: Bryn, and Port Talbot. *With a modification to start the service from Abergwynfi, one return journey daily. Revised fare: all districts, 3/6d weekly.*   *Refused 23/7/1947.*

TGR 3427/5   **Maesteg** to **Old Park**, was not reapplied for.

In the meantime, two brand new Bedford OB coaches, and a second-hand Albion 'Viking' were purchased, but refusal of the workers service licence above, combined with the proprietor D.J. Thomas' ill health, it was decided to terminate the PSV business. The two Bedford OB coaches were quickly sold off to D.J. Thomas' sister-in-law, Martha Thomas, of Llynfi Motor Services, in April 1948, together with the E & T licence TGR 3427/3.

Sadly, D.J. Thomas passed away on 11th April, 1948, and the Cream Line (Maesteg) Ltd., business was placed into Voluntary Liquidation in March 1949. The garage and haulage business passed to D.J. Thomas' eldest son, William Edgar Thomas.

Above: This is a letterhead for the business of William Edgar Thomas, dated 20th June 1950, some two years after he took control of his father's Garage and Haulage business.   *(Courtesy of Cardiff Transport Preservation Group).*

FORM P.S.V. 4/G  CERTIFICATE No **G** 03016

ROAD TRAFFIC ACT, 1930.
CERTIFICATE OF FITNESS.

I, the undersigned, a CERTIFYING OFFICER duly appointed by the Minister of Transport, hereby certify, in accordance with the provisions of the Road Traffic Act, 1930, that the vehicle described below fulfils the prescribed conditions as to fitness in respect of its use as a ...*STAGE*... carriage.

DESCRIPTION OF VEHICLE.
Index mark and registration number (See Note below)... *TX 6435*
Make, model and year of manufacture of chassis... *Thornycroft 1928.*
Chassis Number... *15392*... Seating Capacity, Lower deck... *20*
Upper deck...
General description:—
(i) Four wheeled or six wheeled... *Four*
(ii) Pneumatic tyred or otherwise... *Pneumatic*
(iii) Single or double decked... *Single*
(iv) Type of body... *Saloon*

This Certificate shall continue in force until... *17th March 1939.*
Date of issue... *12th March 1936.*

Fee £3

A. Simpn
Certifying Officer.

NOTE.

If the vehicle does not appear to have been registered under the Roads Act, 1920, that fact will be indicated. In such case the holder of this certificate is required to notify the index mark and registration number of the vehicle to the Commissioners immediately after it has been assigned and to send or deliver this certificate to them for endorsement accordingly.

Above: This Certificate of Fitness (CoF), issued to D.J. Thomas' Thornycroft 'A1', (TX 6435), on 12th March, 1936, would have been the equivalent of a MoT certificate in those far gone days. When this vehicle was new to D.J. Thomas, in 1928, it would have received a 5 year CoF, and afterwards, renewal time would be reduced, normally to a 3 year period, dependant upon condition. However, as vehicles aged, renewal time would decrease to annually. However, this CoF was probably the last one issued to TX 6435, as it was last licensed by D.J. Thomas (Cream Line Services), in September 1937, and scrapped by a Cardiff breaker in March 1938. *(Courtesy of Cardiff Transport Preservation Group).*

Known Vehicle Details for D.J. Thomas, T/A Cream Line Services, Maesteg.

Reg Nº	Chassis	Body	Seats	Remarks
L 1611	Enfield	Torpedo	5	Ex private owner, 9/1918.
L 1298	Alldays & Onions	Tourer	4	Ex Express Motor Co. Aberavon, 3/1921.
L 5820	Ford 'T' 20hp	Tourer		New 10/1919.
L 6048	Daimler 20hp	Platform Lorry		Ex -?- 2/1920. Licensed Hackney.
L 6065	Ford 'T' 20hp	Van		Ex -?- 2/1920.
L 5054	Thornycroft 'J' 35/40hp	Lorry		Ex -?- 7/1920.
L 6402	Peerless	Lorry/Bus		New 3/1920.
L 6561	Ford 'T'	Tourer		New 3/1920.
L 7982	Ford 'T'	Tourer		New 8/1920.
L 8026	Ford 'T' uw 18cwt.	Platform Lorry		New 10/1920. Dark Blue.
NY 480	Ford 'T' uw 14¾cwt.	Tourer	5	New 10/1921. Livery Black.
NY 1240	Ford 'TT' uw 30cwt	Lorry		New 4/1922. Supplied by Bridgend Motor Co.
NY 1241	Ford 'TT'	Tipper Lorry		New 4/1922. Supplied by Bridgend Motor Co.
NY 1242	Ford 'TT'	Tipper Lorry		New 4/1922. Supplied by Bridgend Motor Co.
NY 1243	Ford 'TT'	Tipper Lorry		New 4/1922. Supplied by Bridgend Motor Co.
NY 3125	Ford 'T' 20-24hp	Tourer	5	New 5/1923. Livery Black. uw 14 cwt.
NY 1497	Crossley (ex W/D 1918 chassis). uw 36cwt	Hearse		Ex Wright, Cardiff, 6/1922. Converted into 14 seat charabanc, 7/1923.
NY 4830	Thornycroft 'BT' 30hp uw 2t 12cwt	John Norman (Cardiff)	B24	New 3/1924, Supplied by John Norman, Cardiff. Livery Maroon/White.
-?-	Thornycroft 'BT'	Strachan & Brown	B20F	New 3/1924. Supplied by John Norman, Cardiff.
XO 2465				Ex -?- 2/1925.
NY 5443	Ford 'T'	Car	4	New 4/1924.
NY 7826	Ford 'TT' 22.3hp		B13	New 4/1925. Livery Maroon/Black. uw 1t 6 cwt.
NY 8789	Lancia 35hp (1921)		B20	Ex -?- Reconditioned bus, acquired 7/1925.
NY 9977	Lancia 35hp (1919)	Coach	C20	Ex -?- Reconditioned bus, acquired 1/1926.
NY 6814	Ford 'BB' (10/1924)	Platform Lorry		Ex F.N. Loughor, Llangeinor, 1926.
TX 509	Austin 12	Tourer	4	New 3/1926. Livery Blue.
TX 1380	Thornycroft 'A1' (FB4)	Hall Lewis	B20D	New 7/1926. Supplied by Hall Lewis. uw 3t ¾ cwt
TX 2320	Ford uw 19¼ cwt.	Platform Lorry		New 2/1927.
UH 3037	Thornycroft or Lancia	Hall Lewis		New 6/1927. Registered by Hall Lewis (dealer).
TX 6435	Thornycroft 'A1' (long) uw 3t 9¾ cwt	Hall Lewis	B20	New 11/1928. Supplied by Hall Lewis. Livery, Biscuit.
TX 8352	Chevrolet 'LQ'	Tipper Lorry		New 10/1929. Livery Green. uw 1t 9½ cwt.
-?-	Vulcan 'Prince' F/C		B40D	
TX 6580	Austin 12	Saloon car		New 1929.
TX 3941	Thornycroft 'A1' (FB4)	Hall Lewis	B20	Ex Phillips. Penrhiwceiber, Glam. 4/1930.
TG 1591	Thornycroft 'BC' F/C		B32	New 5/1931.
NY 2169	Austin 22.4hp	Car	6	Ex Private car owner, Wm. Aherne. Cardiff. 9/1930.
HE 3839	Thornycroft 'A9' (1928)		B20	Ex Yorkshire Traction, 1934.
TG 8669	Fordson 'BB'	Tipper Lorry		New 11/1934. Livery Red/Black.
ANY 716	Thornycroft AE 'Handy'	Wadham Bros.	B20F	New 6/1935. uw 3.5t. To Lloyd, Pontrhydfendigaid.
ATG 491	Thornycroft AE 'Handy'	Thurgood	B20F	New 3/1936. uw 3t 8 cwt. To Brewer, Caerau, 9/39.
WO 3449	Thornycroft A6 (1929)		B25	Ex Enterprize. Abercarn, via Western Welsh.
WO 3450	Thornycroft A6 (1929)		B25	Ex Enterprize. Abercarn, via Western Welsh.
TX 9497	AEC Regal (5/1930)	Metcalf	B32R	Ex T. Davies (Osborne Services) Neath, 6/1937.
BTG 82	Bedford	Tipper Lorry		New 7/1936.
CTG 109	Bedford 'WTB'		25	New 7/1937.
CTG 251	Thornycroft CF 'Dainty'	Thurgood	B20F	New 7/1937. To Brewer, Caerau, by 6/1945.
ENY 681	Bedford 'WTB' Mk II	Thurgood	26	New 6/1939.
WN 4457	Dennis 'EV'	South Wales Tpt.	B32R	(Originally SWT), ex Griff Hughes, Caerau, 3/1941.
FNY 443	Bedford 5 ton	Tipper Lorry		New 7/1943.
GNY 856	Bedford OB	Duple 'Vista'	C29F	New 5/1947.
GTG 322	Bedford OB	Thurgood	C29F	New 5/1947.
PK 9850	Albion 'Viking' PR28	(1929)	31	Ex L. Adnams, London, via Jones -?- 10/1947.

WILLIAM JOHN, MAESTEG

William John, of 25 Alfred Street, Maesteg, was another early Hackney Carriage operator in Maesteg. He acquired his first motor vehicle, L 5968, a 1916 Talbot 20 hp lorry, with a detachable 10 seat charabanc body, from Maesteg charabanc operator, Sydney Thomas Jenkins, of 18 Castle Street, in August 1920 (see page 12). By January 1921, it was licensed as a 14 seat charabanc, and was later increased to 20 seats. He operated this vehicle until October 1924, before it passed to a new owner at Hillington, West Norfolk.

Records show that he received his first Hackney Carriage licence, and drivers licence from the Maesteg Authority, on 28th February, 1922, by such time, he had already established himself on the Maesteg to Caerau route.

When competition intensified in the mid-1920s, William John's brother, Frederick James John appeared on the scene, with a licence issued by Maesteg UDC, in October 1925, to operate the Maesteg to Caerau route. More about the notorious F.J. John's business on next page.

On 12th February, 1929, another family member, Arthur Price John, of 17 Upper Street, Maesteg (previously a resident of 25 Alfred Street), was issued with a drivers licence, and a Hackney Carriage Licence, for a 1921 Austin Coupe, registered, L 8512.

By January 1930, Arthur was operating another motor car, TA 5556, on licence Nº 40, from 20 Castle Street, Maesteg. As previously mentioned, Maesteg UDC, licensed motor cars as omnibuses. It was a unique feature that continued under the Ministry of Transport's command in April 1931, when all licensing issues passed to the Traffic Commissioners. At that point in time, Arthur John applied for continuation of the stage carriage service operated by him during the preceding year, between Maesteg (Bus Station) and Caerau (Blaenllynfi Hotel). It was applied for on his licence application number, TGR 351/1. After a hearing held at Bridgend Crown Court, on 8th July, 1931, the licence was refused, and he ceased operating.

Returning to William John, who had also moved to 17 Upper Street, Maesteg, in March 1928, he also applied for continuation of the stage carriage service operated by him during the preceding year, Maesteg (Bus Station), to Caerau (Blaenllynfi Hotel), via Castle Street, High Street, Picton Street, Tonna Road, and Caerau Road. His application, on TGR 354/1, was heard at the same Crown Court hearing, and granted.

After much conflict, William John, and all other joint operators of the Caerau service, signed an agreement on 1st September, 1933, to faithfully observe the agreed timetable and fare table, and by December 1933, he had moved to 17 St Michaels Road, Maesteg. In February 1934, however, he was granted a licence to operate a former Red & White Services, Albion SPLB24, 20 seater bus on the Caerau service (WO 1457), instead of motor cars!

Consequently, motor car competitors on the Caerau route, Elias Williams (TGR 445/1), and Wm. Morris (TGR 1036/1), retreated, and cancelled their licences on 25th April, 1934, with Ellen Hamer (TGR 333/1), and David Pratt (TGR 334/2), cancelling theirs on 11th May, 1937.

Brewer's Motor Services purchased William John's share of the Caerau route during the wartime hostilities in 1940, for £1,000, with Ministry of War Transport approval.

FREDERICK JAMES JOHN, NANTYFFYLLON

Frederick James John, of 36 Barnardo Street, Nantyffyllon, Maesteg, was a brother of established operator, William John, mentioned opposite. He was granted his first Hackney Carriage licence for a motor car, on 23rd June, 1925, and was issued a licence to run a bus on the already congested route between Maesteg and Caerau, in October 1925.

Two months later, in December 1925, he asked the Maesteg Licensing Committee, for a licence to operate one bus on the Maesteg to Bridgend route. The route, already operated by South Wales Commercial Motors (SWCM), Cardiff, since February 1921, and M.D. Morgan, of The Mason's Arms, Bryncethin, Bridgend, since September 1924, was granted to him.

In July 1927, David Morgan gave up his challenge on the Bridgend route due to harassment from SWCM, and sold his share of the service, with two Lancia 20 seat buses, to Fred John.

However, Fred John quickly became a thorn in the Licensing Committee's side! He was defiant, and always at the forefront of any dispute involving local operators.

By April 1928, he had built a new garage for his vehicles at 49 Picton Street, Nantyffyllon, and on 5th June, 1928, he asked the Licensing Committee for permission to run a service from Maesteg Bus Station, to the Cross Inn, at Cwmfelin, via Castle Street and Garth.

A week later, the Licensing Committee invited Mr John, and a representative of SWCM, to attend a meeting, where both agreed to modify their jointly operated Maesteg to Bridgend service, to run alternatively via Castle Street, and Bridgend Road, one week, and Commercial Street, and Llwydarth Road, the following week, with immediate effect. At the same meeting, complaints of punctuality were received from workmen of Tondu Engineering, who were regularly late for work, due to late departure of F.J. John's 7.00 am journey from Maesteg.

Within three weeks of operating the new arrangement above, the Licensing Committee asked both operators to revert to the original route, due to complaints. That issue prompted Mr John to ask again, for a service from Maesteg to Cross Inn, but it was immediately refused. However, the prevailing difficulties regarding alternate routes in the district of Garth, were finally mutually agreed upon by Mr John, and SWCM, on 20th November, 1928.

Meanwhile, on 26th June, 1928, competitors A & F Brewer asked for a licence to run Maesteg to Bridgend. It was refused, but Brewer's continually reapplied for it until 1931, before finally giving up. The stumbling block was the continued refusal by Bridgend and Penybont Councils.

On 25th September, 1928, adventurous Mr John, then applied to [1] run a service between Maesteg and Treorchy, and [2] run a 40 minute service from Maesteg (Town Hall) to Maiden Street, Garth, via Bridgend Road. The Maesteg to Garth application was postponed, but Mr John was asked to submit timetables for the proposed Maesteg to Treorchy service.

At the same meeting, SWCM Ltd., applied to extend their Bridgend to Maesteg service to Treorchy, and Upper Rhondda, or alternatively, a separate service between Maesteg, and Upper Rhondda, via the Inter-Valley Road. SWCM were also asked to submit proposed timetables, but on 27th November, informed the Licensing Committee that they had withdrawn plans for this service, in view of the gradient and nature of the ground on the Cymmer side.

Fred John however, took the planned route to Treorchy no further.

Due to various complaints and licensing issues, Fred John was only granted a 3 month licence for his six buses in January 1929, and during that period, SWCM complained of the way he was running the joint Bridgend service. Additionally, the Hackney Carriage Inspector reported he was running a bus that had not been inspected. He was given a 3 month probationary period, and warned that his licences would be reviewed and possibly withdrawn, but were reissued for another 3 months, and upon expiry in July 1929, were extended to 31st December.

At a Licensing Committee meeting in June 1929, competitors A & F Brewer were granted a licence to operate a 'new' route between Maesteg and Caerau, via Coegnant Rd, Hermon Rd, and George St, and a fortnight later, Mr John asked for a licence to run the same route, which was refused. He then influenced joint operators of the Maesteg-Caerau service, to complain to the Council, regarding the unfairness of Brewer's receiving the new service. The Committee allowed Brewer's new service to continue, as they were the first, and only applicant.

Additionally, Mr John applied to Porthcawl UDC, on 2nd July, 1929, for permission to extend his Maesteg-Bridgend service to reach Porthcawl, at 40 minute intervals, daily. The Council ultimately asked him to submit a timetable, so that a decision could be made, and in September 1929, told him to confer his timings with competing operators. Nothing further was heard!

Above: This is a view of the original Bridgend Bus Station, captured in the 1920s, when South Wales Commercial Motors Ltd, 'dominated' the area. The Commer charabanc, owned by South Wales Commercial Motors, was departing for Ogmore-by-Sea, Southerdown, and St Brides, whilst their Commer single decker, L 6471, was loading for Cardiff. *(Courtesy Byron Gage).*

On 1st August, 1929, competitors SWCM Ltd, together with the Great Western Railway Co. (Road Motor Services); Western Valleys Motor Services Ltd; and Lewis & James, of Cross Keys, amalgamated to form a new company registered as Western Welsh Omnibus Co. Ltd.

Bearing in mind Frederick John's insolence, the Maesteg Council received a letter from the National Union of General & Municipal Workers, on 26th November, 1929, regarding Mr John's refusal to discuss trade union rates of pay and conditions with his employees. At the next Committee meeting, a deputation of employees were permitted to attend, in order to complain about the conditions they were working under. The Committee considered the complaints received from the employees, and it was decided that Mr John be informed prior to renewal of his licences, that his employees must be engaged for reasonable hours.

Fred John replied to the Council on 23rd December, 1929, stating that men in his employ, worked two different shifts, and average hours worked were 48 and 52 per week, respectively.

Three weeks later, on 21st January, 1930, the Licensing Committee discussed a letter received from Western Welsh OC, stating they had decided to purchase the bus business of F.J. John, subject to Council approval.

The transfer of F.J. John's licences was immediately refused, and at a meeting held a month later, the Maesteg Licensing Committee, invited representatives of Western Welsh, together with Messrs Brewer, and D. J. Thomas.

At this meeting, the application of Western Welsh, for transfer of F.J. John's licences was again discussed, and the Committee interviewed D.J. Thomas, and Mr Brewer, regarding their outstanding applications to run a Maesteg to Bridgend service. It was afterwards decided, that the licence held by F.J. John, in respect of his Maesteg to Bridgend service, be granted to WWOC, on conditions: [1] that they undertake to run a half hourly service instead of the 20 minute service previously authorised. [2] With consideration to 'congestion' on the Maesteg to Caerau route, that particular licence of F.J. John, was not transferred to WWOC. [3] Messrs Brewer, and D.J. Thomas, were informed that the Council were prepared to grant their licences to run Maesteg to Bridgend, making a 15 minute service jointly with Western Welsh. [4] That the operators on the Maesteg to Bridgend service be asked to agree to an interchange of return tickets. [5] That the licences to the new operators be granted on condition that they undertake to observe Trade Union rates of wages and hours for their employees.

A week later, on 18th February, 1930, it emerged that Penybont Council, had granted transfer of F.J. John's licence to WWOC only, resulting in further meetings between all three Councils. WWOC were granted transfer of F.J. John's licence on 8th April, 1930, to run a *half hourly* service, but Brewer's and D.J. Thomas were still not included into the service. The transfer did not go ahead, as Maesteg Licensing Committee unanimously decided that the refusal of Penybont RDC, and Bridgend UDC, to grant licences to A & F Brewer, and D.J. Thomas, was bias, with both authorities' apparent desire to grant a monopoly to Western Welsh. Maesteg Council then made an appeal to the Ministry of Transport to hold an inquiry.

Note: A similar issue arose on the Bridgend to Porthcawl route in 1926, when Penybont and Bridgend Councils were giving preference to South Wales Commercial Motors, over joint operators of that service, Francis Motors and D.J. Weeks, until Porthcawl UDC intervened.

In September 1930, there were further complaints of irregular running on the Maesteg-Caerau route, and after a meeting between the Licensing Committee and the operators, new timetables were provisionally approved on 23rd October, with the exception of Fred John.

On 29th October, Frederick John, together with his brother William John, and Fred Pratt, objected to the proposed new timetables, and it was reported on 11th November, that Fred John was defiant, and had failed to comply with the new timetables. The Committee then asked the Hackney Carriage Inspector to inspect Frederick John's buses – but no defects were found.

Fred then involved the Motor Omnibus Proprietors Association with his timetable dispute, and the MOPA drew up an alternative timetable for the Licensing Committee, which was rejected.

A short while later, on 10th February, 1931, Fred asked for permission to extend his Maesteg to Bridgend service through to Caerau. The application was deferred, but in the meantime, Western Welsh were still badgering the Maesteg Licensing Committee for transferral of Frederick John's Maesteg to Bridgend licence.

Fred John then asked the Maesteg Council, for permission to install a 500 gallon petrol tank at his garage premises, 49 Picton Street, Nantyffyllon. Permission was granted in March 1931.

However, when the Road Traffic Act 1930, was introduced in April 1931, Fred John conformed to the new licensing rules, and applied for renewal without change, of both stage carriage services operated by him during the preceding year. They were applied for with his allocated operator identification number, TGR 584:-

TGR 584/1   **Maesteg (Bus Station)** to **Caerau (Blaenllynfi Hotel)**, via: Nantyffyllon.

TGR 584/2   **Maesteg (Bus Station)** to **Bridgend**, via Aberkenfig.

TGR 584/2 was objected to by Western Welsh, but after a County Court hearing at Bridgend, on 8th July, 1931, both licences were granted to Fred John. TGR 584/2 was authorised as previously operated, to run jointly with Western Welsh (TGR 441/29).

Authorisation for inter-availability of weekly and season tickets between Frederick James John, and Western Welsh, on the Maesteg to Bridgend service was granted on 17th April, 1933.

On 23rd March, 1932, the following 'new' licence was asked for:-

TGR 584/3   **Excursions & Tours** starting from Caerau.
             Tours to run from Easter to October.   *Granted 2/5/1932.*

In October 1933, the following 'new' workmen's stage carriage service was asked for:-

TGR 584/4   **Caerau** to **Crynant (Cefn Coed Colliery)**,
             via: Nantyffyllon, Maesteg, Bryn, Port Talbot, and Neath.
             To run on working days throughout the year, on a 3 x shift system.
             Fares: Men, 8 shillings per week.   Boys, 5 shillings per week.

An objection was legitimately received from a comparatively new local competitor, Lewis & Jacob, of Maesteg, as they already held a licence for the same stage carriage route, TGR 1795/1. After numerous postponed hearings at Neath County Police Court, and a lengthy appeal to the Ministry of Transport, the application was finally refused in January 1938.

Returning to January 1935, Western Welsh made another offer to purchase Fred John's entire business, and again asked the Traffic Commissioners for transfer of Mr John's three licences; Maesteg to Caerau, TGR 584/1; Maesteg to Bridgend, TGR 584/2; and the Excursions & Tours licence, TGR 584/3. Western Welsh applied for those licences, on application numbers TGR 441/208, 441/209, & 441/210 respectively, and was heard at Crown Court on 20th February, 1935. TGR 584/2 was finally granted to WWOC, in May 1935, and incorporated into their established Maesteg to Bridgend licence, TGR 441/29, three months later, in August.

The application for Fred John's Excursions & Tours licence, TGR 584/3, was immediately refused, and the ongoing issue regarding transfer of the Caerau service, TGR 584/1, was finally refused in January 1938. Fred John's licence for the Maesteg to Bridgend service, TGR 584/2, was surrendered on 24th July, 1935.

The final outcome was that Western Welsh only acquired F.J. John's share of the Maesteg to Bridgend service, together with four Thornycroft buses, in May 1935. Mr John retained his other buses, and continued running his share of the Caerau service, together with E & T's.

However, Frederick John's address changed to 65 Picton Street, by March 1937, and renewal of his E & T licence, TGR 584/3, continued until outbreak of WW2, when it was suspended. The licence TGR 584/1, passed to Brewer's Motor Services in July 1943, together with his last remaining vehicle, TG 8764, under a MOWT directive, for rationalisation of services.

Known Vehicle Details for FREDERICK JAMES JOHN, NANTYFFYLLON.

Reg N°	Chassis	Body	Seats	Remarks
L 6406	Belsize 25hp (3/1920)	Flat Lorry		Ex -?-
NY 7672	Ford 'T' (3/1925)	Car	5	New Last licensed 1/1928.
NY 2377	Maxwell (1/1923)	Car	5	Ex -?-
NY 8955	Lancia (8/1925)		26	New Last licensed 1929.
NY 9824	Lancia (11/1925)		20 to 26	New Last licensed 1931.
TX 163	Lancia 35hp (2/1926)		B26	New Last licensed 11/1930.
TX 1171	Lancia 35hp (6/1926)		B20	New Last licensed 10/1929.
TX 3954	Thornycroft 'UB' (7/1927)	Hall Lewis	B32	New. To Western Welsh OC (370), 5/1935.
NY 6854	Lancia (10/1924)		B25	Ex M.D. Morgan, Bryncethin, Bridgend, 7/1927, with his business. Last licensed 8/1929.
NY 9522	Lancia 35hp (10/1925)		B20	Ex M.D. Morgan, Bryncethin, Bridgend, 7/1927, with his business. Last licensed 1929.
TX 7602	Thornycroft 'UB' (6/1929)	Hall Lewis	B30 to 32	New. To Western Welsh OC (373), 5/1935.
NY 8789	Lancia 35hp (-/1921)		B20	Reconditioned bus in 7/1925. Ex D.J. Thomas. (Cream Line) Maesteg, 6/1929. Last lic. 1929.
BX 8121	Thornycroft 'SB' (7/1927) Also quoted as 'UB'	Hall Lewis	B26	Ex Morgan Bros, Betws, Ammanford, by 5/1930. To D. Thomas, Llangynwyd, 7/1935. Last lic. -/36.
NY 9277	AEC 'Blenheim' 412 (8/1925)		B26	Ex T. Rowe. Southerndown, 10/1930. To F. Preston, Cardiff, as lorry, 10/1933.
TX 5837	Thornycroft 'UB' (7/1928)	Hall Lewis	B31	Ex W.L. Davies, Clydach, 5/1931. To Western Welsh OC (372) 5/1935. To Breese, Merthyr, -/38.
DE 6511	Thornycroft 'A1' (5/1928)	Hall Lewis	B14F	Ex J.R. Ford, Pembroke, 9/1933. To J.T. Trickery, Pyle, as lorry 1935. Last licensed 12/1935.
BO 9401	--?-- (1925)			Ex S. Taylor. Park Hotel, Cardiff.
TG 8764	Thornycroft 'Handy' 'AE/FB4' 24hp (12/1934)		B20F	New. Sold to A.E & F.R. Brewer, Caerau, 1/7/1943, with the Caerau service.
TX 3306	Thornycroft 'UB' (7/1927)	Vickers Also quoted as Hall Lewis	B32	(New to Rhondda Motor Services, Tylorstown). Ex Red & White MS, Chepstow (142), 6/1932. Sold to Western Welsh OC (371), 5/1935.

GRIFFITH HUGHES, CAERAU

Hackney Carriage operator, Griffith Hughes, of 110 Llwydarth Road, Maesteg, was born in Maesteg on 22nd December, 1902. He acquired his first motor car in January 1921, and his first driving licence was issued by the Maesteg Authority, on 31st May, 1921. His first Hackney Carriage licence was issued on 28th February, 1922, when he joined around twenty-five other motor car operators on the controversial Caerau route, with a second-hand, 1918 Ford 'T', five seat motor car, registered L 5820.

Hughes was an owner driver, running just one vehicle. His first bus in February 1928, had a 1924 Italian built 'SPA' chassis, (Sociedad Piemontese Automobili). This vehicle, registered BX 5196, had been new to J. James & Sons, Ammanford, in January 1925, and arrived here via J.M. Bacus, Burry Port. It operated with Griff Hughes for several years.

By 1931, Hughes had two Hackney Carriage licences, one motor car and one bus, and was operating from 20 Picton Street, Nantyffyllon, the same street as competitor, Fred John.

When responsibility of PSV licensing passed to the Ministry of Transport in April 1931, Griff Hughes was issued with operator reference number TGR 343, and was permitted to continue running a motor car on this number. The only licence he applied for in April 1931, was for continuance of a service operated by him during the previous year:-

TGR 343/1 **Maesteg** to **Caerau** via Nantyffyllon. *(Operation by a motor car)*.

This licence was granted on 8th July, 1931, with ten special conditions, which were applicable to *all* operators running *motor cars* on the said route, as follows:-

[1] The authorised service shall be operated on the following route only: Castle Street, High Street, Picton Street, Tonna Road, and Caerau Road. [2] The standing places for this service shall be the Hackney Carriage stands at Caerau, Nantyffyllon, and Maesteg, which are at present being used by vehicles operating between Caerau and Maesteg. [3] The licensee shall only be entitled to take up passengers at the said standing places at Caerau, Nantyffyllon, and Maesteg, respectively, and shall not be entitled to take up passengers at any other place. [4] The licensee shall immediately after setting down passengers, take his/her place in rotation at one of the said standing places, and vehicles on the stand, shall at all times leave in order of rotation. [5] Not more than six vehicles shall be allowed to stand at the same time at any of the said standing places, and, if upon arrival at any of the said standing places, the licensee finds that there are already the authorised number of vehicles standing there, the licensee shall immediately proceed to one of the other standing places. [6] Fares to be charged on the said route shall be as follows:-

Maesteg (Town Hall Square) to Stand at Caerau.	2½d
Maesteg (Town Hall Square) to Stand at Nantyffyllon.	1½d
Stand, Caerau, to Stand, Maesteg.	2½d
Stand, Caerau, to Stand, Nantyffyllon.	1½d
Stand, Nantyffyllon, to Stand, Maesteg.	1½d
Stand, Nantyffyllon, to Stand, Caerau.	1½d

[7] The Licensee in operating the authorised service, shall observe and conform to statutory and other legal obligations and provisions applying thereto, or to vehicles used on the service,

and in particular, shall not permit any such vehicle to be driven at a speed which is dangerous to the public, and shall not race with other vehicles used on the same route. [8] Not more than one vehicle shall be used by the licensee in operating this service, and that vehicle shall be of the type set out by the licensee in his/her application for this licence or a similar type. [9] The licensee shall at all times observe and carry out the instructions of the police inspector in charge at Maesteg, and shall observe and perform all directions, and instructions issued by the Maesteg UDC, and in the event of any disagreement as to such instructions and directions, the matter in dispute shall be referred to the Traffic Commissioners for the South Wales Area. [10] The licensee shall observe and perform all terms and conditions of an agreement in writing, dated the 15th day of October, 1931, and signed by him/her.

In July 1931, two more licences were applied for:-

TGR 343/2 **Excursions & Tours** starting from Caerau. *All tours to run throughout the year. Maximum number of vehicles to be used on any one day, to be one.*
Granted 16/10/1931.

TGR 343/3 **Maesteg (Bus Station)** to **Caerau (Blaenllynfi Hotel)** *(Operation by a bus).*

TGR 343/3: Was granted 16th October, 1931, with same conditions as TGR 343/1 opposite.

TGR 343/2: When renewal of this licence was sought after on 8th March, 1933, Western Welsh objected to it, and after a hearing at Bridgend Crown Court, on 3rd April, 1933, it was granted with one special condition: Not to advertise any Excursions & Tours.

On 1st September, 1931, an agreement was signed between the six remaining joint operators of the Caerau service, A.E & F.R. Brewer; David John Thomas (Cream Line); Griffith Hughes; Frederick James John; William John; and Fred Pratt, for a fare table and timetable to be faithfully observed and performed at all times.

By January 1933, Griff Hughes' address was given as Blaenllynfi Hotel, Caerau, which was directly opposite Brewer's garages. Griff had become licensee of the Blaenllynfi Hotel.

In subsequent years after licensing responsibilities passed to the Traffic Commissioners, issues became far less common, but on 31st March, 1937, Griff Hughes, and D.J. Thomas (Cream Line Services), applied for permission to introduce weekly tickets on their services, TGR 343/1 and TGR 432/1 respectively. The tickets, 12 single journeys (12 tripper), for 1/6d, and unlimited number of journeys for 2/6d, would only be interchangeable with the services of Griffith Hughes, and D.J. Thomas. Their application was objected to by Brewer's Motor Services, and was refused on 15th September, 1937, on the grounds of monopolizing.

On 18th January, 1939, Hughes applied for a RSL to continue the workmen's stage carriage service, previously issued to Clifford Randall, 10 Woodlands Terrace, Caerau. (Randall had earlier been a competitor on the Maesteg to Caerau route, from 1930, to November 1932):-

TGR 343/4 **Maesteg** to **Nantewlaeth Colliery (South Pit)**, **Glyncorrwg**, via: Caerau, and the Mountain Road between Caerau, and Cymmer, *with revised fares.*

Objections were received from Lewis & Jacob, Maesteg, and G.S. Herbert, Maesteg. The licence was granted on 29th March, 1939, with the following conditions:-

[1] Not more than one vehicle to be used in operating the authorised service, and such vehicle shall be specially approved of in writing, by the Traffic Commissioners, as being suitable for use upon this route. [2] The vehicle operating this service shall be brought to a standstill before commencing the descent on either side of the hill between Caerau and Cymmer, and shall afterwards descend the hill in second or bottom gear, until the foot of the hill is reached. [3] The authorised service shall be run in both directions over the new viaduct at Cymmer.

A later application for revision of timetable was refused on 16th August 1939.

During WW2, the Ministry of War Transport introduced a rationalisation of services to conserve fuel, oil, and rubber. Official records of these changes were not retained for security reasons, but under a MOWT directive for rationalisation of services, Griffith Hughes' business was absorbed by Brewer's Motor Services in 1945.

Known Vehicle Details for GRIFFITH HUGHES, CAERAU.

Reg Nº	Chassis	Body	Seats	Remarks
L 5820	Ford 'T' (1918)	Tourer	5	Ex R. Elizabeth Phillips. Maesteg. 1/1921
BO 2381	(1919)			Ex R. Powell. Llanishen. Unknown date.
NY 911	Chevrolet 20hp	Car	5	New 3/1922.
NY 7255	Ford 'T' 22hp	Car	5	New 1/1925.
BX 5196	Sociedad Piemontese Automobili	Bus	B---	Ex J.M. Bacus, Burry Port, by 2/1928.
TX 2219	Standard 13.9hp	Car	5	Ex H.J. Uphill. Caerau, 1/1929.
TX 1822	Austin 12.8hp	Car		Ex D.W. Price. Maesteg, 10/1932.
VJ 1252	Dennis 'G'	Bus	B14	Ex J. Jordan. To Brewer's, Caerau, by1945.
WN 4457	Dennis 'EV'	South Wales Transport	B32R	Ex South Wales Transport, 3/1939.

Above: This Thornycroft A6, **TP 6601**, fitted with Wadham Bros, B20F bodywork, was acquired by **Fred Pratt of Caerau**, to operate his share of the Maesteg to Caerau service. It was a former Southdown Motor Services vehicle, purchased from the Swansea dealer, Jeffries, in October 1935. More about the Pratt family's business opposite. *(Courtesy of Cardiff TPG).*

M E PRATT & SON, CAERAU

The business of **Martha Ellen Pratt** is a little confusing, due to the fact that vehicles and road service licences were issued in the names of other family members.

The business commenced in June 1920, when Mrs Pratt, of 53 Hermon Road, Caerau, was granted the transfer of an existing Hackney Carriage licence, held by **David John Hamer**, of 56 Gelli St, Caerau, together with a vehicle, registered L 4708.

In May 1925, the licence passed to **Fred Pratt**, of the same address, and by July 1925, he was running a brand new Graham-Dodge, 20 seat bus, NY 8795, on the Maesteg to Caerau route.

In December 1926, he had two licenced vehicles on the route, after purchasing a 24hp Dodge 6 seat motor car, NY 7459, and in December 1929, he asked the Maesteg Licensing Committee for a licence to run another bus on the route. The licence was at first deferred, but in January 1930, licence Nº 33 was issued to a second bus, a Dennis 'G', registered AX 9735, and licence Nº 35, was issued to the motor car NY 7459.

By September 1930, Fred Pratt had moved to 94 Castle Street, Maesteg, and a month later, influenced by Frederick John, and his brother William John, objected to a proposed timetable on their jointly operated Maesteg to Caerau route.

In the meantime, **David John Hamer** (mentioned above), recommenced operating from his original Caerau address, and was issued with a new Hackney Carriage licence, in June 1928. Fifteen months later, Hamer asked for a licence to run a bus on the Maesteg to Caerau service. The application was continuously rejected until November 1930, when he finally received a licence to operate between Maesteg and 'The New Institute' at Nantyffyllon only, and on 27th January, 1931, he was issued a licence for a bus registered UH 1616, in his own name, and a car, TX 214, in his wife's name, **Ellen Honor Hamer**.

Dissatisfied with the outcome of his licence application on the Caerau route, he made a second request in February 1931, to run an additional bus between Maesteg and Nantyffyllon on Fridays and Saturdays only. The licence was granted for the period until introduction of the new Road Traffic Act, in April 1931.

However, when responsibility of PSV licensing passed to the Ministry of Transport in April 1931, David John Hamer, applied for continuation of this licence in his wife's name, Ellen Honor Hamer. Mrs Hamer was issued with operator reference number TGR 333, and the application read: to continue the stage carriage service operated by her during the past year, according to her published timetable:-

TGR 333/1   **Maesteg** to **Caerau**, via Nantyffyllon.   *Granted 16/10/1931*, for a motor car.

It will be noted that the original licence, issued by the Maesteg UDC Licensing Committee, in David John Hamer's name, had been issued to operate between Maesteg and Nantyffyllon, for a two month period only.

Returning to the Pratt family once again, when responsibility of PSV licensing passed to the Ministry of Transport in April, 1931, **David Pratt & Co**, of 56 Gelli Street, Caerau (same address as Ellen Honor Hamer), applied to the Traffic Commissioners for a licence to continue the stage carriage services operated by them during the past year:-

TGR 334/1 **Maesteg (Town Hall)** to **Nantyffyllon**,
via: Rock Inn, and Tonna Road. *Fridays and Saturdays only.*

TGR 334/2 **Maesteg (Town Hall)** to **Caerau**, via: Nantyffyllon.

TGR 334/3 **Excursions & Tours** starting from Caerau and Maesteg.

After a hearing at Bridgend Crown Court, on 8th July, 1931, TGR 334/1 was refused, whilst TGR 334/2 and 334/3 were granted.

Concurrently, **Martha Ellen Pratt & Son**, of Riverside Cottage, Castle Street, Maesteg, applied in April 1931, for the following licences:-

TGR 406/1 **Maesteg (Town Hall)** to **Caerau**, via: Nantyffyllon.

TGR 406/2 **Excursions & Tours** starting from Maesteg (Town Hall), and Caerau.
To run throughout the year.   All Tours within South Wales TA.

TGR 406/1 and 406/2, were granted on 8th July, 1931, and on 29th July, 1931, continuance of the following workmen's stage carriage service operated during the past year was asked for:-

TGR 406/3 **Maesteg (Cerdin)** to **Caerau Colliery**, via Nantyffyllon.

TGR 406/3 was granted 16th October, 1931.

More licence changes were asked for on 6th December, 1933, when **Fred Pratt**, of Riverside Cottage, Castle Street, Maesteg, applied for the licences previously held by M.E. Pratt & Son, on a new application number, TGR 1862:-

TGR 1862/1 **Maesteg (Bus Station)** to **Caerau (Brynllynfi Hotel)**, via Castle Street, High Street, Picton Street, Tonna Road, and Caerau Road.

TGR 1862/2 **Excursions & Tours** starting from Maesteg .

TGR 1861/1 and 1861/2, were granted on 28th February, 1934. The conditions attached to TGR 1861/1, were identical to those of Griffith Hughes' licence TGR 343/1 (page 266 above).

On 1st February, 1934, **Fred Pratt** asked for **Martha Ellen Pratt's** workmen's stage carriage licence, TGR 406/3, Maesteg (Cerdin), to Caerau Colliery. It was asked for on application TGR 1862/3, but at the same time, it was reapplied for with its original number TGR 406/3, due to adjourned hearings. The licence was finally granted two years later, on 27th May, 1936, and from 26th May, 1937, was modified to start from Bridge Street, Maesteg.

All licences held under **Ellen Honor Hamer** (TGR 333/1, motor car licence), and **David Pratt** (TGR 334/2, motor car licence), were cancelled on 11th May, 1937, whilst the licences of **Fred Pratt** (TGR 1862/1, 2, 3), continued until the outbreak of World War 2.

Fred Pratt's licence, TGR 1862/1 was absorbed into Brewer's Motor Services' Maesteg to Caerau service, TGR 267/1, during WW2, under the directive of the Ministry of War Transport in 1940, to conserve fuel and rubber.

Other Competitors in the Maesteg district between 1914 and 1939.

Albert Edward Bayliss, 29 Cwmdu Street, Maesteg.	1929 to 1939
Thomas Buckley, 20 Ivor Street, Maesteg,	1919 to 1939
Arthur Davies, 45 West Street, Maesteg.	1933 to 1939
David Thomas Davies, 1 Coronation Terrace, Nantyffyllon, Maesteg.	1923 to 1925
Henry R. Evans, 15 Talbot Street, Maesteg.	1919 to 1923
Thomas O. Gould, 15 Turbeville Street, Maesteg.	1920 to 1927
David Grey, 25 Homfrey Street, Maesteg.	1924 to 1925
Reginald Edwin Greenslade, 18 Duke Street, Maesteg.	1933 to 1934
David James Griffiths, 86 Hermon Street, Caerau.	1921 to 1929
Griffiths Brothers, Ty Derwen, Llangonoyd, Maesteg.	1925 to 1937
William Griffiths, 18 Temple Street, Maesteg.	1928 to 1930
Henry Charles Herbert & Sons/Herbert Bros, 100 Commercial St, Maesteg.	1919 to 1939
Alexander Horn, 5 Caerau Road, Caerau.	1932 to 1934
Caradog James, 39 High Street, Nantyffyllon, Maesteg.	1919 to 1935
Sydney Thomas Jenkins, 18 Castle Street, Maesteg.	1919 to 1921
Arthur Price John, 20 Castle Street, Maesteg.	1929 to 1931
Daniel Jones, Newtown Stores, 174 Caerau Road, Caerau.	1918 to 1922
Thomas Joshua, 240 Bridgend Rd, Maesteg, to 36 Dyffryn Road, Caerau.	1921 to 1932
Lewis & Jacob, The Garage, Court Street, Maesteg.	1933 to 1981
Gwilym Loveluck, 19 Maesteg Road, Llangonoyd, Maesteg.	1921 to 1926
Robert Moore, 24 Hermon Road, Caerau.	1920 to 1921
John Haydn Morgan, 25 Ewenny Road, Maesteg.	1930 to 1946
M.D. Morgan, Masons Arms, Bryncethin, to The Garage, Bryncethin.	1924 to 1927
William Morris, 55 High Street, Nantyffyllon, Maesteg.	1931 to 1934
Albert Murphey, 144 Caerau Road, Maesteg.	1921 to 1926
Neath Omnibus Co., 4 Queen Street, Neath.	1922 to 1938
Clifford Randall, 23 Dyffryn Road, to 10 Woodlands Terrace, Caerau.	1930 to 1939
Wengar Rees, 12 Coronation Terrace, Nantyffyllon, Maesteg.	1921 to 1928
William David Richards, 297 Bridgend Road, Maesteg.	1929 to 1937
Lily Seldon, 73 Bethania Street, Maesteg.	1931 to 1944
South Wales Transport Co Ltd., Swansea.	1923 to 1988
South Wales Commercial Motors Ltd., Cardiff.	1922 to 1929
David Thomas, 4 Llan Road, Llangynwyd.	1930 to 1969
Edgar Thomas, 19 Bridgend Road, Maesteg.	1919 to 1924
Glyn Haydn Thomas, 33 Salisbury Road, Maesteg.	1935 to 1937
Evan Arthur Thomas, 9 Wesley Street, Caerau.	1914 to 1925
Henry Thomas, 10 Golden Terrace, Maesteg.	1920 to 1922
United Welsh Services Ltd. (initially Chepstow). To Swansea in April 1940.	1939 to 1970
Haydn James Uphill, 9 Grosvenor Terrace, Caerau.	1922 to 1968
Western Welsh O C., 253 Cowbridge Road West, Cardiff.	1929 to 1971
Elias Williams, 6 Greenfield Terrace, Caerau.	1922 to 1934
Iorwerth Gwilim Williams, Spelters Stores, Tonna Road, Caerau.	1929 to 1931
Nehemiah Williams, 13 Picton Street, Nantyffyllon, Maesteg.	1925 to 1930

Above: Another local competitor, Lewis & Jacob, Maesteg, bought this Duple 'A' bodied Dennis 'Lancet III', 35 seat coach, brand new in May 1950, and ran it until May 1962. *(Copyright Byron Gage).*

This completes the story of 'The Maesteg Rivals', which is a great story of enterprise and achievement. It's a story briefly and simply told, but between its pages lies a record of public service difficult to surpass. Between its pages also, are thousands and thousands of unwritten stories of men, women, and families, who worked, lived, and died in that service. It's a tribute to them all.